Walking in His Steps

for David,

with best wishes,

Peter

(September 2002)

Walking in His Steps

A Guide to Exploring the Land of the Bible

PETER WALKER
AND
GRAHAM TOMLIN

Marshall Pickering
An Imprint of HarperCollins*Publishers*

Marshall Pickering is an Imprint of
HarperCollins*Religious*
part of HarperCollins*Publishers*
77–85 Fulham Palace Road, London W6 8JB
www.christian-publishing.com

First published in Great Britain in 2001
by HarperCollins*Publishers*

1 3 5 7 9 10 8 6 4 2

A catalogue record for this book is
available from the British Library

ISBN 0 551 03254 5

Printed and bound in Great Britain by
Creative Print and Design (Wales), Ebbw Vale

CONTENTS

List of Figures

KEY DATES IN THE HOLY LAND

(divided according to the various rulers of Jerusalem)

ANCIENT ISRAEL (1003–587 BC)

1003	King David founds Jerusalem
970	King Solomon dedicates the Temple
722	Fall of Samaria and Northern Kingdom of Israel
587	Fall of Jerusalem to Nebuchadnezzar

THE PERSIANS (538–332)

538	First Jews return from Babylonian exile

THE GREEKS (332–168)

168	Antiochus Epiphanes desecrates the Temple

INDEPENDENT JEWISH KINGDOM (168–63)

168–4	The Maccabees revolt

THE ROMANS (63 BC–AD 313)

37–4	Reign of Herod the Great
c. 6 BC	Birth of Jesus
AD 30 or 33	Jesus is crucified

63	First Jewish Revolt
70	Fall of Jerusalem
132–5	Second Jewish Revolt under Bar Chochba
135	Hadrian refounds Jerusalem as 'Aelia Capitolina'

THE BYZANTINES (313–637)

325	Emperor Constantine summons the Council of Nicaea
335	Eusebius gives oration at the Dedication of Holy Sepulchre
c. 384	Visit of Egeria; Jerome resides in Bethlehem
451	Council of Chalcedon: Jerusalem becomes a patriarchate
614	Sack of Jerusalem by Chosroës of Persia
637	Caliph Omar captures Jerusalem

THE ARABS (637–1099)

691	Abd al-Malik builds the Dome of the Rock
1010	Caliph el Hakim desecrates Holy Sepulchre
1048	Emperor Constantine Monomachus restores Holy Sepulchre
1054	The Great Schism between the Eastern and Western Church
1099	First Crusade

THE LATINS (1099–1187)

1187	Battle of Hattin; Saladin takes Jerusalem
1188–92	Third Crusade

THE MAMELUKES (1247–1507)

1291	Fall of Acre
1453	Fall of Constantinople

THE TURKS (1517–1917)

1537–42	Suleiman the Magnificent rebuilds Jerusalem's walls
1808	Fire destroys much of Holy Sepulchre
1841	Anglicans found a bishopric in Jerusalem
1897	Zionist conference in Basle

THE BRITISH (1917–1948)

1917	Balfour Declaration
1948	End of British Mandate; declaration of the State of Israel; Jordan controls Old City of Jerusalem and the West Bank

THE ISRAELIS (1948–PRESENT)

1967	Six Day War; all Jerusalem under Israeli control
1973	Yom Kippur War

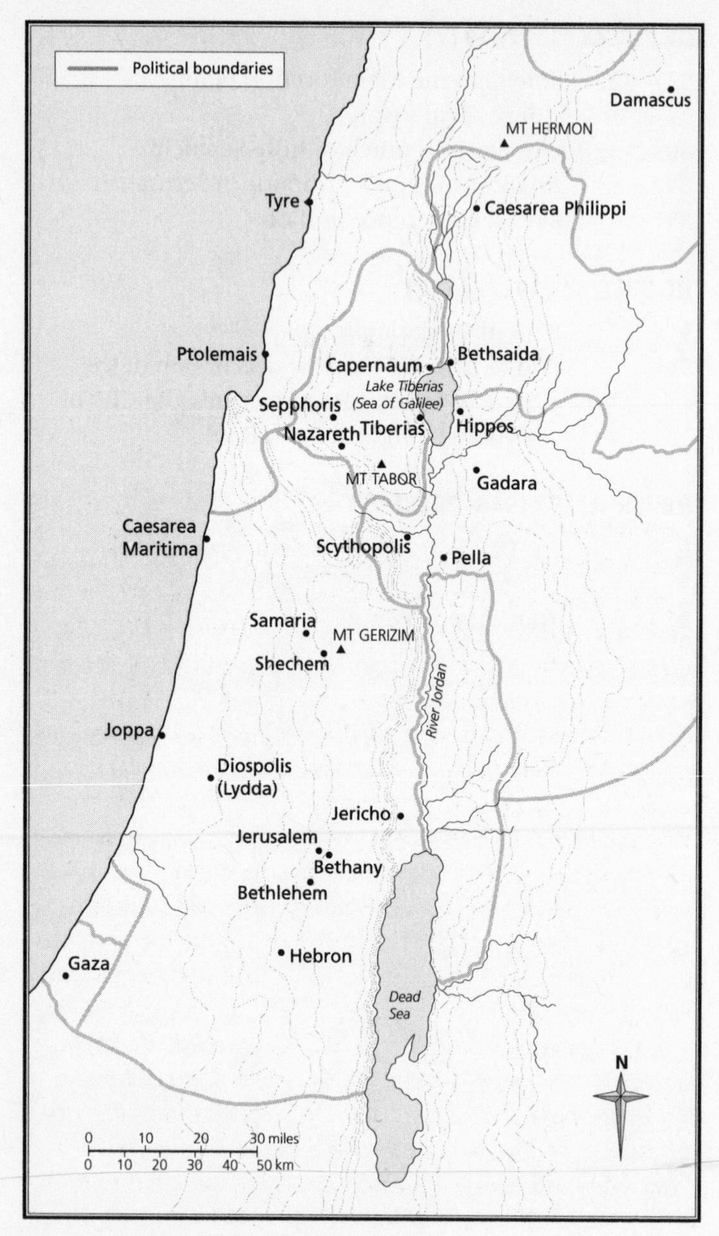

Figure 1. Palestine in New Testament times

PREFACE

This book began in a late-night conversation in the heart of Jerusalem itself. We were leading a study tour of students from the college where we both teach, and had arrived at a hotel just outside the city walls, weary from a long day's journey. As the night wore on, and the sounds of the city rumbled on outside, we started talking about our first encounters with the land of the Bible, and how we had reacted to them. We discovered that our experiences had been very similar, and began to suspect that many Christians visiting the Holy Land went through much the same emotions as we had. We both agreed that our experiences had been, in their different ways, profound and, to use a rather overworked term, life-changing. To visit the land of Jesus Christ, the land of the Bible, had been exhilarating, depressing, disturbing, fascinating, and deeply moving, but never boring. We had never read the Bible in quite the same way again. Yet there was something about the whole experience that hadn't felt right, and as the conversation went on, we began to identify what it was.

We had both been nurtured within the evangelical traditions of the Christian Church. It was to this style of Christianity that we owed our own life in Christ. It was here that we both felt not just more comfortable, but more in tune with the heart of the gospel itself. For us, this tradition had, for all its flaws, held tightly to some vital principles of Christian truth at times when others in the Church might have been tempted to forget them. It had held on to such central Christian themes as the Lordship of Christ, the centrality of the cross, the need for personal faith, the key role of evangelism and the divine authority of the Bible. We also reflected that most Christians visiting the Holy Land today come from a similar background – North and South Americans, Europeans, Africans and Asians who share the same approach to Christian faith and the same values.

On our first visits to the Holy Land we had encountered the pilgrimage mentality. We were taken to be pilgrims, visiting a holy land, with holy places, which were in some way more holy than other places. These 'holy sites' had seen churches erected on them at the slightest excuse, and their interiors decorated in what seemed to us the most gaudy and over-elaborate way. Church services we encountered involved incense, intoned liturgies, monks, priests and patriarchs, all dressed in peculiar ecclesiastical garb, with very little congregational involvement.

In short, the whole thing looked very odd. The whole experience of travelling to the land and visiting the sites associated with the events of the Bible was couched in a language and mentality which we felt was somewhat foreign to us. In our evangelical background, pilgrimage was not an idea we had come across very often, and when we had, it had been frowned upon as a rather suspect practice, all bound up with justification by works, not faith. The idea that some places are more holy than others, indeed the idea that any particular object can be 'holy', was also quite suspicious. Doesn't the New Testament call God or people holy, but not things? Surely Christ is to be found everywhere by his Spirit, not in particular places? Again, the proliferation of monks and monasteries looked decidedly fishy to people brought up to believe that Henry VIII had done us all a big favour by dissolving the monasteries in England, ridding the country of an unbiblical and corrupt way of life.

So the conversation continued as to how, despite our awkwardness with the idea of holy places and all the paraphernalia of pilgrimage, we had come to be leading a kind of 'pilgrimage' of our own. We still held to, and felt ourselves part of, that evangelical tradition, and thought its distinctives were vital both for us and for the whole Church. We still felt uneasy about some aspects of the 'Holy Land' idea, yet we couldn't deny that we had found our first visits to Israel/Palestine one of the most uplifting and stimulating things we had ever done in our Christian lives. There must be thousands of others who visit the Holy Land each year on a tour with their local church, or on a visit organized by one of the many tour companies, who experience the same unease, and perhaps thousands of others who maybe aren't even aware of the jarring between their theological background and their experiences in Israel. Perhaps some of these might like help to think such things through? So we decided, that night, that one day we would write something which tried to help biblical Christians approach a trip to the land of the Bible; and here it is.

This is not a tourist guidebook. Nor is it a work on the sociology of tourism and pilgrimage. Nor is it an archaeological text. There are plenty of other works which will tell the visitor what to look for at different sites, and how they have come into being. Instead it tries to help thoughtful Christians, eager to be true to the Bible, to think through what they are doing when they go on a trip to Israel. Any decent tour company will give all kinds of instructions on how to prepare for a visit to Israel – what to bring, to wear, how to get currency, visas, and so on. Yet so often the more important spiritual and theological preparation just doesn't get done. And that's what this book is all about.

In setting out to write it, we felt there were important theological, historical and spiritual questions to be pondered when embarking on a trip to the Holy Land. So, Part One tries to construct a biblical theology to guide us through the complex issues surrounding the theme. Part Two tells the story of Christian involvement in the land of the Bible, and explains the mark which Christians have left upon the land. Part Three tries to introduce readers to what they might encounter there, especially the people, the landscape and the spiritualities. In between each part we have tried to picture these thoughts going through the mind of two imaginary visitors. Creating Tom and Sarah has been fun – perhaps their emotions and reactions will somehow connect with yours, and even provide some light relief from the hard thinking going on elsewhere.

We are aware that this is a somewhat hazardous task. Some will feel we lean too far in arguing a case for pilgrimage, others will feel we are not 'catholic' enough. If we help both be more true to Christ and his Word, we will be content. We are both very positive about the value of visiting the Land of the Bible; we also want to encourage a thoughtful and responsible approach, which will help visitors integrate a little better what they see and do with what they believe.

A word about us. We both teach theology at Wycliffe Hall, Oxford, a theological college of the Church of England, and part of Oxford University. One of us (Peter) has written extensively on the Holy Land, has led many groups around it, and is a specialist on the New Testament and biblical theology. The other (Graham) is a historical theologian with interests mainly in the Reformation and the early Church.

We are profoundly grateful to all those who have helped in the writing of this book, either through conversation or through reading early drafts of chapters. Perhaps the best books are communal efforts, and this certainly feels like one. In particular, we'd like to thank the rest of the staff at Wycliffe, along with students past and present such as Matthew, Andrew, Helen, Robin, Roy, Paul, Penny and Steve. Friends in Jerusalem and elsewhere have made their contributions, such as Bill Broughton, Bishop Kenneth Cragg, David Gill, Steve Notley, Stephen Sizer and Bodil Skjott. Amy Boucher Pye and Elspeth Taylor of HarperCollins were always helpful and stimulated us to new ideas. Terry Clark graciously offered the use of his excellent photographs. Any opinions or remaining mistakes are, of course, ours not theirs.

Wycliffe Hall
Oxford

Pentecost 2000

THE PILGRIMS' TALE (1)

It was the badges that did it. Sarah had been looking forward to this moment ever since she'd signed her name on a cheque made out to 'Holytour Pilgrimages Ltd'. The airport looked clean, busy, efficient and she felt important and alive as she arranged her bags close together so she could keep an eye on them, and sat down on a grey-cushioned bench next to an escalator. Alongside her sat a suited businessman with shiny shoes, a teenage American complete with snowboard and baseball hat the wrong way round, and a tanned woman wearing a fur coat and reading an Italian newspaper. Out of the corner of her eye she saw a small group of people waiting quietly by the check-in desks, all wearing an identical orange badge. She looked down at the small orange disc pinned to her pullover, and yes, it was the same as theirs. A shiver of excitement ran through her as the realization sank in – she really was going to the Holy Land.

It was the badges that did it. As Tom wandered around the airport terminal, he began to notice a steadily growing number of slightly odd-looking people, all appearing lost, all wearing the same small orange badge. It dawned on him that he had seen a similar badge in the bottom of the envelope containing his flight tickets, itinerary and invitation to take out extra insurance. He had thrown it away, thinking it was a tacky 'free gift' from the tour company. 'What kind of sad people would choose to wear one of those?' he'd thought absently as it had dropped into the kitchen swing-bin. He'd always hated the idea of package tours. They raised memories in his mind of school trips to Brighton and flocks of sheep being harried by sheepdogs. Now, the awful truth settled in his mind. He was one of the badge-wearers. These were to be his companions for the next two weeks.

Resigned to his fate, Tom awkwardly tried to juggle his camera over one shoulder, swing a rucksack over the other, while picking up his black leather suitcase. He began to move slowly and reluctantly towards the badge-wearers. As if trying desperately to escape, he looked across to the large automatic sliding doors leading out of the airport lounge, anywhere but at the small gaggle of people by the check-in desk. Not looking where he was going, he instantly stumbled against someone, spilling his camera from his shoulder, sending it hurtling to the ground with a frightening smack.

'Sorry – I'm really sorry – I wasn't looking ...' he mumbled. She was a young woman, with fair shortish hair, clear skin, a pleasant eager smile, and a bright orange badge on her pullover.

'That's OK,' said Sarah, 'is your camera all right?'

'I guess so – at least I suppose I won't know until I try to use it,' Tom replied, turning it over in his hands ruefully. As he glanced at her, he was pleasantly surprised. His attitude to the badges was beginning to shift – almost imperceptibly, but a definite shift.

'Are you by any chance going to Israel?' he asked.

'Mmmm, yes, I am – how did you know?'

'Oh, just kind of ... guessed,' he lied.

'How about you, where are you going?'

Tom took a deep breath. 'Well, funnily enough, I'm going there too – are you with this Holytour Pilgrimages thing?'

'Yes!' Sarah broke into a broad smile. 'You mean we're on the same trip, how amazing! But where's your badge?'

'Oh, I'm afraid I, er ... lost it,' he lied for the second time in a minute.

They exchanged names, shook hands politely, and made their way together to the check-in desk. After they had seen their suitcases depart along the conveyor belt and been given their boarding passes, they still had an hour and a half until departure, so he offered to buy her a coffee. They walked towards the Expresso Hot Drinks bar in the corner of the lounge, Tom secretly relieved at this delay to the inevitable joining of the tour party.

'I've been looking forward to this so much – it's brilliant, isn't it?' Sarah started, when he returned to a table, bearing steaming coffee and two Danish pastries.

'Yes, I suppose so,' he added, without enthusiasm.

'Aren't you dying to get there?' she asked. He paused, staring at the swirling coffee as he slowly stirred it with a spoon.

'To be honest, no. I don't really know why I'm here – I'm not at all sure about this pilgrimage thing anyway. I have this friend called Barney, see? He goes to the same church as me. He persuaded me to go. Said it would be really good and build up my faith, all that sort of stuff. I had nowhere else to go on holiday this year, so I said I would. He had this brochure from Holytour Pilgrimages or whatever they're called. We paid the fare, then – wouldn't you know – last week he goes down with glandular fever and leaves me to go on my own.'

'Sorry about that,' Sarah added.

After a few moments' silence, Sarah felt the need to say something. 'Don't you think it will be great to see the places where Jesus walked, and where all those things in the Bible happened – you know – David and Goliath, walking on the water, the Resurrection?'

'Well, it would be OK if you knew where they actually happened,' replied Tom. 'But everyone knows it's all guesswork. No one knows for sure where Jesus did this or that. Anyway, it'll all be full of kitsch tourist junk, you know – they'll try to sell us Jesus table mats, electrically operated Virgin Marys. Wouldn't be surprised if someone tried to sell us St Paul's bedroom slippers.' Sarah narrowed her eyes and looked closely at him.

'Bit cynical, aren't you?' she asked.

'I'm sorry. I didn't mean to be cynical. I am a Christian, and I do believe it all, but I'm just not sure that I really need to go to Israel. Can't I believe it just as much by staying here? I mean, I've heard all kinds of stuff about how hardly anything looks like it did in Jesus' day. They've stuck ugly churches everywhere so you can't even imagine what it was like. All this pilgrimage nonsense went out with the Reformation anyway ...' He tailed off, embarrassed at being such a wet blanket, and yet also strangely wanting to make an impression.

'Well, I'm looking forward to it anyway,' Sarah countered. 'I just think it will, you know, make it seem more real. Someone in my church came back and said it was the best thing they'd ever done – they would never be the same again. I'm fairly new to all this. I've only been a Christian a year, but I suppose ever since I started reading the Bible, I've wanted to ... see it all, I suppose. I'm sort of hoping it will make me feel nearer to God.'

Tom was torn between going along with Sarah's eagerness, and his own scepticism. 'Yes, maybe you're right,' he sighed. Sensing a chink in his armour, she pressed on: 'Surely we'll ... feel God's presence a bit more. Maybe we'll be able to get closer to him. It must be easier to feel closer to Jesus in the place where he lived – it's hard sometimes to feel that here.' This was too much for Tom.

'You know that bit where Jesus says that it doesn't matter where you worship, in Samaria or Jerusalem, but that the important thing is to worship in spirit and truth?'

'Yes, I think so,' she answered, uncertain whether she did or not – it sounded vaguely familiar.

'Well, I just think if that's true, what's the point of going to Israel? I can worship him just as well at home, in spirit and truth. I can't see the point.'

Again, silence followed, as they both sipped coffee and took a bite of Danish pastry. She looked straight at him.

'If you're feeling that negative, why are you going then?' she asked quickly.

'Good question. Partly because I don't want to waste my money – if you cancel this late you don't get it back.' He wondered whether he should say the next bit. 'Maybe … well, maybe God wants me to go, somehow.'

'Just what I was thinking,' Sarah added with just a hint of triumph in her voice. 'These things don't just happen, you know. Maybe you're here for a reason. Maybe you need to learn something. And maybe God can't teach you in any other way than by going there.' She smiled at him over the top of his coffee cup. Despite himself, he smiled back.

'We'd better go and join the party. Thanks for the coffee,' Sarah said, as she rose, picking up her bag and striding off in the direction of the El Al desk. Tom followed meekly behind. She threw herself into the group, shook hands, introduced herself, smiled at everyone. Tom held back, stood just a few feet away – part, but not part of the group. The flight was called, the orange badges began to pick up hand luggage, press tickets into inside coat pockets, finger passports nervously. A dark-haired, slightly balding man in his fifties, wearing a dog-collar, brown shoes and a red anorak suddenly emerged from the middle of the group in front of them.

'Excuse me … Can you all listen, please? I'm Roger,

your tour leader,' he announced in a high-pitched voice. Tom's heart sank. 'That means I'll be looking after you during the trip. We'll have an American guide called Tony when we get there, but if you have any problems, please see me. I'm sure we'll have a wonderful time. Shall we pray before we go?' Tom cringed with embarrassment as the group bowed their heads in full view of the whole airport lounge, and Roger prayed a long and sentimental prayer about following in the footsteps of Jesus, journeying mercies and deep fellowship. After they all mumbled 'Amen', Sarah, who was standing next to him, glanced sideways, saw Tom's flushed and anguished face, and laughed: 'Come on, it can't possibly be that bad.'

As they were ushered through the departure lounge on to the plane, Tom tried to stay close to Sarah. She was the only one he knew, the only one who seemed vaguely normal. He could somehow let himself be carried along on the coat-tails of her enthusiasm, especially as he couldn't muster much of his own. Tom sat down, fastened his safety belt, picked out the in-flight magazine, flicked through it and found a feature on 'Israel – Land of the Bible'. It showed pictures of blue skies over the Sea of Galilee, narrow crowded streets in the Old City of Jerusalem, pilgrims praying in churches, Arab shepherds leading sheep over barren rocky hills. He returned it to the pocket in front of him, sat back in his seat and closed his eyes. He thought about his faith, how he would never dream of giving it up. He'd been a Christian for years, it was part of his life, church was woven into the fabric of his time, his friendships, his understanding of himself. Yet somehow lately it had become just a little stale. God seemed distant, irrelevant to his ordinary life, way off in heaven somewhere, and he could go for hours, days even, without seriously thinking about what God wanted of him. Perhaps Sarah was right. Perhaps his reluctance to go on this trip was something to do with his spiritual drifting, his inability to connect God with the rest of his life. Perhaps he was even afraid that this might happen. Perhaps the land of the Bible might just reconnect things for him.

Sarah looked out of the small aircraft window on to the tarmac, as the plane taxied to its runway. She thought back to the time a year or so ago, when a friend had invited her to a course on Christianity. She had gone along, intrigued but sceptical, and had gradually been convinced, not just by the arguments of the speakers, but by the quiet integrity and goodness she'd sensed in the people she met. Since then, this relationship with Jesus they'd talked about had become more and more important to her. By now she couldn't get enough, was bursting to know more, so the chance of a trip to the land where Jesus walked had been irresistible. Yet the conversation with Tom had unsettled her. She felt drawn to him, sorry for him even. He seemed to want to talk, but his hostility to the trip, and his many questions, had made her begin to wonder. Would she really meet Jesus in a new way in Israel? Would God become real to her, or would it all be a big let-down as Tom suspected it would? What would the land of the Bible mean for her?

As the plane stood at the end of the runway, the engines roared, the body of the plane straining like a huge dog waiting to be let off the lead. Suddenly brakes were disengaged, it gathered pace, passengers were pressed back into their seats as it raced down the runway. Inside, a host of emotions, hopes and fears jostled for attention in the minds of both Tom and Sarah, as the plane slowly took to the air – a small pocket of expectation destined for the Holy Land.

Part One

THE VITAL QUESTIONS

Christian Approaches to the Land

Chapter 1

PILGRIMS OR TOURISTS?

So, you're going to the Holy Land? Perhaps, like Sarah, you've booked to go, are eager to get the best out of your trip, and have picked up this book to help you prepare. Or maybe, like Tom, you have all kinds of questions about this 'pilgrimage' idea, are really not sure of the value of visiting the 'Holy Land', or don't know quite how a land can be 'holy' at all. Perhaps you've been to Israel, have come back with all kinds of questions about your experience. Now you want to think through what it all means, and how you can make sense of what you've seen. Perhaps you've never been, have never seen the point of going, and wonder what the fuss is about anyway?

Christians have been drawn to the land of the Bible ever since the time of Jesus himself. As we shall see, there is a long history of Sarahs and Toms, those who have travelled towards the land of Israel/Palestine with hope and anticipation, fear or suspicion. In making that journey, some Christians have seen themselves as pilgrims, some as crusaders, some as guests, some as tourists. Today, many go to the land to support the modern state of Israel; others are instinctively hostile to its policies towards the Palestinians. Can we make sense of this confusing mixture of motives and expectations? Can we develop a responsible, biblical and mature approach to pilgrimage today, aware of some of the abuses, yet alive to the possibilities? Can Tom overcome his doubts? Will Sarah's hopes come true?

On tours to the Holy Land, the authors have sometimes asked tour members whether they think of themselves as tourists or pilgrims. The question usually leads to furrowed brows and puzzled expressions. 'Would I describe myself as a tourist or a pilgrim? I guess something between the two,' said one. 'Certainly more than a tourist, but the idea of pilgrimage tends to conjure up the danger of venerating the site rather than the person of Jesus Christ and the God whom we worship.' 'I'm unhappy with the word "pilgrim", but can't think of a better term for it,' said another.

At the very least, these reactions remind us that pilgrimage is different from tourism. On most holidays, we are tourists, enjoying a place for its beauty, its restful qualities or historical significance. At other times, we travel not just out of idle curiosity, but out of a sense that some places have a deeper significance for us than others. They affect us at a much more profound level because they touch parts of our lives that are more sensitive, closer to the heart. When a war veteran visits the site of a battle in which many friends died, or a refugee returns to the village where she grew up after many years away, 'tourist' isn't really the word to use. 'Pilgrim' might be a better one.

When Christians visit the lands of the Bible, they approach the sites of events which to them are of more than passing historical interest. Christians look on the life of Jesus, his death and his resurrection not just as historical occurrences, but as episodes which have had a profound effect upon them. Calvary is not just the place where a rebellious Jewish rabbi happened to be executed along with many others somewhere in the 30s AD. It is the place where forgiveness and freedom were won for us. Visiting Calvary touches us at a deeper, spiritual level – it is not just part of history, it is also part of *our* story, the story of every Christian believer. It tells us who we are – someone deeply loved, forgiven and accepted by God. When we stand before the rock of Golgotha, or the tomb of Christ, we are not just tourists. We need a better word. Perhaps 'pilgrim' is as good as any.

Yet it will come as no surprise to discover that the whole idea of pilgrimage has been viewed with suspicion by large sections of the Christian Church. As Tom pointed out to Sarah, the idea of pilgrimage took a severe knock at the time of the Reformation in the sixteenth century. Some telling criticisms were made then, which need to be taken seriously as we begin to think of a responsible approach to the subject today. They might also help us spot the theological and spiritual pitfalls which await the unwary Christian traveller.

PILGRIMAGE IN THE MIDDLE AGES

Towards the end of the Middle Ages, pilgrimage to holy places was extremely popular. Tours were made not just to Jerusalem and the Holy Land, but also to sites of well-known miracles, or appearances of saints to ordinary believers. Pilgrims travelled miles across Europe and beyond to see, touch or even kiss bones, clothes or tufts of hair belonging to long-dead saints, as a sign of their devotion to God and a desire for his power.

In Wilsnack, near Berlin, in 1383, fire raged through one of the city churches. As the citizens picked their way through the charred remains, someone discovered a few 'hosts', pieces of communion bread which had not only miraculously survived the fire, but also now showed a drop of blood (Christ's blood, of course) in the centre of the wafer. In Regensburg, a demolition worker involved in the destruction of the synagogue in the city was injured by falling masonry. On touching a statue of the Virgin Mary, he was remarkably healed, and in the following years over two hundred miracles followed, associated in some way or other with the site. These two became huge centres of pilgrimage across Germany, so that when a shrine was opened in Regensburg in 1519, dedicated to the 'Fair Virgin of Regensburg', within a couple of years fifty thousand pilgrim's badges had been sold to visitors. At a similar shrine at the small Swiss town of Einsiedeln, reports said that a hundred and thirty thousand badges were sold in a fortnight during 1466. When you think that the total population of an average German city of the time was about ten thousand, that is big business!

It was precisely this kind of trade that drew the fire of reformers such as Martin Luther and John Calvin at the start of the sixteenth century. Right from the start, the movement they inspired, the Reformation, pursued a hostile campaign against pilgrimages as part of the whole system of human religious 'works' which were performed in some way or another to merit grace and salvation.

Luther's rediscovered doctrine of Justification by Faith proclaimed that people are brought into a right relationship with God ('justified') not on account of what they have done for him, but on account solely of what Christ has done for them. Reconciliation with God comes not through doing lots of religious things, but by a simple trust that, just as the Bible says, God justifies precisely those who know they don't deserve it. As a result, all these human 'works' – pilgrimages to holy places, having masses said for the soul, penitential acts, collecting mementoes or relics of the saints – were instantly rendered at best useless, at worst dangerous for true Christian life. As Luther saw it, the theology of his time gave people the impression that they could be justified by human activity and make some kind of contribution to the 'deal' whereby salvation was acquired. When tied in with this, the fashion for pilgrimage encouraged people to feel that by visiting holy places, they were somehow doing something meritorious before God. Luther was afraid that it was encouraging people to trust for their salvation in possession of a pilgrim's badge.

Calvin also thought that pilgrimage was something which had thankfully been left behind with the rest of the old Church. Under the papacy, he wrote, we Christians were 'running about in all directions, and wearying ourselves with long and toilsome pilgrimages to various saints' (*Commentary on Isaiah*, 30.6).

In the light of the reformers' critique of pilgrimage, many biblical Christians today inherit this same suspicion of the idea of pilgrimage to places which are thought to be more holy than other places. After all, didn't Jesus say (as Tom knew well) that it doesn't matter whether we worship in Samaria or in Jerusalem; all that matters is that we worship in spirit and truth (John 4:20–4)? How then can Christians who wish to be faithful to the Bible, and perhaps also the Reformation heritage, approach the idea of pilgrimage? Can there be such a thing as a 'holy place'? Should pilgrimage be consigned to the garbage-heap of church history along with indulgences, inquisitions and hairshirts?

REVISITING THE REFORMATION

In 1520, as the debate over his theology was gathering steam across Europe's universities and episcopal palaces, Martin Luther wrote an open letter to the political leaders of the Germans, entitled 'To the Christian Nobility of the German Nation'. In it, he voiced his opposition to contemporary pilgrimages. He put forward two main reasons why he thought they should be discouraged. A decade before, as an obscure Augustinian monk, Luther had visited Rome on a small business errand connected with his monastic order. He later spoke of his disillusionment with the corruption and irreverence he found there. This experience seems to have coloured his attitude to the practice: 'At Rome, men do not find a good example, only pure scandal.' More often than not in Luther's eyes, pilgrimage to Rome did more harm than good, when visitors actually saw what a decadent, degenerate and dirty place the medieval city was. Besides this, Luther complained that people tended to think that a pilgrimage earned extra credit in the eyes of God, as an especially pious and prestigious act, a sign of being really serious about God and religion. To him it seemed that people were spending small fortunes on trips to holy places, while leaving their families and neighbours cold and hungry at home. God's clear command to care for neighbours and family was being ignored in favour of a spurious and expensive spiritual exercise which God never told us to engage in.

A few months later, Luther expanded on this theme in another important treatise, known as 'The Babylonian Captivity of the Church'. The work was essentially a manifesto for reform, with detailed proposals of what needed to be done radically to rebuild the church. Included within this was the startling proposal that all places of pilgrimage such as the shrines at Regensburg and Wilsnack should simply be demolished. Luther utters his common complaint that this is just a money-making scam, a means of fleecing the pockets of poor pilgrims by avaricious clerics. Yet he has a deeper reason for objecting to the whole pilgrimage industry of his time. As usual, it is best to let Luther speak for himself:

> let every man stay in his own parish; there he will find more than in all the shrines, even if they were all rolled into one. In your own parish you find baptism, the sacrament, preaching and your neighbour, and these things are greater than all the saints in heaven ... Let him stay at home in his own parish church and be content with the best; his baptism, the gospel, his faith, his Christ, and his God, who is the same God everywhere. (*Address to the Christian Nobility*)

Luther objects to pilgrimages because they detract from the crucial importance of the local community of believers, as the place in which the Christian life is to be lived out. They encourage Christians to become dissatisfied with the channels of grace God has provided in every local church, (the Bible, the sacraments, Christian teaching, and of course other people,) which in fact make up all the ingredients needed to live the Christian life. Pilgrimages encourage the feeling that these are somehow not enough, that unless the sinner goes on pilgrimage to collect his pilgrim's badge, he or she will somehow be missing something important when it comes to the judgement day.

Despite his doubts about pilgrimage, however, Luther doesn't disallow it altogether. He concedes that there may be good reasons for going on pilgrimage, and recommends that the aspiring pilgrim should ask the advice of his local priest or master. To go on pilgrimage out of curiosity 'to see other lands and cities' is not discouraged; Luther is dubious about them 'not because pilgrimages are bad, but because they are ill-advised at this time'.

Calvin's critique was directed more against the idea of holy things than against pilgrimages as such. In his *Treatise on Relics*, he pours ridicule upon the veneration for St Peter's slippers, the shoulder-bone of St Paul or the three different bodies of Lazarus available to pilgrims in different places. For him, the trade in 'holy things' is based on a pernicious mixture of duplicity and credulity. However, Calvin too has a deeper objection:

> Now, the origin and root of this evil, has been, that, instead of discerning Jesus Christ in his Word, his Sacraments, and his Spiritual Graces, the world has, according to its custom, amused itself with his clothes, shirts, and sheets, leaving thus the principal to follow the accessory. (*Treatise on Relics*)

His fear is that a preoccupation with trivia will lead to the worship of trivia, rather than adoration of the true God. Subtly but inevitably, they will deflect attention away from Christ himself, and the places where he can really be found ('his Word, his Sacraments, and his Spiritual Graces'), on to things which once had some kind of association with him or his followers.

On closer inspection, then, it appears that the reformers had four major objections to pilgrimage. The first was connected to the tendency to see pilgrimage as a necessary 'work' which somehow contributed towards one's salvation. Too often, late medieval Christians went on pilgrimage to a holy place thinking that in some way their salvation depended upon it, that it made it more likely that God would have mercy on them. For the reformers this made pilgrimages part of the problem rather than the solution for the late medieval church. For them, salvation starts when we stop trying to do things to impress God, and simply trust his Word which promises forgiveness and mercy, a quite basic point which large parts of the late medieval church had forgotten.

The second objection was a matter of economic justice. Far too often, unscrupulous clerics or greedy businessmen on the lookout for a quick profit had exploited the piety, or naïveté, of innocent believers. Money was being thrown away on the pilgrimage industry rather than spent on the more godly tasks of caring for the poor or family members.

Beyond this lay a third concern, the tendency of pilgrimage to holy places and holy things to lead people away from the local church and the rich resources for salvation God had provided there.

A fourth objection was that pilgrimage led people to worship the wrong things. It led more often than not to a concentration on trivia, the worship of objects rather than of the Living God, the creation, not the Creator. Yet it is significant that despite being profoundly aware of these dangers, still the reformers did not in principle rule out pilgrimage as such. Is it possible then to reconstruct an approach to pilgrimage which avoids these four pitfalls?

REVISITING PILGRIMAGE

Pilgrimage was indelibly associated in the reformers' minds with the attempt to win God's favour. As such, it was futile, or even fraught with spiritual danger, encouraging Christians to trust in their own religiosity rather than in the mercy of God. This first point is quite simple, and needs to be remembered by every visitor to the Holy Land. If you think that somehow God will think more of you for going, or less of you for not going, then for God's sake, and your own, stay at home. An Israeli stamp in your passport may get you into the land of Israel, but it is of no use at all at the gates of heaven. God does not make a favourite of the person who has lots of religious credit points in their spiritual *curriculum vitae*. As the reformers insisted, God justifies not the godly, but the ungodly; not those who have done their best, but those who know they have *not* done their best; not those who trust in their religious activity to curry favour with God, but those who trust in God's willingness to forgive the sinful. This is basic teaching which we need to get clear in our heads before any pilgrimage, or indeed any spiritual activity – it is the source of spiritual contentment and joy, and forgetting it leads to anxiety, self-absorption and a very fretful life.

In many religions of the world, pilgrimage is pretty well obligatory. Every adult Muslim, for example, is expected to undertake the 'Hajj' or pilgrimage to Mecca. Many pilgrims battle through unbearable heat to arrive at Mecca in time for the holy season of Ramadan: some go for sacred studies, some to die in the holy city. In Hinduism, the Upanishads regard pilgrimage as a means of obtaining merit or spiritual gain – to die in sight of the river Ganges is to attain release from the cycle of reincarnation. Some forms of Christianity have approached this level of expectation of pilgrimage to Jerusalem, yet it is hard to justify such a demand from the New Testament. Christian pilgrimage may be helpful, but it certainly isn't compulsory.

Having said all this, it is quite possible (after all, millions of Christians do it every year) to visit the sites of the events of the Bible without a sense that this is in any way necessary for salvation. The reformers' critique of pilgrimage is directed against the abuse of the practice rather than the practice itself. Naturally, if it's not there to impress God, we still need to ask why do it anyway, but we're coming to that!

Second, pilgrimage was, and still is, open to exploitation. Mark Twain, after his visit to the Holy Land, admitted it wasn't all it was cracked up to be. In fact much of his experience was downright miserable. He wrote of how the visitor's 'life is almost badgered out of him by importunate swarms of beggars and pedlars, who hang on the strings to one's sleeves and coat-tails, and shriek and shout in his ears ...' Not a lot has changed. One of the authors, on a visit to the church of the Holy Sepulchre in Jerusalem, while walking behind the 'edicule', the construction built over the site of the tomb of Christ, was beckoned in conspiratorial tones by an old Coptic cleric: 'You want to see the real rock of the tomb of Christ?' Knowing the original rock itself was hidden underneath the edicule, he was intrigued, and showed cautious interest. The monk led him towards a corner of the edicule, and lifting a curtain which hid a small piece of rough stone, 'You touch!' he ordered, as he grabbed his hand and led it towards the rock itself. Then came the sting. 'Two shekels!' he announced, still holding his arm in a vice-like grip, determined not to let go until the price was exacted.

Perhaps such things have always been present. Perhaps it was a right and proper redistribution of wealth from the

West to the East – the monk looked like he needed the two shekels more than this relatively well-off westerner. Perhaps it was a deserved slap on the wrist for letting curiosity run too far. Yet inevitably we feel something is wrong when other people's religious desires or motivations are used for selfish financial ends. Such an experience leaves you feeling cheated and cheapened, as if something important has been defiled. Visitors to the Holy Land need a healthy dose of scepticism about some of the things they are shown, and it is often difficult to distinguish between genuine pilgrimage and the money-making industry which surrounds it. Yet such abuse is strictly speaking a parasite on pilgrimage, not essential to it. With a proper sense of proportion and keeping a critical eye out for religious kitsch, it is possible to avoid the spurious industry surrounding the pilgrimage or tourist trade. Just because some exploit it for their own ends does not mean pilgrimage in itself is inherently wrong, any more than buying a used car is forbidden because there are many disreputable used-car salesmen around.

Third, pilgrimage can lead to a dissatisfaction with the ordinary local church with all its quirks and frustrations. Many a congregation has sent their minister off on a sabbatical trip to the Holy Land, hoping it would liven up his ministry, only to endure for years afterwards sermons liberally laced with stories which begin with the inevitable line 'When I was in the Holy Land ...' Used sparingly, such stories can be useful, but they can subtly convey the impression that you can't *really* understand the Bible unless you've been to Israel, and that life back at home is a disappointing anticlimax. Calvin's and Luther's reminders to us are wise: God has given all we need for living the Christian life in the local church. The Holy Spirit is there to transform, the Bible to teach, the sacraments to embody God's Word and presence, and our neighbour is there to love and care for.

Pilgrimage is no more necessary for living the Christian life than it is necessary for salvation. In terms of salvation, like any other human activity, it is strictly speaking irrelevant. Yet in terms of the Christian life, while not necessary, it might still be helpful and beneficial, in the same way that singing hymns or going to a Bible study or to a Christian festival or retreat centre is not necessary for salvation, but may still be a help and encouragement in living as a Christian. In a later chapter, we will show how a trip to visit the sites of Jesus' life, death and resurrection can send us home with a greater sense of God's presence and reality everywhere, especially back at home, than we ever had before. In fact, one of the tests of whether pilgrimage is undertaken in the right spirit or not is whether or not it enhances an appreciation of God's provision for our needs and his nearness at all times and in all places. Holidays often leave us feeling flat when we return, far from the beach, the mountains, the relaxed leisurely sense of being away from home. A good 'biblical pilgrimage', if we can call it that, sends you back eager to encounter the God who promises to be present and near wherever we are, with a heightened sense that he is with us wherever we go.

Fourth, and perhaps most importantly, is pilgrimage synonymous with idolatry? Does it necessarily lead to the worship of things rather than God? Calvin wasn't the only one to sense this danger. People like Tom sometimes think the idea of pilgrimage carries within it, like a virus, the danger of venerating the place, rather than the God who was once revealed there. Naturally, this is a real concern, and it's quite possible for the natural interest in sites, stones and archaeology to deflect attention from the real point of the trip.

On his visit to Palestine, Mark Twain complained: 'wherever they ferret out a lost locality made holy by some scriptural event, they straightway build a massive – almost imperishable – church there, and preserve the locality for the gratification of future generations'. Especially for Protestants, used to simple church architecture and fostering a suspicion of images and ornamentation, the style of building found on 'holy sites' in Israel can be off-putting. Even those used to such decorative styles can be disappointed to find that the sites look nothing like what was imagined, or even what they would have looked like in Bible times. Jerusalem has been destroyed and rebuilt so often over the years, that it is estimated that present-day street levels are roughly six or seven metres above the level on which Jesus and his contemporaries would have walked.

Added to that are the churches. The Holy Sepulchre in Jerusalem might well mark the exact spot where Jesus died and was buried, but it looks nothing like it today. Many a visitor has felt profoundly let down by what appears to western eyes as a gaudy, over-ornate mess surrounding the site of the crucifixion and resurrection. It's common then to retreat thankfully to the Garden Tomb, which although a much more recent claimant as the site of the events of Easter weekend, at least looks roughly how it might have looked in the first century. It's a relief to find that in Galilee, the lake and the surrounding hills can't have changed that much over two millennia. Yet even here, the supposed sites of the feeding of the five thousand, the appearance to Peter by the lakeside, and the Mount where the Sermon was preached, all have large sturdy churches erected on them. For many, this habit of slapping a church on any possible holy site lessens the imaginative impact of being in the very places where these events occurred. So what are we to make of this tendency to identify the 'exact spot', and rapidly build a church on it?

There are many ways of celebrating something. Some people like to celebrate special days (for example birthdays) with elaborate parties, decoration and colour, some with fine food, wine and tasteful music, others with delicate simplicity and minimum fuss. What do you do with a special place? Take for example the place where many believe the salvation of the world was enacted, the site of Jesus' cross and tomb. Once you have identified a probable site (which is roughly what happened in the fourth century) then what do you do with it? Most western visitors to the Holy Land might have wished that they had done nothing. Leave it as it is, preserve the site as it originally appeared, so we can in our imagination drift back to recall the agony of Good Friday and the joy of Easter Day as if we were there. Nineteenth-century European visitors to Jerusalem, such as Edward Robinson and General Gordon, were not as a rule impressed by the dilapidated Holy Sepulchre. When a location to the north of the city was discovered which contained some early tombs and whose rock formations looked like a skull, they did just what *we* might expect. They (and those who have looked after the Garden Tomb since then) tried to preserve the site as a garden, as it might have looked on the day Mary, Joanna and James' mother crept in solemnly to anoint Jesus' body for burial, only to find events had overtaken them. As a result, western visitors often find the Garden Tomb more appealing and spiritually more refreshing than the Holy Sepulchre, despite the latter's longer claim to be the exact location.

But it's important to realize that much of this is simply a matter of taste and culture, rather than anything objective and inherently superior. Another way to celebrate the importance of these events, and this, it seems, is the way more favoured in eastern Christendom, is to mark the place as special by decorating it, making it seem grand and important, making a fuss of it. If this is the place where our salvation was won, it deserves to be celebrated with gold, silver, jewels and imposing buildings, in other words with the best we can offer. In fact, those who built a church over the traditional site of Calvary and the tomb of Christ didn't have the choice of leaving it as it was. It had already been irrevocably changed – the emperor Hadrian had built a pagan temple to the god Jupiter over it, which itself had to be demolished first.

The resulting decoration of the site may not be to the taste of western Protestant Christians, but the habit of covering sites with ornate ecclesiastical decoration is by no means intended to trivialize or destroy them – exactly the reverse. It is intended to mark the spot as special, as a place where God touched the earth through his Son Jesus, or through his great acts recorded in Scripture. The early Christians who built these 'basilicas' thought these events were not just normal events. Jesus' birth was not like other births, his death not like other deaths. These locations marked the site of the birth and death of God's royal King. So they wanted to make these places look not just like any old site, but to mark them as unique and striking to the visitor. The result may not always be to our taste, but we should at least recognize the motivation as genuine and respect it for what it is. The Christians who decorated these sites were not trying to encourage idolatry, but simply to mark as special the places where the events of their salvation had taken place. We will revisit this important question later in more detail.

There are dangers in every truly Christian activity. Personal prayer can be distorted into a purely private relationship with God which dispenses with the need for Christian fellowship. Evangelism can become a manipulative means of demeaning and dominating other people. Pilgrimage too has its dangers, and the reformers' critique should make us cautious. They helped clear out of the way a load of junk which had become attached to the practice of pilgrimage over the years. They also alert us to some of the dangers into which the unsuspecting Christian might fall, even today. They remind us of the central and indispensable place of the local church in God's purposes, in which God has given us all the things we need. It raises big questions about pilgrimage to locations of supposed miracles not connected with the Bible. Yet the critique stops short of a total rejection of pilgrimage to the land of the Bible, and we have seen how the dangers do not necessarily negate the benefits. The task still remains, however, of constructing a thoughtful biblical theology of pilgrimage. We too need to ask the questions Tom and Sarah did – what exactly do we think we are doing when we step on a plane to fly to Israel as Christian visitors?

To do that, we need to go back to the Bible itself. The Bible has a lot to say about the promised land, Jerusalem and the Temple. What difference has the coming of Jesus made to all this? How does the New Testament view 'holy places' and the 'Holy Land'? And what does that mean for our understanding of pilgrimage today? The next chapters try to answer these very questions.

Chapter 2

JESUS – THE TRUE HOLY PLACE?

Not everyone in the city was happy. When Jesus entered Jerusalem, he caused quite a stir. Making straight for the Temple precincts, he set about overturning the tables of the moneychangers. It was a deliberately provocative act by which Jesus intended to bring his ministry to a climax. It was designed to send a powerful message to the Temple authorities and to the Passover pilgrims. It showed Jesus' protest at some of what was going on in the Temple courts. It also revealed Jesus' understanding of his own Messianic authority.

It is also a key event for us as we consider how the Bible sees holy places. For this was the moment when the Holy One himself went into Jerusalem's most holy place, announcing that God was now doing a new thing. What was that new thing? Who exactly was Jesus? And how might this affect our view of holy places?

JESUS AND THE TEMPLE

This so-called 'cleansing of the Temple' is widely recognized as one of the key episodes which triggered Jesus' subsequent crucifixion. All the Gospel writers record it

(Mark 11:15–17; Luke 19:45–6; Matthew 21:12ff) and John even brings it deliberately to near the very beginning of his Gospel (John 2:13–22), so that his readers can understand from the outset just who this Jesus is. Here we get a vital clue as to the identity and purpose of Jesus.

The Temple cleansing: a sign of the end

But what was Jesus saying in this prophetic act? Was he just correcting a few financial misdemeanours? Did the Temple authorities simply need to 'get their house in order'? Mark makes plain that there was more to it than this. In his account he sandwiches the cleansing between Jesus' act of cursing the fig-tree and his explanation of that act. This cursing was itself another powerful prophetic piece. And why did Jesus do it? To show that his coming to the Temple was like an owner coming to his garden in search of fruit. When he found it was barren and lacking in fruit, there would indeed be dire consequences.

Jesus' overturning of the tables was a 'portent of destruction', a sure sign of what now lay in store for the Temple. And if there was any doubt about this, Jesus soon spelt it out explicitly: 'not one stone', he told his bewildered disciples, 'would be left upon another' (Mark 13:2). Here evidently was a 'holy place' that had gone sadly wrong.

Jesus: the ultimate sacrifice, the divine presence

Yet there was more. When the apostles looked back on this event, they could see further layers of significance. For a start, the Temple was the divinely instituted place of *sacrifice,* the place where God's people could be assured of being forgiven. But a few days later Jesus would offer up his own life to death, and very soon his followers were seeing *this* instead as the ultimate sacrifice. The cross, not the Temple, now became the means whereby Jesus' followers could approach God with confidence.

If so, then Jesus' overturning of the tables pointed forward to a time when the whole sacrificial system, divinely ordained as it was, would no longer be necessary. What had been enacted for centuries in the Holy of Holies on the eastern hill within the city would soon be fulfilled by the giving of Jesus' own life on another hill just to the north-west of the city. Jesus' death would bring to an end the need for the Temple sacrifices. No wonder the Temple curtain was torn in two when he died (Mark 15:38). Moreover, Jesus had already claimed the astonishing right to forgive people's sins (Mark 2:10). Now he made it clear what that meant for Jerusalem's Temple. He himself was operating a kind of one-man counter-Temple movement. So inevitably there would be a clash once he actually arrived in Jerusalem.

The Temple, however, was also the place of God's divine *presence*. In the Old Testament this was the dwelling-place for God's Name (Deuteronomy 12:5; 1 Kings 8:29), the place of his divine 'glory' or *shekinah.* Years before, in 587 BC, Ezekiel in his prophetic vision had seen this *shekinah* depart from the Temple at the time of its first destruction (Ezekiel 11:23). So there was some debate in Jesus' day as to whether the divine presence had ever fully returned. Yet that remained a guiding concept – this was the place where, if anywhere, Israel's God had made his dwelling.

Seen in this light, Jesus' words take on a powerful new meaning. When questioned by what authority he had performed this radical demonstration, he enigmatically replied: 'Destroy this temple, and I will raise it again in three days' (John 2:18–19). It made little sense at the time. Yes, the Messiah was expected to restore or rebuild the Temple: was this what Jesus was meaning? Or was he claiming that he himself could single-handedly bring about the overthrow of this massive Herodian construction? That, at least, seems to have been what some people thought later at his trial (Mark 14:58).

But John tells us there was something deeper still: 'the temple he had spoken of *was his body*. After he was raised from the dead, his disciples recalled what he had said' (John 2:21–2). For John, Jesus was taking this opportunity of standing in the Temple to point to the existence of another, greater Temple – himself, his own body. So another reason why that physical Temple was soon to be destroyed was because a rival Temple had appeared on the scene. Jesus himself was that Temple. He too was about to be destroyed, but for him, unlike the physical Temple, there would be a restoration or resurrection 'in three days'.

Jesus: the true Temple and 'holy place'

It is a mind-blowing claim – sheer madness, unless it happened to be true. But John gives it a high priority in his Gospel so that his readers get the point. If previously the Temple had been the place of God's dwelling on earth, that place was now Jesus. Jesus was the embodiment of Israel's God. He was, as it were, God on earth – or, as expressed in later terminology, 'God incarnate'.

And if we doubt what John meant, we simply turn back to John 1:14: 'The Word became flesh [incarnate] and made his dwelling among us. We have seen his glory, the glory of the One and Only, who came from the Father, full of grace and truth.' When John spoke here of the Word 'dwelling' he actually used the word 'tabernacled'. This was a deliberate reference to God's presence in the wilderness tabernacle (or Tent of Meeting) which then continued in the *shekinah* presence located in the Temple. In other words, John has taken this long-established notion of God's dwelling in his Temple, and said that Jesus now is that Temple. It is an authentically Jewish way of making the claim that Jesus is God's divine presence on earth. Or, if you prefer, Jesus is the most 'holy place'.

John is not alone in making this remarkable claim for the person of Jesus. The other Gospel writers clearly have the same thought in mind when they recount the irony of people mocking Jesus on the cross: 'so, you are going to destroy the Temple and build it in three days' (Mark 15:29). Yes he would, but it would be a different Temple – his own body, raised on the third day. Matthew goes further, recounting (12:6, 42) Jesus' claim to be 'one greater than the Temple' and 'one greater than Solomon' (the builder of the first Temple). Paul declares that 'in Christ all the fullness of the Deity lives in bodily form' (Colossians 2:9). And in the penultimate chapter of the New Testament we learn that the New Jerusalem seen in John's vision has no temple, 'because the Lord God Almighty and the Lamb are its temple' (Revelation 21:22). Though in a different context, the same claim is being made: Jesus, the Lamb who died, is also the true Temple of God, the ultimate 'holy place'.

The implications: Temple, Church and 'holy places'

So within the New Testament Jesus himself is portrayed as the true Temple. This solid conviction would then have major repercussions for the way Christians regarded Jerusalem's Temple. They might use it for a while for preaching the message about Jesus the Messiah, but increasingly they saw it as theologically redundant. The reality of God's presence and the true place of sacrifice had now been revealed in Jesus and his death. This is expounded in most detail by the author of Hebrews, who writes to some Jewish Christians to ensure that they do not lapse into their former ways of viewing the Temple. 'Jesus has appeared once for all at the end of the age to put away sin by the sacrifice of himself'; so we can enter the heavenly sanctuary 'by the new and living way' he has opened up for us. The Temple as part of the old covenant is 'close to destruction', but Christians have, as it were, a quite different 'altar' through which they can now approach God (Hebrews 9:26; 10:20; 8:13; 13:10; see further Walker, *Jesus and the Holy City*, ch. 6). No doubt this was all very surprising. Presumably they had expected the Old Testament pattern to be continued in a straightforward, 'literalistic' way. But now they were convinced that Jesus was the true fulfilment and goal of the Temple.

It would also enormously transform their understanding of the Church. If Christ was the true Temple, then by extension those who believed in him could be considered as 'God's Temple' (1 Corinthians 3:16–17). Those who came to him were 'like living stones being built into a spiritual house to be a holy priesthood, offering spiritual sacrifices acceptable to God through Jesus Christ' (1 Peter 2:5).

But for our purposes this teaching is also vital, because it is the New Testament's starting point for any discussion about 'holy places'. Are there any such places now? What do we mean by that term? All such questions must be answered by remembering this key biblical conviction: Jesus is the true holy place.

NEW TESTAMENT CONCERNS

If we are seeking the presence of God, we will find it in Jesus. So if anyone thinks a 'holy place' provides a distinctive means of approaching God, or is a place where God is somehow more present than elsewhere, then there would be New Testament grounds for questioning that claim.

John's Gospel: holy places and spiritual worship

Intriguingly, the apostle John seems to portray Jesus as the true holy place precisely in order to contradict any such false notions. As W.D. Davies noted in *The Gospel and the*

Land, the opening chapters of John's Gospel can be read as a salvo against any false ideas concerning 'holy places'.

For example, Jacob's ladder had been associated with Bethel (the 'house of God': Genesis 28:11ff). But now Jesus' disciples will see 'heaven open, and the angels of God ascending and descending on the Son of Man' (John 1:51). Bethel is not the place from which to gain access to God: Jesus is. And in the passage Tom quoted at Sarah, the Samaritan woman is told not to get hung up about whether Mount Gerizim or the Jerusalem Temple is the true 'holy place' – the 'place where we must worship'. Jesus responds to her, 'you will worship the Father neither on this mountain nor in Jerusalem. God is spirit, and his worshippers must worship in spirit and in truth' (John 4:20–4). In other words, now that Jesus has come, any previous focus on particular 'holy places' (be they Bethel, Gerizim, the Temple or wherever) is no longer valid or appropriate. These have been fulfilled in Jesus. He is the reality to which they point.

In fact this passage in John 4 becomes the key New Testament text which relates to our particular concern. It lays down clearly the essence of true worship – what it is that 'the Father seeks' from us (v. 23). God is not an idol, nor ultimately located in any fixed building or place, but rather 'is spirit'. Our response, therefore, is not determined by geography but is rather an 'affair of the heart' – we must worship 'in spirit'. This does not mean we cannot use physical places to aid our worship. But such physical trappings are essentially secondary and any theology which gives an implicit priority to particular places or objects runs the risk of inverting God's intention for true worship.

Jesus and the Holy Spirit are not confined to particular places. As John recorded these words, he knew of the remarkable spread of the Christian gospel far away from its original homeland. Jesus had spoken these words by a well in the middle of Samaria, but now there were people throughout the empire and beyond who were worshipping the God of Israel through this same Jesus. How could they do so? Precisely because of the gift of his Spirit.

If the Spirit had not been given, then access to Jesus (himself the way to the Father) would have been restricted to those in the immediate vicinity of Jesus. But now this 'apostolic monopoly' was broken. There was no longer any necessity of being in the very places associated with Jesus' physical presence. Now that the Spirit had been given, every believer could meet with Christ personally – even those who had never seen him. 'Blessed', said Jesus, 'are those who have not seen and yet have believed' (John 20:29). In a similar vein, the apostle Peter could speak with amazement of the believers scattered through what is now Turkey: 'without having seen him, you love him!' (1 Peter 1:8).

The Universal Christ: known through his Spirit and Word

So physical distance from Jerusalem is no problem, because Christ is now a living reality, knowable throughout the world by his Spirit. In a profound sense, he is everywhere. No one need be debarred for reasons of geography. No special privilege adheres to those resident in or visiting the Holy Land. Christ can be just as near and real to those in far-flung lands, because he is no longer bound to any one place. This is an amazing aspect of the Christian gospel, too easily taken for granted. And it is an aspect which must not be subtly compromised by any implication that God is nearer or somehow more accessible in one particular location when compared with another – be it the Holy Land or any other supposed holy place.

In that sense New Testament worship is non-territorial. There are no holy places because Christ alone is that holy place which provides access to God. There is a profound 'desacralization of place'. Or, if that suggests to anyone a secularization of the geographical world, one might equally say that *every* place is a holy place – but only if this means that God can be encountered and worshipped in any place by those who worship him in spirit and in truth, through Jesus and the Spirit. Every place can be a holy place, if it is the place where God is worshipped.

So one of the overriding emphases of the New Testament is that, precisely because of what God has done for us through Jesus in Jerusalem, God is no longer place-bound. Before Jesus' coming, there had been a necessary focus on a particular area of the world, but no more. Instead, the New Testament emphasizes the universal availability of Christ – his total accessibility to those who come to him in faith. There are no second-class citizens; believers have all come 'to fullness of life in him' (Colossians 2:10). No one has greater access to him by reason of birth, nationality or geography. So the promise of salvation, as Peter declares right at the outset, is both for those who are near and 'for those *who are far off,* all those whom the Lord our God calls to him' (Acts 2:39; cf. Ephesians 2:13). It does not matter where you are, whether in Jerusalem, Colossae or Spain. There is only one essential place to be – in Christ.

But how do individuals gain this access to Christ? In the first instance it is through responding in faith to God's Word. 'How are people to believe in him of whom they have not heard?' asks Paul. 'So faith comes from what is heard, and what is heard comes by the preaching of Christ' (Romans 10:14–17; cf. 1 Peter 1:23–5). It is the proclamation of Christ which leads to faith in him, and the divine response is the bestowal of the Spirit of Christ (Romans 8:9b). And after that, how is this relationship with Christ sustained? It is through the Word of God, as it comes to us in its various forms, in preaching, in sacraments, through Bible study, through the godly wisdom of other Christians, the many ways in which we let the 'word of Christ dwell in us richly' (Colossians 3:16). The Good Shepherd continues to speak to his sheep and they must follow their master's voice (John 10:16). If we wish to abide in Christ, not losing that privileged access, we must 'keep his commandments'; 'you will be my disciples', Jesus had said, only 'if you abide in me, and *my words* abide in you' (John 15:7–9). Access to this universal Christ is thus made possible by the gift of the Spirit of Christ as we respond in faith to the word of Christ.

In an important sense, therefore, geography ceases to be relevant. As we saw Luther pointing out in the last chapter, the resources necessary for conducting the Christian life and enjoying God's presence are now freely available throughout the world. The fundamental way we encounter God remains constant regardless of location – namely by God's Spirit at work within us and through our increased obedience to his Word. So we must reject any idea that any particular place can somehow by itself become a new vehicle for the channelling of God's grace and blessing. That indeed would be a form of place-idolatry.

So, when examined, the New Testament does have some important things to say about how we might view the 'holy places' of the Bible. Before asking what this means for us as we visit the places associated with the life of Jesus, it is worth noting three more general emphases within the New Testament which might help us to view these places in an appropriate way.

Three priorities: The exalted Christ, the cross and the gospel

First, concerning *the person of Jesus*. Here the primary New Testament emphasis is upon the risen and exalted Christ, rather than on the historical Jesus. 'Seek the things that are above, where Christ is now seated at the right hand of God' (Colossians 3:1). The New Testament has a bedrock conviction that Jesus' life did not terminate in the cul-de-sac of a Palestinian grave. His life history moved on to include his powerful Resurrection and glorious Ascension. So where is he now? Not in Jerusalem, but in heaven. And the New Testament is shot through with this vision of the glorified Christ – the one who has been here but is so no more, the 'Lamb upon the throne', the one who will return in great glory (e.g. 1 Thessalonians 1:10; Revelation 5:6). 'If once we regarded Christ from a human point of view, we regard him thus no longer' (2 Corinthians 5:16).

This would then explain why the earliest Christians seem to have been little concerned about visiting the places of Jesus. Of course, the historical Jesus remained vitally important. There are, after all, four Gospels given over to recounting his life. His story is rooted in history. But it did not end there. Our ultimate focus must rest on the risen and ascended Christ. Any interest in the places of Jesus must not shift this primary focus.

A second question concerns the role of the *Incarnation* within the New Testament. For our attitude to the places of Jesus will inevitably be affected by the way we view God's coming into human history in Jesus Christ.

Clearly the Incarnation is vital within New Testament thought, but it leads up to the climax of the story, God's work of redemption and salvation, focused in the cross and resurrection of Jesus. Christmas is wonderful, but it is only the beginning of the story, a story which climaxes at Easter. Bethlehem is important, but Calvary is central. Incarnation reveals to us what God is like, atonement tells us how God rescues us. Hence the frequent references to Jesus' 'blood' and to his death for us on the cross (John 1:29; 1 John 4:10; 1 Peter 2:24; Hebrews 7–10; Romans 3:24; 5:6 etc.). Any focusing on the places of Jesus would need to ensure that this New Testament priority was not lost. If the Incarnation on its own does not save anyone, how much less the places of the Incarnation! The centrality of the cross must be preserved, and our evident need not just for revelation but for redemption.

Finally, the general dynamic of the New Testament is outward-looking. Its prime concern is the spread of the gospel and *mission*. Its direction is centrifugal, not centripetal, as the gospel message goes out to the world. The general pattern is out *from* Jerusalem, not back towards it (Acts 1:8). So one does not sense that the early Christians were continually harking back to the land of Palestine. Mission and outreach are primary, spreading the good news of Jesus to 'all the earth'. So something is amiss if our focus on the places of Jesus becomes vaguely nostalgic; and especially if they somehow encourage a mentality where the concerns of mission are drowned.

So in each of these three areas, we can sense that the primary focus of the New Testament lies elsewhere. We are to look *up* believing in the exaltation of Christ. We are to look *back* rejoicing in the cross of Christ. And we are to look *outwards* spreading the gospel of Christ. But does that mean then that we should have no interest whatsoever in the places of the Gospels? Not necessarily. It may all be a matter of priorities.

APPROACHING THE PLACES OF THE BIBLE

How then are we to view the places associated with the life of Jesus? Before we can consider this, we need to ponder another problem: what if the designated place is now not thought to be the authentic site? Does this affect its supposed holiness?

When you visit a 'holy site', looking for the exact spot, if you are at all like Tom, you will be unable to rid yourself of the nagging doubt that no matter what the guidebooks say, they might have got it wrong. It's one thing to be told these events really happened, quite another to be told that we know exactly *where* they happened (whether it's Elijah's cave, Zacchaeus' tree, the site of the transfiguration, or the place of Jesus' ascension). How do we know? Did someone chalk the spot immediately for future reference?

Levels of scepticism rise even further when you find out how some of these sites were discovered. Some sites confidently pointed out by guides today were identified for the sake of Byzantine pilgrims in the fourth century. Others can only date their origins back to the Crusader period, when the demand from pilgrims created a cottage industry of Holy Site Identification. During this period, curious medieval pilgrims had travelled over continents to see the exact sites, and didn't want to go home until they had.

In some sites, we can be fairly sure that we are close to where things really happened. The site identified as Peter's house in the ruins of Capernaum by the Sea of Galilee is a pretty good bet as the real thing. When you walk up the recently exposed first-century steps at the southern end of the Temple Mount in Jerusalem, you can be sure that you are walking where Jesus once walked. Having said that, the number of sites where the identification of location and event is as near as certain is really very small.

If the holiness of a site depends on it being the actual place where Jesus or any other biblical character did this or that, then we have a problem. If we simply can't be sure of most of the sites we're shown, then on these grounds, their claim to be indubitably 'holy' is at least questionable. Tom has a point.

'Holy places': four false starts

Is it right, then, to call these sites 'holy'? It all depends on what you mean. As we have seen, certain ideas can clearly be dismissed at once – even if they have popped up at different times throughout church history. No, these places are not mysterious channels by which we can get through to God in a way that is not possible in other places. Christ is accessible throughout the world. No, Christians do not *have* to visit them; they are not 'necessary for salvation' and certainly do not bestow any supposed merit on pilgrims. All the resources for faith are available elsewhere.

If 'holy' is used to denote some *special presence* of God uniquely tied to these places, then again the answer must be 'no'. For in the New Testament God's presence is now found uniquely in Jesus, and then through his powerful Spirit as he operates in the lives of his people.

'Holiness' in this first sense properly refers to the work of God in and among persons. There may be times and places when Christians, either on their own or with other Christians, may sense God's presence in a distinct way (which, of course, is always hard to explain to the sceptic). But while such 'divine presence' must necessarily occur in a particular place, there is nothing about that particular place as such which contributes to that manifestation. It has more to do with the Spirit among God's people and Jesus' promise to be with us, like the *shekinah* of old, 'whenever two or three meet together in my name' (Matthew 18:20). A place may indeed have been the location for such a divine presence on some occasion. Yet that does not require that this should ever occur there again. 'The Spirit blows where he wills' (John 3:8).

Nor are these places 'holy' as though God has somehow conferred upon them a *unique status* just because they were the locations of various biblical events in the past. Any such 'ontological' view, which seeks to give these places an inherent status of sanctity, is ruled out by the New Testament doctrine of Jesus as the true holy place. Long ago there was one such place which did have such a status. It was Jerusalem's Temple. But Jesus now is that Temple. In the light of his coming, no other place – not even the place formerly occupied by Jerusalem's Temple – can be elevated in this way. Such divine decrees are no longer to be expected.

Third, some suggest that we should see these places as *sacramental*. In developed Christian theology a sacrament is a divinely appointed means of grace – a place and an event in which God has promised to be present and active in and for his people. Baptism and communion fall clearly into this category, because of the express commands and promises of Jesus. Roman Catholic theology has added several others, including for example 'holy matrimony'. Perhaps the 'holy places' of the Gospels should be seen similarly as a sacrament?

There is always a danger in stretching terminology too far. It is important that the authentic sacraments are not devalued through applying this language inappropriately. These 'holy places' are not divinely appointed means of grace in the same way as, for example, Holy Communion. Jesus said 'this is my body'; he did not say 'this is my place'. God may use these sites to bless his people, but the same can be true of a beautiful sunset or an honest friendship. To use sacramental terminology would be to imply once again that there was some necessary or intrinsic connection between God and these 'holy places' in the present. But that claim could never be sustained.

Finally, some suggest we should see these places as 'holy' for a slightly different reason – what might be called the *representative* approach. After all, we recognize that Sunday may appropriately be called 'the Lord's day', even though all time is sacred. Perhaps, then, we should think in a similar way about places? Certain places might be termed 'holy' as a sign that in fact all places are in some sense sanctified.

This certainly is a more attractive option. It has the merit of ensuring that we do not end up 'secularizing' the geographical world. After all, if no place is allowed to be holy, then the cynic might argue that we should go to the opposite extreme and argue that this material world should all be dismissed as godless. If there is no sanctity, perhaps all is secular? No, the Christian faith has a far more positive view concerning the goodness of creation and the reality of God's work in his world. But that vision of God's work in the world is precisely what may be compromised if one starts speaking of certain places as 'holy' in this representational sense. The intention is good but the unfortunate result is that it implies a second-class status for places not termed 'holy'.

Some suggest, therefore, that it might be best to abandon the concept of 'holy place' altogether. They would argue that 'holiness' properly belongs to God in any case and cannot be transferred to inanimate objects. Usually, New Testament writers see it this way (but see 2 Peter 1:18). When the adjective is not applied to God, it is applied to his people who are 'holy' in his sight – the forgiven 'saints' (Romans 1:7 etc.). Much better, therefore, to avoid all such language which tries to connect this personal and ultimately divine concept of 'holiness' with inanimate geographical places. This kind of holiness and places are simply in different categories, and should not be mixed.

HOLY PLACES TODAY

Is this right? Should the language of 'holy places' be abandoned altogether? Not necessarily. In what follows, we want to suggest some possible ways of understanding 'holy places' which tie in with the theology developed above. Let us explore two ways of thinking of places as 'holy', two ways in which we might helpfully approach and appreciate these special sites in the Christian story.

Holiness and history

One approach is to suggest that calling a place 'holy' is simply a way of acknowledging the significance to us *as human beings* of what has happened there in Christian history. We have already seen how the coming of Jesus 'desacralizes space'. These sites are not so much special in *God's* sight, but they are *to us* within human history and for reasons of our Christian memory and association. In other words, their 'holiness' is more historical than theological. Just as the site of any famous battle is a significant place within political history, so perhaps 'holy places' are sites which are significant within *religious* history. Our attitude to them, therefore, if not marked by veneration, should certainly be marked by a profound respect.

On this model, then, these places remain just like any other place. Yet it also allows that, because of what happened in them, they have gained a new significance for us. After all, in one sense a piece of material with particular colours (e.g. red, white and blue) is just that – a piece of material; but in another sense, once someone realizes that it is the flag of their own nation, it takes on a new meaning and significance. 'Holiness' may then just be the best shorthand for expressing this altered significance.

The term 'holy place' can be misunderstood and used in unhelpful ways. Yet it is important to acknowledge the significance of these places and the powerful experience which many people have when they visit them. After all, our faith is a dynamic one in the Living God and in the Risen Christ. So, even if these places are 'holy' simply because of their history and what they mean to us, it remains a powerful experience to visit them in the very presence of the One who worked there in the past and who is alive today. What gives these biblical sites their extra potency (compared, say, with a site of secular history) is that they can bring together in a unique way two vital strands in our faith: its foundation in past historical events and its experience of the Living God in the here and now. So for people of faith, those who have encountered God in Jesus Christ, such places can deepen their imagination and renew their faith in striking ways as they reflect on what their Lord did in this location.

Places and people

A second approach might be to think of the countless Christians who for centuries have come to these very places to remember and meditate upon these events. If holiness belongs to people not places, we might think of the 'holiness' of such a place as instead deriving from the faith, devotion and love of the Christians who have prayed and pondered the significance of the event right here. You might say it 'rubs off' on the Christians who, over the years, have found their way to this very spot, to remember this very event in the vicinity of the place where it happened.

So too much curiosity about exact locations can lead to missing the point. It would be possible to identify all the authentic locations of all the events in the Gospels, see, feel and touch them all, and still go home none the wiser. On Mount Tabor, it is better simply to use the place to allow the event of the transfiguration and its significance to penetrate into our minds and hearts, considering all that it says about Jesus' hidden glory and destiny. Of course we can meditate on the meaning of the transfiguration in personal Bible reading at home, or in a house group study. Yet to do so on Mount Tabor, in a place where Christians have done that for centuries, which is at least near or similar to the exact location where it happened, is bound to intensify and enrich such meditation. This helps us get around the problem of worrying whether or not a particular location is the actual site of the original event or not. In one sense it doesn't matter – it still carries a significance for us due to the thousands of Christians who came there before us.

It's not unlike what happens in an ancient cathedral, dedicated to the worship of God for centuries. The New Testament has no sacred 'buildings', but now, for good reasons, we have these special buildings in which the

Christian community has met and prayed over the years. As we step inside we become aware of the great 'cloud of witnesses', those who have lived, prayed, worshipped in these very places in the past. As we do so, our minds are concentrated on their God and ours. We do not 'come into God's presence' when we enter a cathedral, but we can become more aware of his presence as we do so.

It is similar when we visit a 'holy place', like Mount Tabor. It is not that God is more present there than elsewhere. Rather, because of its association with the transfiguration, and because generations of Christians have come to meditate at this very site over the centuries, it has a power to concentrate our minds and hearts upon Jesus' glory, his majesty and love, and therefore to refresh and reinvigorate our faith. In that sense it might be thought of as a 'holy place'.

So perhaps it is legitimate to label as 'holy' those places which have been important in Christian history and reflection. But we must be careful not to attach to that term meanings which are ruled out by the New Testament. In chapter 4 we will return to examine the related theme of pilgrimage, but for now we close with three brief stories from the Bible which relate closely to our theme.

Three Bible episodes: Jeremiah and Jesus

The first is Jeremiah's sermon in the Jerusalem Temple, as recorded in Jeremiah 7. The people of his day were convinced that this Temple was a safe sanctuary, because it was the place chosen by God. Indeed it was, but they were wrong to presume upon this. In fact it had become for them something of a talisman, perhaps even an idol – a smokescreen which effectively came between them and obedience to the commands of the Lord. As a result, Jeremiah had to proclaim the 'word of the Lord'. He solemnly warned that it would be destroyed, just as Shiloh had been. Even this genuinely 'holy place' was not immune to the judgement of God, when the religiosity of his people had come to defile its true purpose. 'Holy places' can be abused, and the 'holy' used as a cover for unholiness. God does not seek those who are in the right geographical place, but those whose hearts are near him.

Secondly, the transfiguration (Mark 9:2–8) was a holy event, if ever there was one – the manifestation of the eternal glory of Jesus. Peter wanted to capture the event in some way, to tie it down to physical space: '"let us make three tents, one for you, one for Moses, and one for Elijah". But he did not know what he was saying.' So the divine voice interrupts him in his tracks, suggesting an alternative and more appropriate form of response: 'this is my beloved Son; listen to him'. Here is the priority of the word of God and of obedience. The correct response to the glory of Jesus is not to try and domesticate it or to pin it down, but rather to worship and obey. As the holiness of God begins to evoke in us a proper counterpart in our lives, we become places of holiness.

Finally, the words of the angels to the frightened women on the morning of the Resurrection must continue to ring in our ears: 'He is not here, for he is risen!' It is a resounding note that must colour our whole approach to these places associated with the life of this Jesus. If we are seeking in them the presence of Jesus, we may first need to reckon with his absence. Like the women, we are looking for him in the wrong place. If he is to be present to us, it will be as the Risen Lord, knowable throughout the world by his powerful Spirit. These words remind us that in the realm of salvation history time has moved on, and we cannot turn the clock back.

And these angelic words bring to our attention that most important truth which has been underlying all our exploration in this chapter: namely that, at the end of the day, it is the person of Jesus that matters, not the places of Jesus. Any significance that they have derives entirely from him;

and any focus on them which subtly bypasses him is at best misguided and at worst positively dangerous. For as the apostle John saw so clearly, Jesus himself is the true holy place. You can believe in the prime importance of the Incarnation and value the places where it occurred, but John suggests this does not lead on necessarily to these places being seen as somehow qualitatively different. Jesus himself is the Temple (John 2:19–21); he is the Word who for a season 'tabernacled among us' (1:14) but then moved on; he is the one now 'lifted up', who has returned to the Father and longs to 'draw all people to himself' (12:32). According to the New Testament, God wants us to focus on the risen Jesus and seek to obey him – wherever we are.

Chapter 3

HOLY CITY AND HOLY LAND?

So not everyone in the city was happy. When Jesus approached Jerusalem, people feared it might lead to the loss of the Temple, 'our holy place' (John 11:48). And they were right. In a profound sense, as we saw in the last chapter, Jesus' arrival spelled the end for the Temple. But his arrival would have a lasting impact on something else too – the city of Jerusalem itself.

In the previous chapter we considered how Christian visitors like Tom and Sarah might begin to think about 'holy places': in what sense, if any, is it right to think of certain biblical sites as 'holy'? Will it be somehow different to be in the places where Jesus once was? Most Christians about to visit the Holy Land are probably aware that this is going to be a key question. What they may not be quite so prepared for is a second question. In some ways it is a very similar question, yet it is actually quite different. Often it creeps up on people a few days into their visit or after a few days in Jerusalem. The question is: how are we to view the city of Jerusalem and this land as a whole? In what ways might it be right to think of these as either 'holy' or special in God's sight? In other words, we move from the issue of individual 'holy places' to the issues of 'holy city' or 'holy land'.

At first sight, of course, this seems a tiny distinction. Surely, you will ask, when people speak of the 'holy city' or the 'holy land' this is just like when they speak of 'holy places'? Is it not just a way of describing locations which witnessed 'holy' events? In fact, however, something new is being introduced under the camouflage of the word 'holy'. For in the Bible both Jerusalem and the Land are set apart from other cities and lands because they are the objects of divine promises. Jerusalem is the 'city of God' (Psalm 46:4; 48:1 etc.) and the Land is the 'land of promise' or 'promised land' (Hebrews 11:9).

So to talk today of the 'holy city' or the 'holy land' often invokes these categories of divine promise and purpose. Jerusalem and the Land, in other words, are not just 'holy' or special because of what we believe happened there in the biblical past (a previous divine presence). They are 'holy' because of what God may be continuing to do in them in the present or for the future (an ongoing status based on divine promise). This outworking of divine promises and purposes is a completely new factor – something which simply does not enter our heads when we are thinking merely about 'holy places'.

So the question becomes: does the Christian God view this particular city and this particular land as somehow different from other places on the globe because of certain promises which he has made in the Scriptures regarding them? For sceptics this might seem a ridiculous question. After all, did God really make such promises in the past? Would the Living God still be bound by something written by a few ancient prophets long ago? For others, this might seem instead a very abstract and academic question – like the debates about how many angels you can fit on the head of a pin.

At least that's how people might think if they are reading this before their departure to the airport. Once you arrive in Jerusalem, however, as Tom and Sarah soon find out, things look rather different.

Suddenly as a visitor you realize that this issue of what your God thinks of Jerusalem and the Land is one of the most potent questions in the region. You begin to see that so much of the conflict in the area, both past and present, can be traced back to the way different religious groups have answered this question and then sought to act out the answer. If this city is special to the God of Islam, it needs to be in Muslim hands. If it is special to the Christian God, we need to fight a Crusade. If the city is close to the heart of the God worshipped by the Jews, then Jewish control is right and proper.

This is not an academic issue. It is an urgent matter, which impinges on every aspect of life in the Middle East. Lots of people in this region of the world believe that their God has some special purpose for the region, and they are insistent on using that conviction to justify their own actions – many of which are deliberately aimed to help bring about those divine purposes.

So once again Tom and Sarah find themselves racing back to the Bible, to rummage through its pages. Can it help them at all with this burning question which somehow has never really bothered them before? After all, how else are they going to answer these big issues – issues that might never have arisen if the Bible had not been written? Others in the tour party, however, start to become a little cynical. Perhaps, they say, this is the point at which we must dismiss the Bible. Is not the Bible, or least its varied interpretations, one of the things that has caused all these problems? They have a point. But if the Bible raises these questions, it may be fairer and wiser to believe that it may also point us towards their solution. What we need is a rounded biblical theology – putting together the biblical material in a way that is coherent and makes sense of the whole.

There is no doubt that in the Old Testament period both Jerusalem and the Land had a special status within God's sight. We saw in chapter 2 how the Temple had a particular role within the divine plan at this stage, being the place he ordained for his presence and for appropriate sacrifices. The same was true of the surrounding city of Jerusalem and the wider Land.

The Temple, the City and the Land seem to have been like three concentric circles within Old Testament thought.

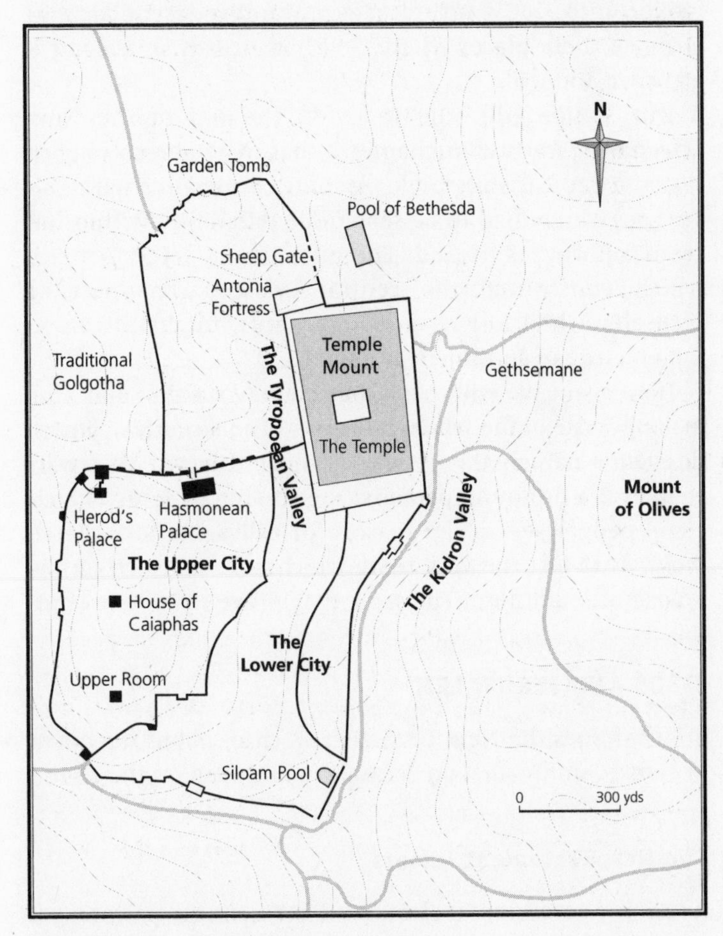

Figure 2. Jerusalem in the time of Jesus

The rabbis spoke of ten degrees of holiness emanating from the Holy of Holies within the Temple (*m.Kelim* 1:6–9). So there was an interconnection between them, each playing a vital role within God's covenant with his people – the Most Holy Place, then the City of God, then the Promised Land. They were places where God revealed himself ('in Judah God is known': Psalm 76:1) and for which he had special plans. And when the Old Testament prophets looked into God's future they naturally described it in terms of these places where God had already revealed his presence and will.

But is this still true today in the era of the New Covenant? We saw in chapter 2 that, with the coming of Jesus, a radical shift took place in connection with the Temple. It now had to be seen quite differently within the eternal purposes of God. The question is: if the Temple, which constituted the central, most sacred part of Jerusalem, had lost its previous status, might the same then be true of Jerusalem and the Land?

Here again we will argue that the key starting point for making sense of the whole Bible must be its central, climactic event – namely the life and teaching of Jesus. We saw in chapter 2 a profound paradox: the coming of Jesus, which some people see as the reason for calling certain places 'holy', is in fact the very thing which may call such terminology into question. The same may prove to be true here.

JESUS AND JERUSALEM

So what does the New Testament teach us about the effect of Jesus' coming, first on Jerusalem, and then on the Land?

The New Testament letters

As soon as we look at the New Testament on this matter, we realize that it has something vitally important to say.

How about this for a startling statement in one of Paul's earliest letters: 'The present city of Jerusalem ... is in slavery with her children' (Galatians 4:25). Something dramatic must have happened to cause him to come out with this negative view of Jerusalem. After all, he himself had gone to Jerusalem for his university training, and almost certainly had shared with his fellow nationalists a strong love of the city. But now it all looks rather different. During his upbringing he would no doubt have looked to Jerusalem as his 'mother city', but now instead he encourages Christians to have their focus on 'the Jerusalem that is above ... and she is our mother' (Galatians 4:26). It is a deliberate contrast, a whole new way of viewing this important city. What could possibly have brought it about?

Paul's blunt statement proved to be the opening of a new approach to Jerusalem which was then followed by other New Testament writers. Perhaps the clearest example comes in the letter to the Hebrews. The writer consciously seeks to wean his readers away from a focus on the earthly Jerusalem; instead they are travelling to the 'heavenly Jerusalem' (12:22). The Jesus they now worship had been rejected by Jerusalem 'outside the city gate' (13:12). So his followers, if they are to show their allegiance to him, must leave Jerusalem behind and instead 'go out to him outside the camp ... For here we have no enduring city, but we are looking for the city that is to come' (13:13–14).

In other words, don't go on pinning your hopes on the physical Jerusalem. That will let you down. That is no longer a focal point within God's purposes. No, turn your attention instead to the heavenly Jerusalem, 'the city with foundations, whose architect and builder is God' (11:10). After all, this – not the physical Jerusalem – was what had inspired Abraham and the patriarchs. They were not focusing on an earthly city or country: 'instead they were longing for a better country – a heavenly one' (10:16). These are striking comments from an author, often himself described as the most Jewish writer of the New Testament, writing explicitly to Jewish Christians. It is a strong challenge to their previous loyalties. They must view Jerusalem differently now.

The same challenge is found in the book of Revelation. Christians are to set their sights not on the earthly Jerusalem, but on the 'Holy City, the New Jerusalem, coming down out of heaven from God' (21:2, 10; cf. 3:12). By contrast the physical city of Jerusalem, the 'city where the Lord was crucified', is described as being no better than the 'great city' of pagan Rome and worthy of being called 'Sodom and Egypt' (11:8). Why? What's happened?

The four Evangelists

The answer must lie in the story recounted by the Gospel writers. Their story, of course, integrally involves Jerusalem. And each writer, even if in different ways, tells that story in such a way that Jerusalem emerges in a strange new light.

Take John for example. His view of Jerusalem is coloured by his view of the 'world'. He sees Jesus as God himself entering his 'world' by coming to Israel ('his own': 1:10–11). So his being rejected and crucified in Jerusalem serves only to highlight the sin of the world. Jerusalem, the place of 'God's own', has become instead a microcosm of the 'world' in its rejection of God's Messiah. In other words, the city of God has become the city of the world. It is the place where Jesus encountered 'the prince of this world' at the time of 'judgement on the world' (12:31). So any previous status that Jerusalem had enjoyed as the place of true worship was now brought to an end through the appearance of Israel's Messiah and the free gift of the Spirit: 'a time is coming when you will worship the Father neither on this mountain [Mt Gerizim] nor in Jerusalem', but 'in spirit and in truth' (John 4:21–4).

Initially, Matthew's view seems more positive. With his innate loyalty to Judaism, he refers to Jerusalem as the 'holy city' (4:5; 27:53). Yet, on closer inspection, this description only serves to highlight a savage irony. In his version of the wedding banquet, those who murder the king's servants are punished with the burning of 'their city' (22:7). 'O Jerusalem, Jerusalem,' says Jesus, 'you who kill the prophets ...' (27:37ff). The supposedly 'holy city' has proved itself to be quite the opposite. Jesus had said that Jerusalem was the 'city of the Great King' (Matthew 5:35); but now the city had rejected that King – the King who had come in the very person of Jesus (25:34). What would that mean for the city?

Matthew's answer is implicit in the way he concludes his Gospel – not in Jerusalem, but on a mountain in Galilee. The Gospel of Mark had highlighted even more poignantly this contrast between Galilee and Jerusalem (see e.g. Mark 14:28; 16:7). Now Matthew uses it too. The risen Jesus speaks in Galilee, proclaiming that God's purposes are now focused not on Mount Zion but rather on him, Jesus, to whom 'all authority in heaven and earth has been given'. And the gospel of God will now burst forth from Jerusalem 'to all nations' (Matthew 28:19).

But it is Luke who, of all the Evangelists, focuses most clearly on the issue of Jerusalem. Indeed the very structure of Luke–Acts is based on Jesus' going up to Jerusalem (Luke), followed by the apostles' going out to the 'ends of the earth' (Acts). Very early in this Gospel Jesus 'sets his face towards Jerusalem' (9:51), 'for surely no prophet can die outside Jerusalem!' (13:33). Jerusalem proves to be the place which 'did not recognize the time of God's coming' and which therefore in the future would experience divine judgement: 'If you, even you, had only known on this day what would bring you peace – but now it is hidden from your eyes. The days will come when your enemies ... will dash you to the ground' (19:41–4; cf. 21:20; 23:28–31).

So in Luke's second volume, the book of Acts, the story moves away from Jerusalem. Even though some of Jesus' followers remained in the city (as a sign that faith in Jesus was not marginal to Judaism), the dynamic of the Christian message increasingly focused elsewhere. This can be sensed in the way Luke gives such space to Paul's traumatic journey from Jerusalem to Rome (Acts 22–8). Almost certainly this reflects the author's conviction that there had been a shift in the centre of gravity. God's purposes were now directed towards the wider world. Jerusalem had had its day.

The New Testament is nothing if not radical. And here we see it being radical concerning one of the most central realities of Old Testament thought – the sanctity and centrality of Jerusalem. All the New Testament writers would have affirmed the vital role which Jerusalem had truly played in the past – they were not saying that had been false – but now they were saying that Israel's God had done a new thing.

Explaining the change

When we ask what caused these predominantly Jewish writers to reach this radical conclusion, we are thrown back once again to consider the life and teaching of Jesus himself. There were other factors at work, of course: the sudden universal spread of the Christian message, the experience of the Spirit, the realization that other Jewish particularities such as circumcision were no longer essential. But at the heart of this matter lies that prophet from Nazareth.

So they came to a new view of Jerusalem, first, through reflecting on Jesus' death outside its walls. The one whom they followed had been rejected by the city. Indeed, they too were experiencing some of that rejection now as his disciples. How tragic, that at the very moment for which Jerusalem had all along been prepared – the Messianic age, the advent of its true and rightful king – the supposed 'City of God' had failed to recognize that king. Some of the power of this can be sensed as they describe the pivotal moment when Jesus came over the Mount of Olives to enter the city. Even before his demonstration in the Temple, this was the long-awaited moment: this was Jerusalem's greatest hour, the arrival of Zion's King seated on a donkey (Zechariah 9:9), but the city did not know the 'hour of its visitation' (Luke 19:44). So Jesus wept.

But there was a second reason for their new approach to Jerusalem. This resulted from what Jesus himself had said and done. People had likened Jesus to Jeremiah (Matthew 16:14), the prophet who long before had pronounced judgement on the city. Jesus had now done the same. He had warned that the city and the nation were now entering their most crucial 'hour'. Judgement was coming. The Romans would not go away but would rather be the agents of God's wrath. Jesus was ushering in a new age, a new act in the divine drama – what in Hebrews would be called 'the time of the new order' (9:10). And in due course this prophet was vindicated. On the third day God raised him from the dead and, within a generation, his solemn prophetic words proved all too true. If the first Christians had a radically new approach to Jerusalem, it was ultimately because they were trying to be loyal to Jesus.

Important lessons

So the story of the city, as with the Temple, speaks of two vital concepts within biblical thought. First, it emphasizes the reality of God's judgement. As in the days of Jeremiah, so now history had repeated itself. For all its fine pedigree, Jerusalem had not been spared God's wrath. And if any Gentile Christians began to think that this left them unscathed, they too had to think again. For Jesus' prophecies had intertwined the coming judgement on Jerusalem with the ultimate end of the age, when he would return (Mark 13). The fall of Jerusalem was thus a warning in advance of the judgement which awaited all humankind. The good news of the gospel, however, was that Jesus in his death had already borne this judgement that was awaiting Jerusalem (dying as Israel's Messiah on a Roman cross). Those who followed him would pass through that judgement and emerge on the other side – in Resurrection life.

Yet this story revealed a second truth at the same time. Paradoxically, all this had come about not just because of the outworking of God's judgement, but also in full accordance with his divine purposes. The story of Jerusalem reveals God's eternal intentions. Now that the New Covenant had been established, it could be seen that Jerusalem's role had all along been to prepare for the events recorded in the New Testament. For example, when the Spirit came, the city's role as witnessing to the presence of God among his people would no longer be necessary. Or again, when the time came for the gospel to go out to 'all nations', the previous particular focus on Jerusalem would have to give way. And ultimately, when the full revelation of God in Christ was made known and the glories of the heavenly Jerusalem unveiled, then Jerusalem's previous role as signposting God's final purposes for the world was clearly brought to an end. The long-awaited reality had come.

And it had come about on the real stage of history, when Jesus came to Jerusalem. It was no abstract ideal but something established in real space and time and enacted in real 'flesh and blood'. Jesus' coming to Jerusalem was, in a mysterious way, the city's undoing – a historical moment with profound ramifications in the spiritual realm. The city could never be the same again. The sign had to give way to the reality. Jesus, not Jerusalem, was now at the centre.

JESUS AND THE LAND

The same shift can be seen with regard to the importance of the Land. If the Temple, the City and the Land were indeed like concentric circles – all intimately connected at a theological level – then this should not surprise us. What affects one will affect the others too. So we begin to see how Jesus' dramatic demonstration in the Temple turns out to have been like a stone thrown into the middle of a pond. It sent shockwaves out in all directions, reverberating through the established system. And the New Testament writers were those called by God to note those shockwaves and to teach what this would mean for the years to come. So how did they view the Land? It was the 'promised land' in the past; was it still a land peculiarly tied up with God's promises for the future?

Initially the New Testament appears not to speak so obviously on this issue. After all, the New Testament only explicitly refers to the Land on a handful of occasions, whereas in the Old Testament it is mentioned over sixteen hundred times. Perhaps they were not very interested? But no, this was a matter which lay at the very heart of Jewish faith. The history of this period makes it plain that people inspired by the Old Testament prophecies were longing for God to fulfil his purposes and to bring about freedom for his people in their promised land. New Testament writers could not suddenly have forgotten about it. If they give the matter comparatively little space, it is far more likely that this is because they have thought about the issue but no longer see it in quite the same way.

Paul and Hebrews

Again Paul and the writer of Hebrews shed light on this issue. In another of his telling 'throwaway' lines, Paul talks of the divine promise to Abraham 'that he would be heir of the *world*' (Romans 4:13). Yet in the Old Testament Abraham was only ever promised the Land (see Genesis 12:7 etc.). What is going on? Evidently Paul now sees the Land-promise in a more universal light, as a pledge given by God that he would one day institute his rule and Kingdom, not just within the Land of Israel, but eventually throughout the world. That day had now at last arrived. So the significance of the Land, just like the Temple and Jerusalem, was inherently temporary. The purposes of the God of Abraham had always been moving towards a more universal goal – the undoing of the sin of Adam and the blessing of 'all peoples on earth' (Genesis 12:3). For Paul the time had clearly come for those universal implications to become real. God's kingly rule could now be exercised over the whole of his world through his anointed Messiah. The Land, the initial focus of God's promises, was now eclipsed by a focus on the world as a whole.

So Paul's focus was not on the Land, but on the world. In fact, in all his other references to the Abrahamic promises he skipped over the territorial aspect of the promise; nor did he list the gift of the Land amongst Israel's promises and privileges (Romans 9:4; cf. 15:8–9). Before his conversion Paul was quite probably a Shammaite Pharisee, a nationalist with a great 'zeal' for the restoration of his nation's political future within their own Land. But now that he had met with the Risen Jesus, he realized he had been looking in the wrong direction. If there had been special blessings associated with being 'in the Land', these were now to be found 'in Christ'. As W.D. Davies put it: for Paul 'the Land had become irrelevant; it is not the Promised Land (much as he loved it) that became his "inheritance", but the Living Lord, in whom was a whole "new creation"' (*The Gospel and the Land*, pp. 179, 213).

The writer of Hebrews too views the Land in a new way – though his emphasis is slightly different from Paul's. For him the divine promises concerning the Land must be seen as part of God's deeper purpose to bring his people home to the 'heavenly country'. Hence the 'promised land' conquered by Joshua becomes an advance sign of the 'Sabbath-rest' which still remains 'for the people of

God' (Hebrews 4:8–9). And the 'land of promise' offered to the patriarchs is a pointer to the 'heavenly country' which was the ultimate goal of their longing and their true 'inheritance' (11:16). The promise concerning the Land had been real and valid in its own terms; but now it could be seen to have always been pointing forwards to something far greater. So he writes to encourage his Jewish–Christian readers to develop precisely this kind of faith which sees beyond the temporary shadows to their heavenly and true meaning. If they had then gone back to focusing on the physical Land (or indeed on Jerusalem or its Temple), then his whole purpose would have been thwarted. He wanted them to look elsewhere – to the place which was truly the place of promise. Their faith was not to be tied up with particular geographical places: instead 'faith is being certain of what we do not see' (Hebrews 11:1).

The same shift in focus can be seen in other New Testament writers as well. Luke gives great space to Stephen's speech in which the martyr emphasizes how God's greatest blessings had been experienced outside the Land (Acts 7); the same would hold true now as the disciples of Jesus were scattered to the 'ends of the earth' (8:1; cf. 1:8). And at the end of the Bible, the author of Revelation uses the word for 'land' seventy-seven times, but clearly uses it in a wider sense as a reference to the whole inhabited world. The focus of the New Testament is universal, not parochial.

The new exodus

So we begin to sense that the New Testament has a new approach to the issue of the Land. But again, if this is so, what has brought it about? One answer lies in the writers' conviction that Jesus has effectively brought about a new 'exodus' for God's people (Luke 9:31; see also 1

Corinthians 10:1–11; Hebrews 12:22ff; Romans 5–7; Revelation 15:3). His death was a new Passover (1 Corinthians 5:7). He himself was like Moses, only greater (Hebrews 3:2–6; John 1:17; John 6–8); he was the deliverer from the slavery of sin and death. But the original Exodus had been the prelude to the arrival of God's people in the 'promised land'. So if Christians now rejoiced in a different exodus, they would inevitably view the Land differently too. A greater exodus pointed to a greater Land.

In speaking of this second exodus, the New Testament writers were using the language and ideas of their Jewish contemporaries. A new exodus was precisely what their friends were looking for. They were longing for an act of deliverance, the coming of freedom. The Old Testament Babylonian exile was in one sense over, but in another sense – so long as Roman Gentiles dominated the Land – it was still going on. Jews longed for an end to this period of exile and frustration. As the Israelites said even when they had just returned from Babylon, 'we are slaves in the Land you gave us' (Nehemiah 9:36). When would the exile be over? When would God perform a new exodus? The first Christians addressed precisely these hopes. But the exodus they started to proclaim was radically different and much deeper. And it did not involve any of the expected political consequences.

A good example of this comes in John's Gospel in the description of Jesus' teaching at the feast of Tabernacles – a feast which was tied up with all sorts of expectations for a second exodus. In characteristic fashion John presents Jesus as the feast's true fulfilment (7:37–9; 8:12). He then proceeds to speak of a quite different kind of 'freedom' (8:32–6) and portrays Jesus as the true 'king of the Jews', whose kingdom is 'not of this world' (18:33–6). In other words, all the hopes associated with any independent political kingdom within the 'promised land' had now been fulfilled – but through Jesus and in a quite unexpected way.

By his death Jesus was the one in whom the 'scattered children of God' could be restored or gathered together as one (11:52). If people were longing for a second exodus, or for a true restoration after centuries of seeming exile, then they need look no further than Jesus.

Jesus' radical Kingdom-agenda

However, the principal reason why the New Testament writers began to see the Land in a new way is because they learnt this from the teaching and example of Jesus. As with their views towards the Temple and Jerusalem, they came to these radical new conclusions only because Jesus himself had given them the lead.

Many people suppose that Jesus' ministry had nothing whatsoever to do with this issue of the Land. They forget that the 'kingdom of God' which Jesus' contemporaries were expecting was not a spiritual kingdom but precisely a political kingdom. And they forget that what prompted this expectation was those promises in the Old Testament that God would one day bring his people out of exile and restore them to their Land. Those texts fuelled expectations then, just as now, of what God would do in the Land. In fact Jesus came at a time when the longings for 'restoration' were reaching fever pitch, when uprising against Rome was very much in the air. So when Jesus came as a prophet announcing the arrival of God's Kingdom, this rang all sorts of political bells. It stirred up again all the longings that God would at last fulfil his ancient promises concerning Israel and the Land. Despite what many in the Christian Church have subsequently imagined, Jesus' message was not exclusively 'spiritual' and 'otherworldly'. No, it made profound connections with the politics of his day.

But, in contrast to what many of his contemporaries would have hoped, neither was he a straightforward political revolutionary. Jesus' Kingdom-agenda turned out to be quite different. On the one occasion he expressly spoke about the Land as such, he said it was 'the meek', not the revolutionaries, who would 'inherit the Land' (Matthew 5:5). For his hearers he indeed made all the right connections but came to all the wrong conclusions. This Kingdom-hope would be fulfilled not by the sword, but through the death of the King; the great act of restoration would be God's raising of Israel's Messiah 'on the third day' (Luke 24:46; cf. Hosea 6:2). The exile, always known to have been the consequences of sin, would be ended when this Messiah had secured the forgiveness of sins. So a new exodus would be achieved, and people from all nations would be 'gathered in' (Matthew 8:11). In other words, Jesus took this cluster of hopes, which in their different ways were all associated with the Land, and pointed to a quite different mode of fulfilment – in him, the Messiah of Israel.

The disciples' lesson

Of course, the disciples themselves seem not to have understood this radical alternative agenda at the time. Some of them may have been originally attracted to Jesus because they thought he was going to fulfil their preconceived notions of what the Messiah would do; they had it all worked out just how God would inaugurate his Kingdom. Gradually, however, they realized Jesus had something else in mind. Instead of a Messiah who would expel the Romans, this one would be crucified by them. Instead of fighting to retain their Land, they were called, if need be, to 'sell their possessions' – including presumably the ownership of land (Luke 12:13; cf. Acts 4:34). Jesus' Kingdom-agenda turned everything upside down.

Even after the resurrection, they are clearly confused and want Jesus to fall in with their own plans. For what was the one question which they were bursting to ask when Jesus began to speak about returning to the Father? 'Lord,' they pleaded, 'are you at this time going to restore the Kingdom to Israel?' (Acts 1:6). In other words, is this not the time when the Romans are going to be pushed out from the Land and Israel will at last know peace and security within her own borders? Will Israel not now at last be recognized as God's agent of rule in his world?

Jesus' reply gave them quite a different agenda: you must be prepared instead to leave the Land, going out to the 'ends of the earth'. You must proclaim that Israel's Messiah is now installed on the throne of David (cf. Acts 2:30) and is exalted by God as Lord of the world. That's how God's Kingdom will be established; that's how people will know that Israel has been restored. And so the book of Acts, in conscious parallel to the book of Joshua in the Old Testament, goes on to tell of the spread of God's rule. But note how the 'land to be possessed' is no longer the promised land of Israel but the whole world.

Conclusions

So no wonder Jesus' followers came to view the promised land in a different light. This was just one part of a cluster of hopes which Jesus had fulfilled in a quite different way. Their focus was no longer to be on the kingdom of Israel in its Land but on the Kingdom of God – God's rule in Jesus over the world.

The New Testament writers did not, therefore, continue to look for a political restoration of Israel. Nor were they wondering about when and how God's promises concerning the Land would be fulfilled. And this was not simply because they had more urgent matters to consider. On the contrary, it was precisely because they believed the great act of fulfilment had already occurred. The Kingdom of God had been established; the new age had started. The promises were not somehow 'on hold', awaiting another season. No, they had been fulfilled in Christ. 'For no matter how many promises God has made,' concluded Paul, 'they are "Yes" in Christ' (2 Corinthians 1:20). He was their true fulfilment. Jesus had become 'a servant of the Jews' to 'confirm the promises made to the patriarchs' (Romans 15:8). God's promises in the Old Testament had now been acted upon and brought to fulfilment by Jesus.

A key point to note here is that the apostles were reading the same Old Testament as we do. The promises relating to the future of Jerusalem and the Land which fuel such speculation in our own day were precisely the same passages which fuelled the passions of Jesus' contemporaries. Jesus' ministry addressed those issues – it did not simply bypass them – but he gave them a different solution. The Kingdom of God had arrived – but in Jesus himself. The disciples gradually learnt their lesson; they learnt to read their Old Testament in the light of its fulfilment in Jesus. We must learn the same lesson and not slip back into those very ways of thinking from which Jesus so painstakingly had to wean his disciples.

This means that Christians cannot go back to the Old Testament as though Jesus had never come – or as though the New Testament had never been written. We must read the Old Testament with Christian eyes – precisely because this is what the apostles did themselves. It was not as though they came up with a whole new set of ideas, turning their backs on the Old Testament. Nor did they see the Old Testament promises as operating in some quite different channel. On the contrary the Old Testament was their Bible – it was open in front of them – and they believed that Jesus was its fulfilment. He was the one who was himself the great 'mystery kept hidden for ages but now disclosed to the saints' (Colossians 1:26; cf. 2:2–3). The same is true today. We must approach the Land and view the promises relating to it in the light of Jesus.

It also means that Christians may want to question those

who claim that these promises are finding an alternative fulfilment in the modern Middle East. If they have been fulfilled in Christ, then is it not derogatory to him, and disobedient to his apostles' teaching, to see them as now fulfilled in a different way? Either God was fulfilling his purposes in Jesus, or he wasn't. You can't have it both ways.

So the New Testament does have a profound, distinctive and yet unexpected approach to this whole issue of the Land. Once again the claim is being made that Israel's story has entered into a definitive new phase with the coming of Jesus. God has indeed worked to fulfil his ancient promises, but the fulfilment is significantly different from what was expected. And in consequence of this, the Land (as with the Temple and the City) could never be the same again.

AND TODAY?

So how are we to view Jerusalem and the Land today? Visiting the land of the Bible is causing Sarah and Tom to think much harder than they expected, and to ask questions which previously had not really occurred to them. What does the Bible say? If this land was the one where God himself 'pitched his tent' (to use the Pope's carefully chosen phrase when he landed at Tel Aviv airport in March 2000), does that make it distinctively 'holy' in the present? If Jerusalem and the Land were the objects of divine promises in the past, does that mean that they retain that status to this day?

The above approach suggests the answer might well be 'no'. Of course, many people reach the opposite conclusion and want the answer to be 'yes' – for a variety of reasons, both spiritual and political. But the great conflicts resulting from that conclusion should perhaps begin to suggest that there is 'a more excellent way'.

Our alternative approach to the whole issue comes about, as we have seen, by putting the historical ministry of Jesus at the centre of all our thought. This, of course, makes eminent sense if, as Christians believe, the coming of Jesus was the central event in all human history – and was therefore the most important episode in the long history of the Holy Land. Get your central focus correct, and all the other issues will begin to fall into their proper place.

So yes, of course, the coming of Jesus to this city and this Land makes them unique. They will forever have powerful historical and religious associations which make them special in some way. But that very coming also transforms them. Precisely because of what Jesus said and did in this one location, these entities can never be the same. The role which they played previously is no longer necessary. The hopes associated with them have been fulfilled in other ways. Why? Simply because Jesus has come. He is the ultimate spiritual reality, the focused presence of God, the fulfilment of divine promise. Shadows and expectation have to give way to reality and fulfilment.

This means that great caution must be exercised whenever Christians are tempted to reinvest Jerusalem or the Holy Land with a distinctive theological status. This is running counter to the whole thrust of the New Testament. Christians of all persuasions fall prey to this temptation. In the history of the Church it has happened most frequently, as we shall see, through believers emphasizing the Incarnation. More recently it has come about through people emphasizing the fulfilment of biblical prophecies. In either case, the motives may be honourable – a love of the land or its people, a devotion to Jesus and the Scriptures – but the consequences are not happy ones. And a deeper reading of those Scriptures and a greater realization of the uniqueness of Jesus can, as we have suggested, lead to the opposite conclusion.

So at the end of the day Tom and Sarah – and indeed all Christian visitors to the Land – are confronted again and again with the sheer brilliance and power of this figure from Nazareth. This was the one who in his own person brought God to humankind and turned the story of Israel and the world inside out. He is the centre and everything else must revolve around him. The Temple, the city, the Land – all have been vitally important. But Jesus is the true holy one. Better then, perhaps, not to call it the 'holy land', but rather 'the land of the Holy One'.

Chapter 4

BIBLICAL PILGRIMAGE?

Jesus is the true 'holy place'. We have begun to piece together what this central insight of the New Testament means for our understanding of 'holy places', a 'holy city' and a 'holy land'. Yet if these have suddenly become less important for Christian believers than we might have thought, does that mean that Tom was right? Is pilgrimage a waste of time? Is it a dangerous, sub-Christian practice? Is there such a thing as a 'biblical pilgrimage'? This chapter tries to suggest how pilgrimage can be a profoundly helpful and positive experience for us, and to explain what we can expect to gain from it as we, like Tom and Sarah, touch down in the land of the Bible.

I. BACKCLOTH TO THE BIBLE

One of the main Christian motivations for visiting the Holy Land, and historically perhaps the oldest, is simply to understand the Bible better. In the first three centuries, the evidence suggests that Christians didn't visit Palestine so much because it contained 'holy places', but out of a historical interest alone, to help in their reading of the Scriptures. 'The man who has seen Judaea with his own eyes and who knows the sites of ancient cities and their names, whether the same or changed, will gaze more clearly on Holy Scripture', said Jerome, one of the greatest of the early church fathers. Origen, the third-century Christian theologian, wrote that he visited the Land in order to 'trace the footsteps of Jesus', and it is clear that his reason for going, as it was for many early Christian visitors, was simply to gain a clearer understanding of the biblical story.

It is a cliché, but still quite true, that you never quite read the Bible in the same way again after a visit to the Land. Visitors often come back with new discoveries: 'I never knew Calvary and Jesus' tomb were so close to each other!' 'I never imagined the River Jordan was so small!' 'I didn't realize Bethlehem was so near to Jerusalem.' 'Why do I always think of the baby Jesus in a wooden stable and a wooden manger, when it was a cave and a stone animal trough?'

Whenever we read the Bible, as with any narrative, we construct a mental picture of the scene in our minds. Once we have been able to picture the contours of the landscape, the shape of the valleys, the dryness of the hills in which the events of the Bible were played out, our God-given imaginations can stretch much further, and at the same time be more firmly rooted in reality. Visitors also find that themes of Scripture immediately make much more sense when read in the land in which it was written.

Take water for example. For most of us, water comes out of a tap. Sometimes it falls from the skies, but then when it rains, we usually complain. In a recent survey, 40 per cent of British people indicated that they do not drink water because it is too 'boring and uninteresting'. Despite occasional water shortages, summer standpipes and drying reservoirs, we take water for granted, assuming it will always be there when we need it, at all times of the year.

So when Jeremiah writes of God as the only true 'spring of living water' (Jeremiah 17:13), and the Psalmist pictures his aching for God as like an exhausted and thirsty traveller in the desert, 'a dry and weary land where there is no water' (Psalm 63:1), these images don't make much impression on us. In the land of the Bible, it is very different.

It is one thing to debate such ideas in a Bible study, or even read them on a page of a book as you are doing right now. It's very different to encounter these images when you are standing hot, tired, with a drying throat in the Judean desert surrounded by barren rocks, valleys and parched vegetation.

When you see a place like Jericho, an oasis of green in a wide expanse of dry rocks and arid wilderness, you suddenly realize how life and water are inseparable. A desert traveller who does not take a good supply of water will not last long. In such a place, water literally means the difference between life and death. Suddenly these pictures, of finding God as like coming across a life-giving spring of delicious cold water in the desert, or stories of the miraculous supply of water as the Israelites staggered on in the wilderness, are filled with meaning.

Compared to the desiccated land of the surrounding nations – arid Sinai, the dry plains of Moab, and the vast Syrian desert – the land of Canaan seemed lush and dripping with goodness to the early Israelite settlers. The fresh, green land of the coastal plain, the *Shephelah* and the Judean hills on which the clouds blown in from the Mediterranean dropped their moisture seemed like a land the Lord had blessed above all others – rich with fruit, wine and bread, precisely because it was well watered by the rains which could be relied upon twice a year, every year. No wonder the spies returned to tell Moses 'it is a good land the Lord our God is giving us' (Deuteronomy 1:25).

Water is just one example among many. Visitors will find their own when in the Land itself. A renewed interest in Bible reading is a very common reaction to a trip to the Holy Land. 'This has extended my ability to imagine the reality of the Gospel narratives – I find I read the Bible much more slowly now – I find myself stopping over small phrases,' said one visitor. 'In the past, when I read the Bible, the characters assumed mythical proportions. This visit has brought them all down to earth. I'm sure it will change the way that I read and think and imagine what was going on,' said another.

The Bible is the most revolutionary book in the world. It uniquely reveals the mind and character of God. Yet it was also written by real people rooted in real human cultures, landscapes, climates and histories. To know just a little of that cultural and geographical backdrop can help make its startling message stand out that much more sharply. To understand the Bible just that bit better is well worth the effort.

II. IT REALLY HAPPENED

Yet there are more than purely educational reasons for a pilgrimage to the Holy Land. As we have seen, the Christian life can be lived just as well by the disciple who never leaves her own town, faithfully seeking to follow the way of Christ where she is. It is tempting, therefore, to think that geography doesn't matter at all; that the important thing is not the physical place, but the spiritual meaning. God can be found everywhere, so there is no need to go to a particular place to find him. As we have seen, these are in an important sense true, yet we also need to recognize some dangers which lie down this path.

Christianity is a profoundly historical religion. It also takes physical things very seriously. It matters for Christians that God intervened in the history of the small tribe of the Hebrews in the ancient Near East to rescue them from slavery and bring them to a full, rich and pleasant land. It matters that Jesus was born on one particular day in one particular year at one particular place on the face of the earth. It matters that he died, and that we can point to the very city, and roughly the very place on the earth where his cross was tilted upright from the ground. It matters that he was raised physically from death, from a real tomb. If these events did not take place within space and time, in real places on the surface of the earth, then Christianity becomes just another set of abstract ideas, floating in the philosophical ether.

The Incarnation, the cross and Resurrection are not just nice ideas or hopeful stories, but real events which once took place. And as such, they tell us authoritatively that God is interested in history. They assure us that God has broken into human life and experience, and that his intervention has made a difference.

The God Christians believe in does not float serenely in heaven untouched by the pain, injustice and passion which make up human experience. Instead, he has known it first hand. He has pledged his deep love for his creation and his abiding commitment to it by entering it, tasting human experience to the full, even death itself, and conquering it. As John puts it, 'the Word became flesh and lived for a while among us. We have seen his glory' (John 1:14).

So in one sense, it is vitally important that Christians remember that if we want to, we can go to particular sites where God made himself known to his people. It is crucial that there is a place on this planet where God once walked in the person of his Son, taught, performed miracles, died and rose again. To suggest that all this was unimportant, that all that mattered was the spiritual reality underlying it, would make Christianity into something very different from what it has always been – a faith which insists God has taken human form, lived a human life and died and risen again for us. Since the coming of Jesus, the Temple, the city and the Land may have lost the significance which they had possessed before. At the same time, however, the existence of a particular place where God definitively revealed himself within human history is crucial for any Christian keen to hold on to the biblical, historic faith.

The sites linked with Jesus' ministry, or even the events recorded in the Old Testament, are places where God intersected with human life, and to that extent take on a significance for us that other places do not have. They are crucial reminders to us of the fact that God has stepped on to the stage of human history, and it is not uncommon for this sense of the historicity of faith to be reinforced by a visit to the Holy Land. One traveller, on a trip led by the authors, described his reaction to the land as 'not so much a spiritual experience, but a physical experience'. Another said, 'Seeing many of the sites where Jesus walked has increased my faith in the Incarnation. Of course, I did believe it before, but coming here has put flesh on those bones.'

Christian pilgrims often return with a much firmer grasp on the historical reality of the Gospel story. These events really happened. Jesus was a real human person as well as the Son of God. He transformed the lives of ordinary Galilean fishermen, not unlike those you see on the lake today. His death was a real human death, with blood dripping on to pale broken rocks, and cries echoing around the small disused quarry which had become the site for crucifixion just outside the walls of the city. These events are real, and God did step into human history, on to the stage of his own play, in the person of Jesus of Nazareth.

III. THE REAL JESUS

But who is the real Jesus? This brings us to a third reason for biblical pilgrimage. For many Christians, Jesus is the one they pray to, worship, love and confide in. For them, the stress lies upon an immediate relationship with the Risen Lord here and now. For others, he is primarily a historical figure whose identity may or may not be reconstructed from the fragmentary accounts in the Gospels.

Who then is he? The Risen Christ, or the Jesus of history?

Perhaps neither of these two options tells the whole story on its own. Neither is adequate as a full Christian understanding of the person of Christ. It is of course perfectly possible to view Jesus purely as a historical figure. There is enough historical evidence outside the Gospels to tell us he lived, died and created something of a stir in Roman Palestine in the first century. In this sense, he takes his place alongside Pontius Pilate, the emperor Vespasian and Flavius Josephus, the Jewish apologist, as figures influencing the history of this part of the Roman Empire at that time.

Yet Christians cannot stop there. The New Testament is incomprehensible without the sense that Jesus rose from death and is somehow still present by his Spirit with his followers after his earthly life. The rousing conclusion to Matthew's Gospel has Jesus promising his disciples that 'I will be with you always, to the end of the age' (Matthew 28:20). Paul spoke of Jesus 'at the right hand of God ... interceding for us' (Romans 8:34). Jesus Christ is not just a historical figure. He is now the exalted Lord, the one whose life could not be extinguished by death, and who is still alive to be known and worshipped today.

On the other hand, it is possible to go to Bible studies, listen to sermons, sing devotional Christian songs and end up thinking of Jesus either as a heavenly spirit, or if he is earthly at all, as some ethereal figure floating around a dreamy Galilean landscape. We rightly speak of a 'personal relationship with Jesus', but this can conjure up pictures of an invisible friend on to whom we project all our hopes and ideals, and who bears little resemblance to any historical reality.

So, if some Christians may be in danger of thinking of Jesus as just another historical personage like Genghis Khan or Julius Caesar, others could be in danger of seeing him just as a comforting presence like Father Christmas or the Easter Bunny. Having an 'imaginary friend' who bears no relationship to reality is a charming childish habit, but an alarming neurosis in a mature adult! If we are to speak of a personal relationship with the Living Christ, as we must, if we are to be true to the New Testament, then it is essential that the Risen Christ we relate to is continuous with the person of Jesus who lived in Palestine two thousand years ago.

When we pray to or worship Jesus Christ, the one we address is not just a first-century Galilean artisan who died and was buried (that would be idolatry). Nor is he a kind of 'ideal person', a mental projection of all our desires and wishes (that would be fantasy). He is the real Jesus of Nazareth, the authentic historical man who now has been raised by God from death, is ascended to the right hand of God, and who holds all authority in heaven and on earth. We can make our distinctions between the Jesus of history and the Christ of faith, but it's extremely important to keep them together as two sides, or even two stages in the career, of the same person.

So the Jesus we worship today is essentially the same as the Jesus who walked in Palestine, and is described in the Gospels. He still cares for the poor and oppressed and the disabled. He still opposes religious and other types of hypocrisy. He still offers forgiveness and a new start to those who, like Zacchaeus, realize they need it. He still says to those caught in shame and degradation, 'neither do I condemn you. Go and sin no more.' If we lose this vital connection between the Jesus in heaven to whom we sing and pray, and the Jesus who walked the busy streets of Jerusalem, we are likely to start projecting all kinds of things on to him which don't belong there. Subtly, we will begin to create a Jesus in our own image, the Jesus who justifies our way of life rather than challenging it, or who can be manipulated to support our political viewpoint against that of our enemies. That's where a pilgrimage can help.

In our daily relationship with Christ we may be tempted to divorce the exalted Lord from the Jesus of history, but we won't be able to do so for long in the land where Jesus walked. The physical surroundings, the sights and sounds constantly remind us of the real humanity and historicality of Jesus.

Qumran, near the shores of the Dead Sea, was the chosen location of a group of Jewish religious radicals in the first century. Documents belonging to this community, usually thought to be a group known as the 'Essenes', famously began to be discovered in 1947 – what we now know as the Dead Sea Scrolls. To stand in the ruins of the community's buildings today, to look across to Jericho and think of Jesus walking from there towards Jerusalem just a few short miles away, is to grasp that Jesus must have known of this group, and many others like them, whom we glimpse in the gospel narratives, such as Sadducees, Pharisees, and Herodians. If we fail to appreciate what Jesus' message meant in its own time, we are in danger of misrepresenting what it means today. Jesus was a real first-century Jewish teacher. The Kingdom he announced was meant to impact upon life there and then, not just some spiritual world to come. To discover that Jesus was on one level at least a historical figure, caught up with the political and religious controversies of his day, can be disturbing and unsettling. It can threaten our image of Jesus as just a convenient, reassuring presence in our lives. It can bring home to us the harsh things Jesus had to say about religious and political power and injustice. It can challenge us to look again at our way of life, and the Jesus who confronts us as well as comforts us.

There is a story of an early Christian desert monk who was 'Monophysite', who in other words espoused a theological position which tended to downplay the real humanity of Jesus, in favour of his divine glory. The story describes how he was 'converted' to the more orthodox belief in Jesus as fully divine *and* fully human on a visit to the church of the Holy Sepulchre in Jerusalem. This story hints to us that a visit to the site of Jesus' death and resurrection, real events within history in a real place, convinced him, and can convince us, if we need convincing, of the true identity of Jesus, grittily human and awe-inspiringly divine. Time spent in the land of the Bible can help us reconnect the Jesus we pray to with the Jesus who walked on earth. It can reacquaint us with the real Jesus.

IV. HE WASN'T THERE ...

Going to the church of the Holy Sepulchre in Jerusalem can still be a perplexing experience. Those who hope to find a peaceful meditative atmosphere, resplendent with the glory of God and glowing with the love of the Christian community, are likely to be disappointed. Architecturally, it is confusing to say the least. A bewildering mixture of styles and periods jostle uncomfortably alongside one another, some bits surviving from Constantine's great basilica of the fourth century, some erected during the Crusader period in medieval times, some nineteenth-century additions, much of it held up by creaking scaffolding and ageing pillars. Six different Christian denominations occupy various parts of the building. Each performs its rites in different languages and it is sometimes hard to hear yourself think above the din of competing chants of monks, priests or patriarchs. The different churches can find it so hard to co-operate that repairs can take years to organize, and because there have been disputes between the denominations in the past, the key to the church has long been held by a local Muslim family. On the surface, the church can be a reminder not of the greatness of Christianity, but of its divisions and weakness. It would take the most determinedly optimistic visitor to suggest that its outward appearance and internal politics bring a vivid sense of the presence of God.

Yet Christians keep turning up every day, visiting and revisiting, drawn to it like a magnet. Why? *Because it is the only church in the world with an empty tomb.* Christians visit it not because Jesus is there, but precisely because he is NOT there. Despite the noise and confusion, there is still a great sense of joy about this church, because it can be a most eloquent and powerful reminder of the Risen Jesus. Christians don't visit it as a shrine to their dead leader, as the place where his bones were laid to rest, and where they can at least be near to the relics of his life, like a museum to a dead war hero. Instead they walk around it with profound gladness because Jesus was once laid there, but he is there no longer. It is very strengthening to Christian faith to go to the place where Jesus' body was laid, and to see for yourself that there is nothing there. The Garden Tomb, another site where people remember the burial of Jesus, makes the very same point with its inscription on the door to the sepulchre: 'He is not here: he is risen'.

To meet Jesus during his life on earth would have meant travelling to Palestine, walking through Galilee, or searching the streets of Jerusalem. Today, stooping low to creep into the centre of the edicule built on the spot where Jesus' tomb is said to have been located (you can only enter one or two at a time, it is so small), reminds us that, as the angel said on the first Easter Day, 'He is not here, he is risen!' That is precisely the point: Jesus is not to be found exclusively in the Holy Sepulchre, or indeed at any special location. Why? Because he is risen. He has also given his followers the gift of the Holy Spirit, through whom his presence is available to all who put their trust in him wherever they happen to be (John 14:16–18). He can be encountered not just in Jerusalem but anywhere. Consequently, leaving the church of the Holy Sepulchre doesn't feel like leaving God behind as you walk back into the courtyard outside. Instead it reinforces the sense that God is present at all times, that the Risen Jesus can be with us wherever we are, whether in the streets of Jerusalem, back in our local church, at work or around the breakfast table at home.

So, in the Land, it is important to remember as we journey around these 'holy places' that God was once here as one of us. Jesus was a real, human, historical figure, who walked human streets, felt human pain, laughed at human jokes. He was fully and gloriously human, precisely because he was so fully and gloriously divine. Yet it is also vital to remember that he is no longer confined to these 'holy places'. He is present wherever his people are. The temples in which he now chooses to live are the bodies of his people, and especially so when they meet together around his table and his Word. He can be found as readily and as willingly in Jarrow, Jeddah or Jakarta as he can be in Jerusalem, but paradoxically, it sometimes takes a visit to Jerusalem to realize it!

SPIRITUAL PILGRIMAGE

If there are many good reasons to visit the land of the Bible, what of the journey itself? A true Christian is never static, always moving, always pressing on to what lies ahead. In the Bible and in the work of later theologians such as John Calvin and John Bunyan, pilgrimage was often used as a picture of the Christian life. Throughout the Bible, a rich vein of imagery sees this life as a long, sometimes arduous, journey towards the 'Jerusalem which is above' (Galatians 4:26). The story of Abraham, and then the wanderings of the people of Israel through the wilderness under the leadership of Moses, and then the entry into the land under Joshua, is one big story of a pilgrimage towards a land promised to them by their God. The eleventh chapter of the book of Hebrews takes up this theme, and sees a deeper meaning beneath the journeying of Abraham, Jacob, Moses and the rest. They were looking not just for a terrestrial home, a place to lay their heads, but a heavenly, spiritual one. In the mind of the writer to the Hebrews, their wanderings became a sign of the journey each Christian takes towards their spiritual home, the 'city with foundations, whose architect and builder is God' (Hebrews 11:10). The heavenly city of the book of Revelation is modelled on Jerusalem (Revelation 21:2), as the goal of all Christians' longing. The search for Jerusalem becomes the search for a true spiritual home, a place where justice, peace and harmony reign, where good desires are fulfilled and goodness and truth, evil and falsehood are shown in their true colours, seen for what they truly are.

Bunyan's *Pilgrim's Progress* develops brilliantly this picture of the Christian life as an arduous journey. Hardships, temptations, losing the way, being attacked by thieves, exhaustion, all the trials of the traveller become figures of the struggles of the Christian life with temptation, opposition, misunderstanding, unpopularity and plain boredom. On the journey lurk all manner of dangers and pitfalls, yet also good companions, along with occasional glimpses of the end, and finally, the glorious arrival at the destination.

Like Bunyan's pilgrim, the Christian is never truly at home within this world. His home is always just beyond the horizon. Stanley Hauerwas and William Willimon use the idea of 'resident aliens' as a telling description of the Christian in a modern secular society. Their point is that Christians really belong to another kingdom. They owe their loyalty to another king, and any national, political or ethnic ties they have here can only ever be temporary and provisional. In a sense Christians don't really belong here. They are, as the song used to say, 'just a-passing through'. The Christian is never quite content. She experiences a strange mixture of true comfort that she is loved by God as she is, fully accepted, forgiven and embraced, yet at the same time, she knows that she still has far to go. Jesus blesses not those who are satisfied with the *status quo*, but those who hunger for justice, those who mourn, who are persecuted for righteousness' sake, and whose poverty of spirit stands as a sharp contrast to the confidence and self-satisfaction all around.

Going on a physical journey or 'pilgrimage' can still teach us much about this aspect of the Christian life. Of course the experience of pilgrimage is very different now from what it was in the Middle Ages when travellers ventured on a voyage to the new Latin kingdom established by the Crusaders in Palestine. Then, the journey would take weeks, even months. It was long and hard, and the extremes of hunger, thirst, cold, heat and bandits were a constant threat to life itself. There was no guarantee on setting out that the pilgrim would necessarily make it all the way there, let alone back again. Now the journey begins in a modern air-conditioned airport. It takes hours, not weeks. We can breakfast in Hamburg and lunch in Haifa. The sense of adventure and journeying is much less stark and fraught with danger than it ever was in the past.

However, it is still possible to retain this sense of pilgrimage as echoing the theme of journeying through the Christian life, and turn a trip to the Holy Land into a vivid reminder of the Christian's lifelong journey to his true home in heaven. Just as the patriarchs' journeys became a figure of the inner journey towards the true heavenly city, so our journeys, undertaken out of a desire to strengthen our faith more and more, can in a lesser way also become a dramatic reminder for us of the Christian life as pilgrimage.

A trip which is not just a well-deserved break to some beach or leisure park, but undertaken deliberately out of a desire to establish and build up faith, can in itself become a valuable means of growth in the Christian life. Leaving home behind reminds us not to settle down too easily, not to become too much 'at home' with the standards and values of the culture around us. Walking through dry desert landscapes can become a picture of the long path of obedience and faith. Sleeping in different beds each night conveys the sense that we are never truly at home in the world, always travelling, moving on, journeying to our true home in heaven. Journeying with good friends, offering small signs of help, sharing the sense of wonder at seeing new things, talking long into the night with an honesty and freedom which are often more possible when away from the mundane and customary: all of this can paint for us a picture of what true fellowship can be. Travelling as lightly as is practical, with fewer belongings than we might normally take on holiday, can prompt us to become a little less attached to the things we think we own, to remember that our life does not consist in the abundance of our possessions.

Being uprooted from familiar surroundings, thrown among strange and alien peoples and cultures, can make us more able to re-evaluate our own 'normal' patterns of life. Being disorientated can sometimes be an opportunity for growth and change, as it forces us to see ourselves, others, and God in new ways. Then, arriving at the final destination, whether Jerusalem or somewhere else, can become a reminder of the great day when we will reach the 'Jerusalem which is above', and see face to face the God who stands at the end of our days, and who alone can fulfil all our hopes.

Pilgrimage is not required of Christians nor divinely mandated. It is not a guaranteed, automatic means of blessing. Yet it can still be an effective means of growth and encouragement for the contemporary biblical Christian. Today, as much as ever, visitors need to steer clear of the dangers which the reformers identified, and remember the vast difference the coming of Jesus as the true 'holy place' has made to our understanding of the Holy Land. Despite all this, pilgrimage has a simple yet powerful capacity to teach us new things about the Bible, to impress upon us the reality of God's work in Christ in the streets and cities of Palestine, and to remind us of some simple yet profound spiritual truths. It can renew a tired faith. It can rekindle spiritual fires that are burning dimly. It can stimulate minds eager to learn and devour knowledge. Most importantly, it can refocus our hearts and minds on the God who broods over all creation, yet who chose to reveal himself supremely in one person at one time, in one place, for all humankind.

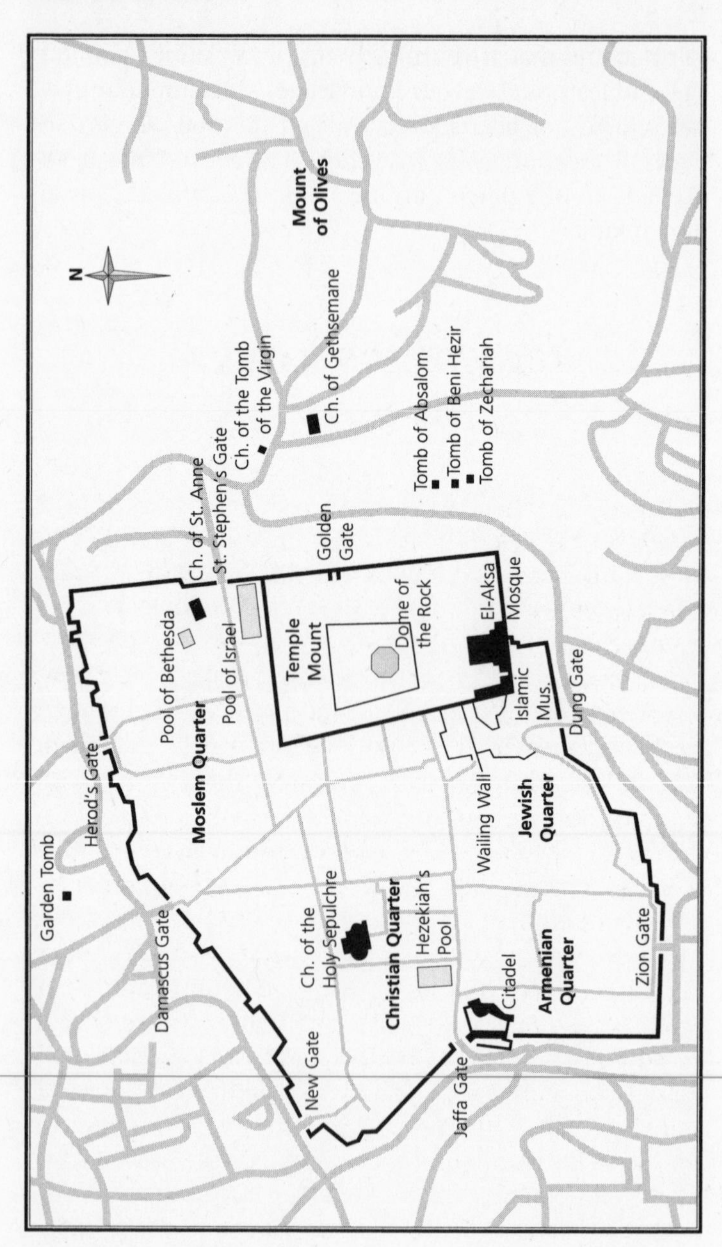

Figure 3. Jerusalem today

THE PILGRIMS' TALE (2)

Sarah woke with a start. She could hear a low metallic wail outside her hotel bedroom. It sounded human, but was in a language she could not make out. She looked at her watch. Six a.m. As she sank back on to the pillow, her mind slowly cleared, and she realized that she was listening to the Muslim call to prayer from a nearby mosque. Late the previous evening they had finally arrived in Jerusalem, and had gazed across from the Mount of Olives at the extraordinary sight of the golden Dome of the Rock, and the Old City behind and around it. It was a picture she had seen many times in books, but nothing prepared her for the sheer vibrancy, colour and noise of the scene. Roger had handed out maps and diagrams and had tried to point out where everything was. He talked about the City of David, Crusaders, Turks and some modest character who called himself Suleiman the Magnificent, who had something to do with the city walls, but she just got confused, and decided instead simply to drink in the view. They had later settled into a hotel not far from the Damascus Gate in Arab East Jerusalem.

She got out of bed and wandered to the window, pulled back the shutters, and peered out over the street. A small group of *Hasidim*, orthodox Jewish men, each wearing a knee-length black coat, a wide-brimmed hat, and long curls hanging beside his face, talked busily as they walked along briskly together. A couple of Arab traders were arranging warm-looking rings of bread for sale to passers-by, as the city began to stretch, yawn, and prepare itself for the new day.

She climbed into bed again and thought back over the past week. Images flooded into her mind: the morning walk through wet, fertile fields by the church commemorating the Sermon on the Mount; sitting quietly on a rocky shore by the still waters of the Sea of Galilee; intense discussions with Palestinian Christians in Nazareth, explaining the injustice they felt at their treatment within the land of Israel; the afternoon they had spent in the powerful silence of the desert; tedious long hours looking out of the window of the bus. Yet here, she felt close to the centre of the world, at the end of her journey: Jerusalem.

After dozing a little longer, she went downstairs, where Tom and the rest of the party were already eating breakfast. They ate quickly, gathered bags, cameras and guidebooks, climbed on to the bus, and were soon driving around the edge of the medieval city walls. Tony, the American guide, described how they were heading around the Mount of Olives towards Bethphage. She had read about it in the Gospels, but had never quite known how to pronounce it. Tony called it *Beth-fa-gay*. After a fifteen-minute drive, they clambered out of the coach, were greeted by an elderly one-legged Arab, the 'guardian of the site', and filed into a clean-looking church, with a bright mural depicting Jesus on a donkey surrounded by palm-waving disciples. Tony sat them all down, and began to speak.

Today's the day when our visit to the Holy Land reaches its climax. Today we focus down on to one single event, which arguably is the most important to have taken place in this land and indeed in the whole of history – the arrival of Jesus in Jerusalem and what happened in those crucial few days which followed.

We are following in the steps of Jesus as he makes his way over the Mount of Olives, trying to imagine what it would have been like to be in the crowds welcoming this Galilean prophet. We are following his journey to the cross.

Here in Bethphage we are right on the edge of the desert. When we go outside the church in a moment we will be able to see the contours of the land descending quickly, down towards the Dead Sea. If you were travelling up in the first century from Jericho on the Roman road, then Bethphage was the first 'outpost' of Jerusalem – the first indication that your journey was nearly over. Here was a tiny hamlet to greet you after your long hike, climbing up over three thousand feet in the course of fourteen miles of desert. Bethany was a slight detour to your left, hidden by one of the several hills which all form part of the Mount of Olives.

So before we set out on our walk into the city, let's reflect on why it was that Jesus ever made that journey up from Galilee through the Judean desert toward Jerusalem. If he had wanted a quiet life, he could have had it in Galilee. Jerusalem was inevitably the place where matters would come to a head. So why did he deliberately enter into the eye of the storm?

Partly, of course, it was because of Passover. Each year vast numbers of Galilean Jews made their way up to their capital city for this festival, one of the three festivals at the heart of Jewish life. So many came, in fact, that they camped outside the city; the Mount of Olives would have been covered with tents – something more like a modern pop festival! But Jesus had other reasons for seeing a visit to Jerusalem at this Passover season as being essential for his life's work. We read in Luke 9:51 that 'Jesus resolutely set out for Jerusalem'. Why? Let me give you four reasons.

First, because Jesus was a prophet – the last in the long line of those called by God to speak to his chosen people. Sooner or later, a true prophet had to come to the capital city. He could not announce the will of the Lord, he could not denounce certain aspects of the contemporary scene, while all the time hiding himself in some backwater. Jesus had to come to Jerusalem to deliver his message from the Lord: 'repent, for the kingdom of God is at hand'.

Second, because Jesus was offering a challenge to the Temple. At the heart of the city lay this enormous institution, the place where God's Name was believed to dwell, the divinely appointed place for receiving God's forgiveness through sacrifice. But now, as seen in the healing of the paralytic, Jesus was claiming to be himself the place where forgiveness was found. 'One greater than the Temple is here,' he claimed, 'one greater even than Solomon', the builder of the original Temple. So Jesus made straight for the Temple when he arrived in Jerusalem. It was not just that the Temple and its authorities were ripe for his prophetic critique. It was also that Jesus himself in his own person constituted a challenge to all that the Temple stood for. If there was a profound sense in which God's presence – or God's Name – was now dwelling in Jesus, then a clash between Jesus and the Temple was inevitable. If you like, 'the city was not big enough for the both of them'.

Third, because Jesus was making a claim to be the Messiah. And the Messiah was the 'Son of David', entitled to royal acclaim in Jerusalem. Sooner or later any royal claimant must go to the capital to press their claim. And that's why what we remember in this place – his choosing to enter Jerusalem on a donkey – is so significant. For it fulfilled the prophecy in Zechariah which told the 'daughter of Zion' (i.e. Jerusalem) that 'your king comes to you, gentle and riding on a donkey' (Zechariah 9:9). Here Jesus was making an enormous claim for himself – to be the true king of Zion/Jerusalem. When one then remembers that in the Old Testament there are verses which suggest that God alone is truly the King of Zion, then it is more staggering still. When Jesus spoke about the 'Kingdom of God', this was not a vaguely nice idea, but a forthright announcement that God was now becoming King – and he was becoming King through none other than Jesus himself! So the King inevitably had to come to his city. But what kind of welcome would he receive when he got there, and what kind of throne would he sit on? And here we come to a fourth reason for Jesus' coming up to Jerusalem:

Because Jesus was called to die. Christian believers sometimes see this as the only reason for Jesus' journey up to Jerusalem, but as we have just seen there are all sorts of other reasons as well. Sceptics, on the other hand, think it macabre or bizarre that anyone could consciously go into a situation actively intending the outcome to be their own death. It does seem strange. Yet there is ample evidence in the Gospels that Jesus did indeed see his forthcoming visit to Jerusalem in this solemn light. 'I must keep going,' he said on one occasion with a heavy dose of irony, 'because surely no prophet can die outside Jerusalem!' (Luke 13:33). 'The Son of Man came ... to give his life as a ransom for many' (Mark 10:45). Contrary to what Simon Peter wanted, he warned his disciples that 'the Son of Man must suffer many things and be rejected by the elders, and he must be killed' (Luke 9:22). Jesus had read of the Suffering Servant in Isaiah and believed it was his own destiny to be that Servant: 'It is written [in Isaiah 53:12], "And he was numbered with the transgressors"; and I tell you that this must be fulfilled in me' (Luke 22:37).

So Jesus came up to Jerusalem with much on his mind, with much to accomplish. Luke refers in fact to his need to accomplish a 'new exodus' (Luke 9:31), a new act of God bringing liberation to his people. So this was going to be a Passover with a profound difference – indeed a new Passover with a whole new meaning. He came to speak God's word; he came to embody God's presence; he came to enact God's rule – he was truly the 'Prophet, Priest and King'. But he also came to die, to give his life for others – the Servant, the Saviour, the Redeemer.

Now we see how much hung on the shoulders of that solitary figure making his way up through the desert here towards Bethphage. Now perhaps we understand why Jesus strode out ahead of the disciples, causing them to be somewhat afraid of him (Mark 10:32). His desire was so intense to fulfil his mission, to undergo (as he called it) his 'baptism'; he could not rest now, he had said, 'until it was completed' (Luke 12:50).

Now too perhaps we may understand why the crowds, as they saw Jesus leaving Jericho for Jerusalem, believed that 'the

Kingdom of God was going to appear at once' (Luke 19:11). There was something about Jesus that made people aware that something enormously significant was about to take place in Jerusalem. And they were right. God was indeed about to establish his Kingdom in a new way. Yet it would not quite be the Kingdom they were looking for, nor would it come about in the expected way. The King must die:

Ride on, ride on in majesty,
in lowly pomp ride on to die.
Bow thy meek head to mortal pain;
then take, O God, thy power and reign.

So Jesus' disciples and the Galilean pilgrims made their way up here towards Bethphage, eager to get their first glimpse of Jerusalem, keen to see what would happen next when this Jesus entered the city. Jesus knew. His strategy was clear. He had planned what might be called a little bit of 'street theatre'. He would ride in on a donkey, and two of his disciples were told to collect it from the 'village yonder'.

We do not know for certain whether the donkey was collected from here or from Bethany over the hill (though the latter is possible, given Jesus' friends there – Mary, Martha and Lazarus: Luke 10:38–42; John 11–12). What we do know is that this was a vital moment in the life of Jesus and in the history of Jerusalem – the City of God, long prepared, now about to be presented with her King. The crowds loved it, the disciples followed, and we too must now follow in his steps to see what happens next.

Let's have our reading from Luke's Gospel (19:28–36) and then we shall sing 'All Glory, Laud and Honour, to thee Redeemer King'.

The group stood to sing the hymn. Afterwards, some remained quietly praying. Sarah sat staring into space, thinking hard on Tony's words, picturing in her imagination the intense figure of Jesus striding through this place, almost frightening in his fierce determination, so different from the warm, comforting Jesus she was used to. Tom shivered as the cold morning air began to bite. He got up, anxious to summon some warmth back into his numb hands. He walked across the church towards a large rock enclosed by a square iron grille. 'What's that?' whispered Sarah, as she crept up close to him. 'It's supposed to be the rock from which Jesus climbed on to the donkey,' Tom whispered back. 'The guidebook says the Crusaders identified it and built a church here.'

'Oh. Do you think it was?' she asked.

'No, of course not,' he insisted emphatically. 'Like I told you, it's all guesswork here. How on earth did they know? A bunch of rowdy medieval French thugs came here and said this was the place, just so they could fleece money from the tourists, if you ask me.'

'But surely you think it happened somewhere?' she replied. 'And if you're going to go on like that all day, you'd better talk to someone else. I want to be really focused today and drink it all in. I don't need your sceptical comments. They'll take away the mood of the day for me. Anyway, you'll miss the whole point if all you're thinking about is whether or not it's the very place.'

She walked out of the church into the courtyard outside. The morning was chilly and damp; a gentle mist hung in the air. Roger led them down a small path towards what he said were first-century tombs behind the church. Tom followed her. 'Sarah, look, I'm sorry. I'll try to be more positive. You're right, I'll try to get into it a bit more.'

They found themselves in a kind of sloped garden. In the side of the hill, there were several small openings into the underlying rock. Tony explained how these were genuine first-century tombs, and one of them even had its 'rolling stone' still in place.

Tom peered through the mist into the darkness of one of the tombs. Somehow he could feel his imagination being liberated. Perhaps it was the quietness of the place, the absence of tourists, or even the fact that he knew this wasn't the real tomb of Jesus – he didn't have to worry about whether or not it was. He suddenly found himself imagining a small group of women creeping up to another tomb on a similar cold morning in Jerusalem two thousand years before. He began to imagine their horror and confusion as they realized the tomb was open, presumably broken into and robbed.

As the rest of the group began to edge back towards the church, Tom remained behind, standing before the empty tomb. All through the trip he had felt awkward about his continued cynicism. He had wondered how on earth all this connected with his real life, the one he lived at home. Now something deep inside him stirred, as the confusion of the women echoed with his, and he began to see how this day just might hold something significant for him. Perhaps the mist would clear.

Roger led them out of the garden, back on to the road. They then walked in silence a few hundred yards up a small rise. Eventually they turned to the right, alongside a stone wall. A group of Italian pilgrims, led by a brown-habited Franciscan friar, were filing out of a door in the wall. When they had all come through, Tom, Sarah and the others stepped inside and found themselves in a circular courtyard, with a graceful octagonal, domed stone building in the centre. Tony assembled them, before continuing his narrative.

From now on, until we reach Gethsemane at the foot of the Kidron valley, it's downhill all the way. We are on the highest point on the Mount of Olives. That's why this area (and particularly the area covered by that small dome behind me) is the traditional place of the Ascension. After all, what better place to remember that event than on a mountaintop?

You may remember there was some fun and games in the fourth century when Eusebius wanted the Ascension to be associated with a cave fifty metres to the south of here (under what is now the Pater Noster church, which we will be passing in a moment). But at the end of the fourth century the Byzantine Christians built this round structure, leaving it suitably open to the sky. The Muslims then put the dome over it in the ninth century, but the different Orthodox churches still use it each year on their Ascension Day, covering this courtyard with lots of colourful awnings.

Luke's Gospel (which we are following today) tells us that 'Jesus went out as usual to the Mount of Olives' (Luke 22:39). So, if this is the hill that Jesus frequented, it was only natural for him to return here for the moment of his final departure.

As a result the Mount of Olives is not just about Palm Sunday. We have to remember what also happened here a few weeks later, when Jesus was 'taken up' in glory. All this gives our walk a whole extra layer of meaning. This is not just the way of the cross; it is also the way of the King, marching towards his throne. The crowds at that time proclaimed him as Zion's King; they were right but only because this Jesus is more than that – King of the world and of all creation. So as we walk in his steps, we also worship the risen Lord of creation.

Luke says that, after a period of around 'forty days' in which he had given his disciples 'many convincing proofs that he was alive' (Acts 1:3), Jesus finally led them out to somewhere near here (Luke 24:50). The word Luke uses for 'led out' had been used before of Moses leading out the people from Egypt and through the wilderness for forty years. It's his way of reminding us that Jesus was a new Moses who had just performed a new exodus, doing a work in Jerusalem for the liberation of his people. So Jesus now leads his disciples out from the city, so that they can be formed into his new people – focused on him; and he tells them that very soon, once they have received the Spirit, they too will be going out from Jerusalem 'to the ends of the earth' with news of this great liberation.

This must have been an incredibly powerful moment for the disciples. Sensing perhaps that Jesus was about to leave them, they blurted out their most burning question: if you are the Messiah, surely you cannot leave us without doing the main thing the Messiah was supposed to do – to restore Israel? But Jesus could leave them – and he did! Because in a way which they would only gradually come to recognize, he had restored Israel through his resurrection – only it was not quite what they had been expecting. And if they were thinking about the nation of Israel being restored as it responded to this message of their crucified Messiah, well, that was their task – to be his witnesses in Jerusalem and then throughout the world. The Kingdom would be restored and implemented as people responded to the proclamation of the King.

So Jesus was taken away from them into a 'cloud'. As elsewhere in the Bible and on the Mount of the Transfiguration, the cloud was a sign of God's presence and glory. This was the moment of his vindication, the time when at last, in the language of Daniel, the 'Son of Man came with the clouds of heaven' and approached 'the Ancient of Days', being 'led into his presence' (Daniel 7:13). It was the time when, in the language of the Psalmist, the Lord God said to our Lord, 'Sit at my right hand until I make your enemies a footstool for your feet' (Psalm 110:1). It was the moment when Jesus finally received his Father's praise for fulfilling his awesome mission, the moment when Jesus received the throne which had eluded him in Jerusalem. 'The head which once was crowned with thorns is crowned with glory now.'

And for the disciples it was a moment of both joy and deep sadness. They perhaps could glimpse Jesus at long last receiving the glory that was his due. And yet the one who had come to be the centre of their lives was now being wrenched away from them. The next time they would see him would be in the age to come. In the meantime they had been left the most enormous task. They were a tiny group. Yet, if Jesus was God's supreme word to his world, then he had clearly entrusted to them the responsibility of letting the whole world know. What if they failed? It appeared that God had no other plans. So while they 'returned to Jerusalem with great joy' (Luke 24:52), they also began waiting upon God for the gift of his Spirit (Acts 1:4, 14) – which they would surely need for the road that lay ahead.

We too need that Spirit if we are to proclaim this Jesus and the world is to know what God has done here in Jerusalem. But we too can now make our own way into the city 'with joy'. We too know that Jesus has been glorified. So although this is the way of the cross, it is also the way of the King: 'Rejoice, the Lord is King!' 'Crown him with many crowns': the lamb who died in Jerusalem is 'on his throne'.

Tom and Sarah waited their turn as each member of the party entered the small domed structure at the centre of the courtyard. 'So this is where Jesus is supposed to have ascended from?' asked Sarah. 'Yes, and the guidebook says you can even see the footprint left behind when he took off – look!' Tom pointed to a small indentation in the rock at the centre of the floor, which appeared vaguely like a foot if you looked hard enough. 'Must have had some backthrust!' he laughed. Sarah glanced at him, but this time he was smiling, and the cloud that had haunted his face for most of the trip had begun to lift. They left the courtyard and resumed the walk, moving downwards now, past the Pater Noster church that Tony had mentioned.

'It must have been really odd for the disciples, don't you think?' asked Sarah.

'How do you mean?'

'Well, having Jesus with them for so long, then him just ... disappearing.'

'Mmm, I suppose so,' replied Tom. 'Still, no different from us, we have to make do with Jesus not being here either. Maybe that's the point of coming here, though – it is beginning to make some kind of sense now. You're quite right, all this "exact spot" stuff is pointless. Back there at the tombs, and when Tony was talking about Jesus going away, it hit me that Jesus isn't here. Well, he is and he isn't. He isn't here in person – maybe that's what I wanted, but knew he couldn't be, so that's why I was so frustrated, if you see what I mean. But he is here. I suppose that's what "risen and ascended" means. He's not here any more in person, but he's still here with us in the Spirit, like the disciples found after he'd gone away.'

'Not sure I understood all that,' said Sarah, as they walked steadily down past some bustling Arab houses. Dogs barked behind a wire fence as they passed, and a group of children stopped their game of football to watch. Suddenly, as they turned a corner, there it was – the city of Jerusalem! Until now it had been hidden behind the houses. As the mists cleared, fresh sunlight caught the golden Dome of the Rock. But it seemed different from the night before. Less exhilarating, more brooding, simmering. Across the Kidron valley, they could see the sturdy walls of the Temple platform. A small ridge ran down to their left on the other side of the valley, which Tom remembered as the place where King David had originally built his city. Tony gathered the group together and spoke once more:

This is always a great moment, the moment when Jerusalem suddenly comes into view! You saw it for the first time last night and so hopefully you've got your bearings now. It is a splendid sight and it stirs the heart. They say that no one coming up to Jerusalem can see the city without their heart missing a beat.

And the same thing happened for those Galilean pilgrims who were with Jesus, as we learn from Luke 19:37–40. Presumably most of them had seen it before, but that did not stop them spontaneously bursting into praise. 'When he came near the place where the road goes down the Mount of Olives, the whole crowd of disciples began joyfully to praise God.' They had probably been on the road for the best part of a week, and now their journey was almost at an end. Here at last was what they had been waiting for – a sight of their capital city, the 'holy city' of the living God, and of the Temple which lay at the very heart of their faith.

But they were also praising God on this occasion for an extra reason, because of 'all the miracles they had seen' – that is, through Jesus. What sparked this new outburst of praise, their 'hosannas', was the powerful combination of Jesus and Jerusalem, the great preacher of the Kingdom of God now entering into the city of the Great King. Surely, they thought, he would now establish God's Kingdom and rule: 'blessed is the King who comes in the name of the Lord!' But what kind of kingdom and what kind of king?

So the atmosphere is electric as we make our way down the hill. You can sense it in the way the Pharisees want Jesus to rebuke his disciples. What the crowds are saying about Jesus is outrageous if it is not true; and it is also political dynamite – best hushed up. But Jesus lets the crowds have their way for a little longer. For, despite all their muddled ideas, they are on to something. This is indeed the moment for which Jerusalem was destined, for which the Mount of Olives was created: 'if the crowd keeps quiet,' replied Jesus, 'the stones will cry out!'

Almost as if trying to hear the shouts of the crowd, the group fell silent as they walked steadily downhill, across the face of the slope of the Mount of Olives. A few stopped to take pictures across the valley. Below them, they could see hundreds of rectangular stone Jewish tombs, some with smaller stones placed on them. A small group of black-coated Hasidim gathered sombrely around one of the tombs.

Sarah too had felt a small gasp escape her lips as a sunlit Jerusalem broke into view. Now, as she walked pensively down the hill, she slowly assembled in her mind images of the city she could see before her with the Jesus who seemed more and more real with each step. She became aware of a group of Greek pilgrims overtaking them on the way down, singing what she supposed was a Greek hymn. At the back of the group was a small elderly man bent low with age, wearing a faded black suit which looked as if it must have been his only suit, brown scuffed shoes, his face creased and wind-beaten. As he walked, he sang with an intensity which took Sarah's breath away. She found herself almost shocked by him. She could not understand a word he was singing. Their lives must have been about as far apart as she could imagine. She had read about how Greek Christians sometimes came to Jerusalem before they died in a kind of preparation for the journey into death itself. Maybe that was why he had come.

It wasn't just the fervour with which he sang. It was the realization that here was someone whose faith was so much older than hers. She had been in some Greek Orthodox churches in Galilee on the first part of the trip, and had sensed a faith whose roots stretched far into the dark earth of the past. He seemed to her a piece of ancient Christianity thrust into the present, as if he had been spirited in by a time capsule.

Tom caught up with her. 'You OK?' he asked.

'Yes,' she replied, 'just suffering from a touch of culture shock.'

'You mean those Greeks?'

'That's right. I guess I thought our worship songs at home were the only way to do it. I've no idea what they believe, but you know I think I can feel what he's feeling – does that make sense?' Tom nodded in agreement.

They continued down the hill, which became steeper as they went. The pair walked behind the rest of the group, each sensing that important things were happening inside the other. It was a feeling both exhilarating and yet disturbing; and their mutual vulnerability drew them together, as if for reassurance that someone else might understand.

They followed the others down some steep steps and found themselves beside a strange-shaped building, carved elegantly like a teardrop. The sign at the entrance had called it 'Dominus Flevit', Latin for 'the Lord wept'. The Italian pilgrims they had met earlier were emerging from the dark interior of the building, so they began to file in themselves. They immediately saw a familiar postcard view of Jerusalem through an iron-grilled window, with a representation of a chalice in the centre. The window drew the eye and focused it unerringly on two small domes in the middle distance. Roger stood up and read in his by now familiar squeaky voice the story of Jesus weeping over Jerusalem from Luke 19. Then in the quiet, Tony stood up and began to speak, starting very slowly:

It's so strange. Suddenly in the midst of the celebration, the person at its centre bursts into tears. Something is profoundly wrong. But Jesus is not weeping for himself. He is weeping for Jerusalem, the city which he loved so passionately. He had addressed Jerusalem before, longing to 'gather your children together as a hen gathers her chicks under her wing, but you were not willing' (Luke 13:34). He longed to be the true Lord of the city and to prevent its inhabitants from setting out on a road which would surely lead to destruction. But now, with his prophet's imagination he saw the city being encircled, not by his own embrace, but by the mighty armies of Rome.

And why was this going to come about? At one level it was because the city's political leaders, fired up with nationalism, could not see the 'signs of the times' and that rebellion against Rome was destined to be disastrous. They did not know the 'peace terms', the 'things that belonged to peace'. If only you, Yerushalaim, the City of Peace, loved real peace!

But at a more profound level, it was because the city was spiritually blind to the significance of what was happening right now under her very nose: 'because you did not know on this day ...because you did not recognize the time of God's coming to you'. This should have been Jerusalem's finest hour, its moment of glory – the City of God welcoming the Son of God. But she missed it; it passed her by. And worse still, she would play a part in Jesus' being rejected and thrown out from her midst – to be crucified outside her walls.

But the 'stone which the builders rejected would become the chief corner-stone'. Jesus would be vindicated. As for Jerusalem and its Temple, 'they will not leave one stone upon another' (cf. Luke 21:6). It was indeed a pivotal point in Jerusalem's history and it all turned on the arrival of this one man on a donkey. It was a unique moment, with awesome consequences. Jerusalem would never quite be the same again.

And as Jesus looks over the city today and over us, what does he see? A city which has missed the source of its true peace, and is blind? It is enough to make you weep. And what would he say of us his followers, the people who claim to have welcomed him? Are we too sometimes equally blind to what God is doing? Let us resolve to be those who 'recognize the time of God's coming' to us, and respond so that Jesus does not once again weep over us.

After singing the hymn 'My song is love unknown', a little too slowly for Tom's liking, they walked out again into the sunlight, over to a small platform, to look across at the city. The domed building stood behind them, a silent memory of Jesus' tears over the city. Tourist buses queued on the road below them, while on the pavement, some young Israeli soldiers in green fatigues strutted past. The Muslim call to prayer rang out from the Al-Aqsa mosque higher up on the Temple platform. Tom tried to imagine what it would be like to be a Muslim or a Jew, and what the city would mean to them. He didn't get very far, as his imagination balked at the vast distance between his experience and theirs. His mind ranged over all that had happened here in the centuries that had passed since the time of Jesus – so much passion and energy, but for what? As the other members of the party began to drift away, he felt himself just beginning to sense some of the frustration lying hidden in Jesus' words about peace and Jerusalem, as they echoed with a piercing irony above the most fought-over city in the world.

Part Two

THE LIVING HISTORY
Christian Involvement in the Land

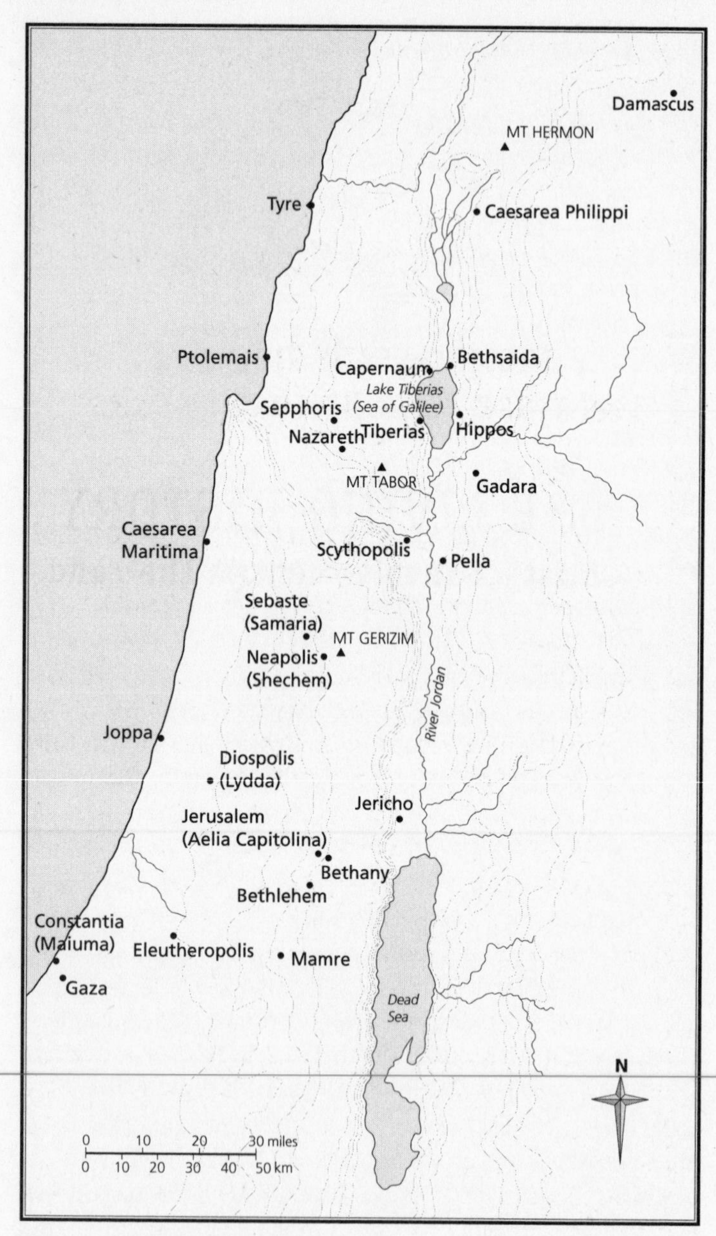

Figure 4. Palestine (AD 70–638)

Chapter 5

FROM RAGS TO RICHES: THE FIRST FOUR HUNDRED YEARS

When Tom and Sarah boarded that aeroplane, they were only dimly aware of the complex issues that a visit to the Holy Land can raise for Christians. Yes, they had had that awkward exchange in the coffee lounge, when they stumbled across their very different expectations; but they had little idea as they did so that they were walking on the tip of a very large iceberg. As they sipped their coffee, they were unwittingly stumbling into a debate which has raged for two thousand years – ever since the coming of Jesus. Just how are Christian believers to respond to the places and the Land where Jesus lived, and to Jerusalem, the city of his Crucifixion and Resurrection?

Now, they have arrived in Jerusalem with a great sense of excitement, but are finding it a bewildering and confusing place. And as they do so, they gradually become aware that, bubbling away beneath the surface, there is a whole string of further questions. Just what do they think they are doing now that they are on this 'pilgrimage' in the land of the Bible?

These are the kinds of questions which we have tried to unpack in Part One. We went back to the Bible to establish a biblical framework within which to answer these questions and then suggested some positive ways in which biblical Christians can approach a visit to the Holy Land today.

THE LIVING PAST

But of course Sarah and Tom are not the first people to have raised these questions, nor are we the first people to have attempted to answer them! Throughout the last two millennia our Christian brothers and sisters have been wrestling with the same questions: How do we celebrate the history and geography of the biblical story while not undermining the spiritual and universal dimensions of the Christian faith? Does it matter who owns Jerusalem and the biblical sites, and what should any such owners do with these places?

Not surprisingly, Christians through the ages have come up with a variety of answers. Some have preferred to emphasize the spiritual nature of Christian faith, some have stressed that the history remains vitally important. Many others have pressed for a more sacramental approach to the Land of the Incarnation, while many in recent times have believed the promised land to be still playing a role within God's prophetic purposes. Each of these different belief-systems has then spawned a bewildering spread of different agendas, each in turn leaving its mark upon this one long-suffering Land.

So Tom and Sarah have come to the Holy Land, hoping above all to walk in the footsteps of Jesus. But now they are here, they find themselves bombarded with layer upon layer of history, each layer fraught with different significance for those who remember it in different ways. 'I came to find Jesus,' visitors have frequently said to us, 'but all I discovered was Herod and Hadrian, Byzantines and Crusaders, Israelis and Palestinians.' They find modern politics, fuelled by religious and ethnic controversy. And they find a church which reflects all that history too, and is inevitably marked by the diversity which comes from having practised the faith in a land where history is ever-present and can never be forgotten. It can be very confusing.

For, despite what some might wish, time has not stood still here and the Land has been home to many people in the intervening years. So visitors need quickly to gain a historical perspective. And, as they do so, they soon discover that history in the Holy Land is *living* history. What happened, for example, in the Crusades nine hundred years ago, still lives on in the minds of people who live here. You cannot live in the Land of the Bible without being affected by its history. And the same goes for pilgrims. Here indeed, as one Israeli video calls it, 'the long past lives'.

LEARNING FROM THE PAST

In this part of the book we move on to describe the history of Christian involvement in the Holy Land. As we go through the different historical periods, we have two questions in mind: First, what has been happening to the Christian church in this land since the time of the apostles? Second, what have Christians thought about the Land and what have they done when they visited? We want the likes of Tom and Sarah to be able to get a handle on the different layers of history. And we want them to see how Christians have responded in quite different ways to the very same questions which they themselves are now beginning to ask.

But more than that, we hope they will also be able to start evaluating those various responses in the light of the biblical picture presented above in Part One. Yes, we are chiefly involved in historical description. But a mindset shaped by the biblical teaching will also find itself asking important questions of that history. For there's lots to learn from the story of Christian involvement in the Holy Land. And remember, those who will not learn the lessons of history are always in danger of repeating its mistakes.

THE NEW TESTAMENT PERIOD (AD 30–70)

Early Christians in Jerusalem

According to the Book of Acts (2:41) the Christian church was launched in a dramatic way with three thousand people responding to Peter's first sermon, the first proclamation of the Resurrection, which he delivered during the Jewish festival of Pentecost. There was an early Jerusalem 'spring-time'. Jerusalem, the centre of Jewish life, was the natural place for the proclamation to Israel of its Risen Messiah, and there were some initial signs that the response to this message would be positive.

Persecution and opposition, however, lay just around the corner. Soon the Christian community was scattered throughout the country (Acts 5). The persecution was probably focused on those Christians with a background in Hellenistic Judaism who had a more radical view about the Temple (such as Stephen; see Acts 6–7). Yet it cannot have been easy for the small community now left behind in the city. Jerusalem was the obvious 'headquarters' for this new Messianic movement, but gradually the apostles themselves moved away. So the local church was overseen by James, the Lord's brother (Acts 15:13; 21:18). A later Christian source, the church historian Eusebius (c. 260–339) tells us that this 'James the Just' was martyred, thrown down from the pinnacle of the Temple by a mob, probably in AD 62 (Eusebius, *Ecclesiastical History*, 2.1). In those final few years leading up to the first Jewish Revolt it was a tense time to be a follower of Jesus in Jerusalem.

The tension can be sensed back in AD 56 when Paul brought up to Jerusalem the gifts he had collected from his

Gentile converts (2 Corinthians 8–9). In comparison with these converts, the 'saints' in Judea were poor – both because of famines in the area (Acts 11:28), and also quite probably because of their vulnerable situation among the wider Jewish populace (1 Thessalonians 2:14–16). Paul knew he was walking into the 'eye of the storm' (Romans 15:25–32). As Jewish nationalism increased, people in Jerusalem would not respond well to anyone like Paul who, through welcoming Gentiles into the People of God, was compromising Jewish identity. Some in James' own congregation, possibly connected to the so-called 'Judaizers', shared these concerns (Acts 21:20; cf. Galatians 5:7; Philippians 3:2). So James was forced to lay down some conditions before he could receive Paul's gift. And, sure enough, Paul was soon seized in the Temple courts – charged (incorrectly, as it happened) with having brought a Gentile into the Court of Israel. He survived because of the intervention of the Roman garrison. Six years later, during a brief spell when there was no Roman governor in Palestine, James would not be so fortunate.

Despite its promising start, the Christian Church in Jerusalem would never be that strong. For the unique claims of Jesus the Messiah brought into question things which Jerusalem held dear – the sanctity of its Temple and the necessity of people entering the People of God by first adopting the mantle of Judaism. James was a brave man when he decreed at the famous Jerusalem conference in AD 49 that Gentiles could enter the new People of God as Gentiles – that is, without being circumcised and adopting the various Jewish rules about food and the Sabbath (Acts 15:13ff). This would not go down well in Jerusalem. Being a Christian in Jerusalem was tough from the very beginning.

So when the Roman armies began to encircle the city in AD 67, the Christian community almost certainly fled the city to a town in TransJordan called Pella (Eusebius, *EH*, 3.5.3). Jesus had told his disciples to 'flee to the mountains' (Mark 13:14); when push came to shove, he implied, their loyalty was not to Jerusalem but to Jesus himself. And, in keeping with his predictions, the Holy City was sacked by the Romans and its Temple completely destroyed in the summer of AD 70. This was indeed a tragic day in Jerusalem's history.

Visiting the Gospel sites

But did believers living in the city before 70 preserve a memory of the various locations associated with Jesus' life – such as Gethsemane or Golgotha?

Almost certainly they knew the Gospel sites well. Yet, strictly, this is only conjecture. In particular, there is no firm evidence of any special interest in Jesus' tomb (though some have wondered if our Gospel accounts of the Resurrection reflect early Christian liturgies recited at the tomb). Apart from a passing reference in Acts 13:29 Jesus' tomb is never mentioned again – it disappears from the scene altogether. Did Paul make a point of visiting his Lord's tomb on his return trips to Jerusalem? Did believers go there to remember the Resurrection? Or were they more concerned with looking forwards, not backwards? It would be intriguing to know. But we don't.

And what about interest in the Holy Land among those who lived *beyond* the bounds of Palestine? We know from Acts 15 that the apostles returned once for a major consultation, but never again thereafter – they had more urgent business than to return for an annual reunion! We also know that Luke, the writer of the Gospel and of Acts, accompanied Paul on that dangerous visit to Jerusalem (Acts 21:17); but their primary purpose was to hand over their collection of money, not to see the 'holy sites'!

From Jerusalem to the ends of the earth

Nevertheless, as a historian, Luke would surely have been extremely interested in what he found in the Holy Land.

Once he had unpacked his bags in Jerusalem it would be surprising if he did not get out his notebook. He refers quite often to the Mount of Olives (Luke 19:37; 22:39; Acts 1:12): did he ever sit on its slopes and contemplate the city spread out before him? And what about those two whole years when Paul was in prison in Caesarea? No doubt he frequently visited Paul, but did he not also take the opportunity to go out round the country on the occasional research trip? For Luke, as indeed for the other Gospel writers, history was vitally important. It mattered that the story of Jesus had happened in real time and space. So even if the Christian gospel was now revealing its remarkable capacity to spread far and wide by the power of the Spirit, an interest in the original geography of Jesus' life could never be jettisoned as unimportant or 'unspiritual'. Christian theology and hope, then as now, was rooted in the soil of history.

The concluding chapters of Acts underline one of its central themes – that the message of Jesus could be known and Israel's God encountered anywhere in the world. How so? Because of the outpouring of the Holy Spirit on 'all people'; the 'promise is for you and to *all that are far off,* every one whom the Lord calls to him' (Acts 2:17, 39). Jesus himself had predicted that there would soon come a day when true worshippers would not need to come to Jerusalem, but instead would be able to worship the Father in 'spirit and in truth' (John 4:21–4). That day had now come, and the spread of the Church into the world far away from Jerusalem was sure evidence of the fact.

BETWEEN THE TWO JEWISH REVOLTS (AD 70–135)

As we move into the period after 70 it is worth noting how things might have looked to any Christian who was privileged to live through most of the first century (such as the elderly apostle John). What would surely have struck them was the incredible transition that had engulfed the world in their lifetime: the coming of Jesus, the spread of the gospel way beyond Palestine, and the fall of Jerusalem. These were momentous events, all interconnected, so they would believe, in the eternal purposes of God. So much had happened so quickly. And, in particular, the Holy Land would be irrevocably changed.

The family of Jesus

What happened for Christian believers living there in the years after AD 70? There will have been small Christian communities up and down the Land. The 'Nazarenes' would continue for several centuries, living as tiny communities in Galilee. There is also an intriguing story about the grandsons of Jude, who seem to have lived in Galilee but were brought before the Emperor Domitian (AD 81–96). Apparently he feared that their connection with this Messiah-figure Jesus might mean they were preparing an uprising against Rome. But when he saw their extreme poverty, he realized that they hardly posed any serious threat worth worrying about.

Some of the believers who had fled Jerusalem during the first Jewish Revolt must have returned to the city. For we know from Eusebius that there was a Christian community in Jerusalem. Its leadership, he tells us, was kept, as it were, 'within the family'. After James' death, other members of Jesus' human family such as Simeon and Justus were elected to lead the Church – a pattern which continued until the early years of the second century (*EH*, 4.5.3–5; 5.12).

The sudden change

Eusebius' list of bishops then continues with other Jewish names until the year 135, when suddenly the leadership of the Church (and indeed all its members) becomes entirely Gentile. Why the sudden Gentile 'takeover'? The answer lies in the second Jewish Revolt (AD 132–135). Not surprisingly there had been considerable unrest in Judea in the years after 70, with many wanting to rebuild the Temple and restore Jerusalem. Matters came to a head when a powerful leader emerged, Simon Ben Chosiba, who was soon recognized by many as the Messiah. Indeed, the famous Rabbi Akiba gave him the Messianic title Simon Bar Chochba (alluding to the 'son of the star' in Numbers 24:17).

The followers of Messiah Jesus were once again in a difficult situation. They were soon given trouble by their fellow Jews for not joining in the revolt. And then, when the revolt was crushed by the Roman Emperor Hadrian, they shared the same fate. In his determination that there should be no further revolts, Hadrian decreed that no circumcised person would be allowed to set eyes on the city. This included, of course, the city's Jewish Christian community. Once again the Jewish Jerusalem church went into exile – this time never to return. Any Christians who lived in the city thereafter would be Gentiles.

Jerusalem itself became a pagan city, refounded by Hadrian as 'Aelia Capitolina' and colonized by military veterans. The city plan was based quite consciously on that of a normal Roman army camp. The city now occupied only the northern half of the city of Jesus' day and a large part of it was given over to the camp of the Tenth Legion. As far as we can tell, the remainder of the city was not even surrounded by a wall. 'Jerusalem' as such was no more – or, at least, it was just a shadow of its former self.

FROM HADRIAN TO CONSTANTINE (AD 135–325)

And so it remained for nearly two hundred years. During this period the Christian community in the city gradually increased in size – though it remained small compared to that in the new provincial capital on the coast, Caesarea. Do we know where they met for worship? Quite possibly just outside the area of Aelia, in a building which had been in the 'upper city' of Jesus' day. Could this in fact be the 'upper room' associated with the events of the Last Supper or Pentecost? Christians, both ancient and modern, have suggested this identification, but we cannot be certain. We know from Eusebius, however, that the Jerusalem Christians managed a small library somewhere in the city and continued to preserve the names of their bishops. They also kept a chair which they claimed to be the 'throne' of their first bishop, James (*EH*, 7.19).

Visitors to the Land

They also welcomed visitors – not a vast horde, but enough to suggest that there were Christians elsewhere for whom the historical roots of their faith were important. One of them, a man called Alexander, came from Cappadocia around AD 200 (Eusebius, *EH*, 6.11.12). He was unexpectedly asked by the local Jerusalem Christians to be their bishop, because the previous bishop, Narcissus, had mysteriously disappeared. To their embarrassment Narcissus then returned a few years later, having been in the Judean desert on an unannounced personal retreat!

Alexander, however, had first come to the Land, we are told, 'for the sake of the places and for prayer'. This is the first explicit link between visiting biblical sites and praying – that combination which in due season would give rise to 'pilgrimage'. Meanwhile, around AD 230 the great Alexandrian scholar Origen settled in Caesarea. Although this was initially for quite other reasons, it gave him the opportunity to investigate some of the biblical sites, such as Bethlehem (*Against Celsus*, 1.51) and 'Bethany beyond the Jordan' (*Commentary on John 1:28*).

Indeed, according to Eusebius' claims (*Demonstration of*

the Gospel, 6.18), visitors came from 'all over the world' to visit Bethlehem and the Mount of Olives; overlooking the ruins of Jerusalem, he says, they reflected on Jesus' solemn words of judgement pronounced two centuries earlier from the same viewpoint. Strictly speaking, Eusebius' exaggerated terminology gives us no idea of how *many* such visitors there were – only that they came from a wide variety of places. Yet there was clearly a steady trickle and a greater volume of devout tourism than the few known names would suggest.

Around AD 290 Eusebius himself composed a kind of gazetteer (the *Onomastikon*) which listed most of the biblical sites. Many of these, he said, were still being 'pointed out' to this day. In another work he mentions a particularly intriguing item: a bronze statue of Jesus kept in a house in Panias (formerly Caesarea Philippi), which reputedly had belonged to the woman Jesus healed (in Mark 5:34; see *EH,* 7.18). Without questioning the authenticity of these sites, we begin to sense that the ancestors of today's unofficial Holy Land guides were already learning the tricks of the trade – pointing out interesting sites and objects to any who were interested!

History and Christian spirituality

So by the year 300 there was clearly in some quarters a continuing interest in the Land of Palestine precisely because of its biblical heritage. Biblical history, and particularly the history of Jesus, were not unimportant. Yet the predominant attitude in the worldwide Christian Church, it must be said, was one which tended to place its emphasis elsewhere. Eusebius himself, though he was the Church's first main historian, was himself schooled in the 'spiritualizing' tendency of his mentor Origen. For such theologians the Christian faith could be distinguished from Judaism and paganism precisely because of its focus on the spiritual realm, and its lack of religious concern for physical objects and places. The sights of the early Church were set instead on 'things above' (Colossians 3:1–2).

In any case, in those days of continuing persecution few had the luxury of going on excursions to the Holy Land. Instead Christian faith was still fuelled by an emphasis on the exalted Christ and the worldwide availability of his Spirit. Jesus' words about 'worship in spirit and in truth' (John 4:24) continued to have a profound effect on his followers. So in the main they were reluctant to reinvent the notion of particular places as 'holy', and their focus was decidedly on the 'heavenly Jerusalem', not the 'Jerusalem below' (Galatians 4:25–6; Hebrews 12:22; Revelation 21:2).

FROM EUSEBIUS TO JEROME (AD 325–400)

Christian thought and practice was in for a sudden shock at the start of the fourth century. Few could have foretold what would happen next. Suddenly there was an emperor who, instead of persecuting the Church, actually supported it. This in turn led to mammoth changes in the Holy Land – the building of numerous Christian churches and a vast influx of pilgrims. By the year 400 the Holy Land would be transformed and so too Christian attitudes towards it.

Constantine and the Holy Sepulchre

The emperor in question was, of course, Constantine. Having ruled in the West from 312, he gained control of the eastern half of the Empire from 324. During the next thirteen years (until his death in 337) Jerusalem was changed indelibly, and developments took place which would set the pattern for the rest of that century and indeed right up until the present. Our chief commentator on this vital period is once again Eusebius of Caesarea. He was now the elderly metropolitan bishop of the whole of

Palestine and would eventually be the one to write Constantine's biography (*Life of Constantine*).

Previous to Constantine the Christian community was liable to spasmodic outbreaks of persecution. Indeed, one of the fiercest bouts came in the early 300s under the emperor Diocletian. In *Martyrs of Palestine*, again by Eusebius, we have a detailed account of what Palestinian Christians had to endure, especially in his home city of Caesarea, the provincial capital. In such circumstances it was not just that tourism was a luxury which few Christians could afford. There was also little opportunity for significant biblical sites to be earmarked in any public way. Worshippers had to be content with the natural surroundings. A cave on the Mount of Olives, for example, was frequented by visitors – possibly used in the first instance just as a convenient, dry, discreet place in which to gather their thoughts.

With the coming of Constantine to power, however, all this changed. In particular, a tradition had developed that the tomb where Jesus had been buried now itself lay buried under one of Hadrian's buildings in the centre of Aelia Capitolina – a pagan temple dedicated to Aphrodite. Bishop Macarius, the bishop of Jerusalem, met Constantine at the Council of Nicea in the summer of 325 and obtained the emperor's permission for the pulling down of this pagan temple and the building of what would come in time to be known as the church of the Holy Sepulchre (or the church of the Resurrection).

This is not the place to describe this event in detail, nor indeed to enter into the vexed questions associated with the issue of the tomb's authenticity (see Walker, *The Weekend that Changed the World*, chs. 5, 7). Yet the whole episode remains one of the most fascinating stories in the history of Christians' involvement in the Holy Land: an ancient archaeological excavation in search of the most significant tomb in the world and one which, contrary to their wildest dreams, was actually successful. A tomb was found and immediately identified as that of Jesus. No wonder local Christians were excited! No wonder Eusebius compared its coming back to light after nearly three hundred years with Jesus' own coming back to life after three days! Not too surprising, either, that people began to describe this location as a 'holy place'. It was truly a sensational discovery, sufficient to cause quite a stir for many years to come (Eusebius, *Life*, 3.25ff).

Constantine ordered the building of a magnificent church complex. The tomb itself was cut free from its surrounding rock and set in the midst of an attractive courtyard, surmounted (in due course) by a spectacular dome; this area became known as the Anastasis (or 'Resurrection'). To its east lay the great basilica, called the Martyrium (or 'Witness'). The whole complex was dedicated in September 335 and Eusebius rushed off to Constantinople to tell the absentee emperor all about it.

Queen Helena and the Triad

Constantine himself never visited the Holy Land, though he said at his baptism shortly before his death that he had hoped to be baptized in the River Jordan (*Life*, 4.62). His mother, however, did. The visit of Queen Helena, despite all the subsequent legendary accretions, is historic fact. She visited in 326 (or soon after) and was instrumental in seeing Constantine's Holy Land Plan move into its second stage: the building of two further churches which would complete a triad of sites marking the three principal events recited in the Creed. The church of the Nativity was begun in Bethlehem and a church commemorating the Ascension (known as the 'Eleona' – from the Greek for 'olives') was built on the Mount of Olives.

Intriguingly, both these further sites were associated with 'caves'. Our earliest sources after the Gospels refer to Jesus being born in a 'cave' (see *Proto-Evangelium of James*,

18 and Justin, *Dialogue with Trypho*, 78, both c. AD 150; cf. Origen, *Against Celsus*, 1.51, from c. AD 240 and Eusebius, *Demonstration*, 3.2.47, *EH*, 7.2.14). This may well be historically correct. There is, in fact, no reference to any 'stable' in the Bible. Palestinian homes were indeed sometimes built out forwards from natural caves, with the cave being the warmest, innermost part of the home – a good place to keep one's precious animals (cf. Luke 2:7). If there was any 'innkeeper', he may have been kinder than we thought!

As for the cave on the Mount of Olives, we noted just above how it may have become popular in the pre-Constantinian period for quite practical reasons. This too, however, is mentioned in early literature (see the apocryphal *Acts of John*, 97). The tradition gradually developed that this cave might have been used by Jesus himself as a quiet teaching place for his disciples. Not surprisingly, however, Eusebius' attempt to identify the cave with the scene of the Ascension failed to catch on in the popular imagination. After all, the Ascension begs to be commemorated in a slightly more open space, not in a cave! So by the end of the century, funds had been raised for a separate small building, suitably open to the sky and located on the summit of the Mount of Olives. This was the 'Imbomon' dedicated in the early 390s AD. It is now marked by the small Muslim cupola some fifty metres to the north of the ruined Eleona church (itself now covered partly by the Pater Noster church).

Other churches

Indeed, by the end of the century several other churches had been built. In Jerusalem there was the 'graceful' small church in Gethsemane, and a quite significant building to commemorate Pentecost on Mount Sion (probably that same site where Christians had been meeting to worship outside 'Aelia' since the second century). Churches built elsewhere to commemorate Gospel sites included those in Nazareth and Capernaum – over the likely homes of Jesus and Peter, respectively. And, even if churches were not yet built on them, suitable sites had been earmarked for hosts of other events as recorded in the Gospels.

Some of these identifications are highly questionable by modern standards (such as Zacchaeus' tree in Jericho!). In general, scholars are inclined to be more sceptical of site-traditions which emerge for the first time only in the fourth century. These include Mount Tabor as the scene of the Transfiguration, the conglomeration of sites on the Sea of Galilee at Tabgha, and the locating of Cana at what is now known as Kefr Kenna. With each of these places the choice was reasonably appropriate but it was also influenced quite considerably by practical considerations of convenience. Given this sudden influx of pilgrims, all of whom wanted to be shown *exactly* where the Gospel events had happened, it would hardly be surprising if local people began to try to meet their demands!

Jerome, Egeria and Cyril

So by the year 400 the face of Palestine was decidedly different from what it had been a hundred years before. In that earlier period, the Christian population in Jerusalem would have been primarily Greek-speaking. Now other Christian communities from the East were beginning to settle there – not least the Syrians and Armenians. And travellers from the Latin West were also being tempted to stay.

The most famous of these is Jerome, who came from Rome to live and work in a monastery in Bethlehem from 386 until his death in 419. Working from the original Hebrew text, he translated the Bible into Latin (the 'Vulgate'), and wrote numerous biblical commentaries. One of the things he also did, however, was to translate Eusebius' gazetteer of sites into Latin. This necessarily involved him in having to note the many changes that had taken place in the intervening one hundred years.

He also wrote numerous letters to his friends back in Italy. One of these describes the exhausting pilgrimage of his friend, Paula, as she insisted on visiting all the 'holy sites' around the country (*Epistle* 108). By that date there was a veritable pilgrimage circuit – no doubt supported by an army of local guides – which included not only Galilee but frequently the Sinai desert as well.

In stark contrast to the period before Constantine, we know of many visitors to the Holy Land during this period:

- the Bordeaux Pilgrim (AD 333), who wrote a handy travelogue of what he saw
- the godly Gregory of Nyssa (AD 380), who was frankly unimpressed and raised questions about the whole enterprise of 'pilgrimage' (*Ep*. 2)
- the heretic-hunting Epiphanius from Cyprus (AD 393)
- the wealthy Poemenia, who financed the building on the crest of the Mount of Olives, and Melania, who founded a monastery nearby with Rufinus
- and some infamous Christians who came to Palestine for refuge (for example, the heretics Arius and Pelagius in 335 and 415 respectively).

Yet the most famous is surely the Spanish nun, Egeria, who made an extended visit from 381 to 384 and whose fascinating account survives to this day (see Wilkinson, *Egeria's Travels*).

In her account we see just how much Palestine had changed in the years since the time of Constantine. Jerusalem, in particular, had become a pageant of liturgical colour. The celebration of Holy Week (the 'great week'), for example, had become an almost exhausting experience. There were numerous services on each day of the week, incorporating various excursions to and from the Mount of Olives. The church of the Holy Sepulchre was in frequent use and packed to the doors with worshippers listening to the Good Friday readings, and celebrating the Paschal vigil.

Much of this innovation can probably be attributed to Jerusalem's Bishop Cyril, who, despite being sent into exile on several occasions during his long episcopate (c. 348–84), seems more than anyone else to have put Jerusalem back on the Christian map. We have a record of his *Catechetical Lectures* which were delivered to his baptismal candidates in the church of the Holy Sepulchre. In these we see his convictions that Jerusalem was still a 'holy city'; it had, after all, been the scene of the Incarnation and Redemption, of Pentecost and the inauguration of the Eucharist. It would also be the place of Christ's return. As such, Jerusalem should have a natural pre-eminence in Christian thinking and Church practice, for 'the prerogative of all good things lies in Jerusalem'. Jerusalem in the first century may indeed have rejected Jesus, 'but this Jerusalem worships him' (see Walker, *Holy City, Holy Places?*, ch. 9).

Cyril had no hesitation in also developing a theology of 'holy places'. The Gospel sites 'all but showed Christ to the eyes of the faithful' and had the power to 'shame', 'reprove' and 'confute' any who were tempted to disbelieve the message of Christ. 'Others merely hear, but we see and touch.' This was strong stuff, a clear promotion both of pilgrimage and also of relics: come to Jerusalem and then, if you can, take something of it back with you!

The collection of relics

The most famous relic of this period was the first one to be 'discovered': the wood of the 'true cross'. Again various later legends have somewhat obscured the issue, but some wood was indeed found during those first excavations in the area of the modern Holy Sepulchre and immediately presented as part of Jesus' cross.

Eusebius was not best pleased with this (see Walker, *Holy City, Holy Places?*, pp. 126–30). Either he was doubtful of its authenticity or else he was wary of how the Jerusalem church might start cultivating a relic trade for its own purposes. Moreover, his theology would almost certainly have caused him to have major questions about the spiritual benefit of such a trade. Yet, despite his attempts to cover it up, his own account of the excavations seems to betray the existence of this relic. Within a few years Bishop Cyril has no qualms in speaking on several occasions of the 'wood of the cross' which, he claimed, had now spread 'all over the world'. By Egeria's day what remained of the relic in Jerusalem was displayed to the faithful on the afternoon of Good Friday. They were able to kiss it, but they were closely watched by the clergy. Only a few years earlier a devotee had tried to bite off some of it to take home with her!

In due course various other relics would be 'discovered' and would find their way to places far from the shores of Palestine. The Holy Land pretty much had a monopoly on the bones of Old Testament characters (such as the patriarch Joseph and the prophets Zechariah, Habbakuk and Samuel). And there was a major sensation when the bones of St Stephen were uncovered in 415 from a tomb not far from the modern Ben Gurion Airport. Bishop John of Jerusalem ensured they were brought to the Sion church in Jerusalem on the martyr's feast day, 26 December. Some years later the emperor Theodosius II would pay vast sums to have the empress Eudocia bring Stephen's bones back to Constantinople. It was all part of the movement whereby Christian visitors would try to take back with them a little bit of the Holy Land – what they referred to as *eulogiae* (or 'blessings').

At one extreme this might be tied up with a fair amount of superstition. Some pilgrims took home small 'tokens' of burnt clay (taken from the soil around the sites) and then ground them up, dissolved them in water and drank them for their supposed miraculous properties. On the other hand, some of it was not so dissimilar from modern tourists taking back various memorabilia of their trip – whether olive wood or Jordan water. In those days Jordan water was also a popular souvenir, but so too was oil from the lamps of the Holy Sepulchre, dried flowers from Gethsemane, or simply dust from Jerusalem's streets. Suffice it to say that this souvenir instinct was one which vendors resident in Jerusalem were not slow to seize upon – then as now!

Celebrating the Incarnation

This development of the Christian Holy Land is quite remarkable for its sheer speed. How would a historian explain it? No doubt many factors were operating – some commercial, some to do with tourism, some shrewdly political, some genuinely spiritual. Clearly Constantine gave it a boost with his own personal agenda: his empire needed some new symbols to bind it together, and there was also something gratifying about the possible comparisons that could now be made between himself and Christ. Meanwhile for the Church there was the need to cement and encourage the new-found faith of the many who were now coming through its doors. Pilgrimage could help these believers know their faith was built on solid foundations. There was also a straightforward desire to celebrate Christ's life in public after nearly three hundred years of waiting on the sidelines. The Christian Church had a long pent-up desire to come out from hiding and express in this world (and especially in the very places where it happened) the great news of salvation accomplished in Jesus Christ.

Yet, at a more theological level, the most powerful reason for this elevation of the Holy Land within Christian imagination was simply the doctrine of the Incarnation. If anyone questioned what was going on, it was the Incarnation that could be appealed to for legitimization. The Holy Land was, above all, a place to celebrate Christ incarnate.

This doctrine, implicit within the New Testament, was the foundation on which the rest of Christian belief was based. Not surprisingly, then, it was the one most criticized and most in need of defence as the Church now entered more openly into the marketplace of ideas. So numerous church councils were convened in due course, at which the great truths about the person of Christ were hammered out. Given this distinctive theological climate, it was only natural that the Holy Land too should come to play a special role within the life of the Church – as a kind of earthly foil to the theological debates about Christ and the Incarnation. It was a means of ensuring that all the discussions concerning abstract theology kept their feet on the ground – at least to some degree.

This focus on the Incarnation is then expressed by those who visited the Holy Land. They were full of wonder that this was the land, unique on the face of the earth, which had been visited by God the Son. 'No other sentiment draws people to Jerusalem,' said Paulinus of Nola around AD 400, 'than the desire to see and touch the places where Christ was physically present, and to be able to say from their very own experience, "We have gone into his tabernacle, and have worshipped in the places where his feet have stood".' Or, as Jerome put it to Paula: 'The whole mystery of our faith is native to this country and city.' It was, as some visitors later described it, 'this God-trodden Land' (see Wilken, *The Land Called Holy*, p. 192).

It was a powerful thought, and one which changed the face of Palestine within a very short space of time. In the years before 325 Palestine was still a backwater within the Empire. One of its pagan governors, Firmilianus, around AD 310 did not even know that there had been a city in his province called Jerusalem! By the end of the century, no one could make the same mistake; Jerusalem and the Holy Land were now centre stage within the thought and practice of the Byzantine Empire. So much had changed in just seventy-five years, and the driving force was the Incarnation.

Tom and Sarah return through time

Imagine if Tom had visited Palestine in AD 300, but Sarah's trip was unavoidably delayed until AD 400. There would have been a vast contrast between their two experiences. Tom would have found a land little touched by Christian devotion, still bearing the marks of the calamity of AD 70 and clearly under pagan rule. Sarah, like Jerome's friend Paula, would have found a land littered with 'holy places'. Once she got used to the Byzantine buildings located over the sites associated with her Saviour, she might have become an ardent fan. And although at first it might have seemed strange, she would probably have found the liturgical celebrations in each of these locations quite moving – hearing the Scriptures and praying with other Christians in the very places hallowed by her incarnate Lord.

Had Tom been with her in AD 400, he might have been a bit more sceptical about the whole thing, being somewhat cynical by nature. He would have noted the potential economic abuse as local traders plied their tourist souvenirs; the dangers of naïve pilgrims being convinced by Christian leaders and local guides that the designated sites were authentic, when quite possibly they were nothing of the sort; the description of Jerusalem as a 'holy city' despite the way Jesus was treated by that city and his strong prophetic words against her; and all this talk of 'holy places' when surely the New Testament encourages us to keep a spiritual focus on the Risen Jesus. Was there not a real danger of idolatry as people pinned their hopes on specific locations and treasured souvenirs? And were people now in danger of seeing a visit to the Holy Land as an essential part of their Christian experience, when again it was nothing of the sort? For as Christ was real in lands far removed from the land of his birth, Christ could be met wherever his people gathered to pray. The Incarnation was, of course, a central aspect of Christian faith, but was this the right way to proclaim it? What would Jesus have made of all this focus on the very spot where his feet had stood?

Tom's concerns are real. They have been expressed many times before, not only by the reformers as they considered pilgrimage in western Europe, but also by people watching developments in the Holy Land back in the fourth century. Jerome, though sitting in Bethlehem, discouraged some would-be pilgrims, assuring them that Christians in Britain had equal access to the door of Paradise (*Ep*. 58). Gregory of Nyssa thought the 'holiness' of the Land was vastly exaggerated; if holiness was measured by the number of believing Christians *per capita*, then far better to stay in Cappadocia (*Ep*. 2)! And Eusebius himself, our chief source describing the great Constantinian upheavals, evidently saw these new developments as a mixed blessing. He and Tom might have been kindred spirits. Sarah, by contrast, might have been more like Egeria, or perhaps like Cyril, the up-and-coming young bishop of Jerusalem who would transform the city with his enthusiasm and colour.

But what were Christians to do? Suddenly they found themselves enjoying the emperor's favour with his permission to make this unique land reflect more truly the Holy One who had blessed it with his presence. Were they to leave it just like anywhere else? Were they to leave it in a first-century time-warp, so that visitors seventeen hundred years later could see it 'just as it was' in Jesus' day? Were they to debar admission to any who might abuse the practice of pilgrimage?

Or had the time come to celebrate? – to celebrate the arrival of Christian faith in the very courts of power, and the return of the rule of Christ in the very Land where he had been rejected? He had been 'in the world, but the world had known him not; he had come to his own, but his own had received him not' (John 1:10–11). But now at long last he was being recognized throughout the world for what he truly was – the King of Kings! The Byzantine Empire would come in time to be celebrated as a manifestation of the rule of Christ upon earth and a foretaste of his heavenly Kingdom. It was high time that his royal flag be raised in Jerusalem. 'A prophet is not without honour', he himself had said, 'except in his own country' (Luke 4:24). Perhaps now the time had truly come when the Nazarene, acclaimed throughout the world, could return to his own country as its rightful king. So the changes made to the Holy Land, and the churches which marked its landscape, were all ways of making good the deficit of the New Testament era. At that time he had been crucified in weakness. Now he was being honoured as Lord of the world.

Chapter 6

THE FLOWERING OF THE DESERT

THE BYZANTINE HOLY LAND

So Tom and Sarah are back in time, experiencing the so-called 'Byzantine' era in the history of the Holy Land – the time when Palestine was under the rule of the Christian emperors based in Constantinople (formerly called Byzantium). With the advantage of hindsight, we can now see this as the great Christian era within the Land, spanning the period from AD 325 to the early seventh century.

It was in this period that the phrase 'the Holy Land' began to emerge. Although it was used a little by Jerome and others to refer to the 'promised land' of the Bible, Christians were hesitant to use it of the contemporary land of Palestine. It was first used in this sense in the early sixth century by some Judean monks in a letter to the emperor. At this time there was a real flourishing of the province as a whole, both the bustling cities and the empty wilderness. This was when both cities and deserts came into their own.

Expansion and peace

The Byzantine era was a time of enormous expansion and material development within the Holy Land. The population rose to perhaps four times that of the biblical period, a level not matched until modern times. To a large extent this was brought about through the influx of people and money associated with the 'holy places'. The population began to decline, however, in the sixth century. This was due to a series of epidemics, probably the result of some chronic hygiene problems in the excessively built-up cities. Yet it was still the most prosperous era in the Land's long history.

Numerous churches were built during these years. If one includes the area to the east of the Jordan, then the total rises to over five hundred. Modern visitors to Kursi (on the east of the Sea of Galilee), to Capernaum, and to Jacob's well near Nablus – to name but three examples – will witness the fruit of this prolific building spree. Perhaps the best idea of the Christian Holy Land during this period can

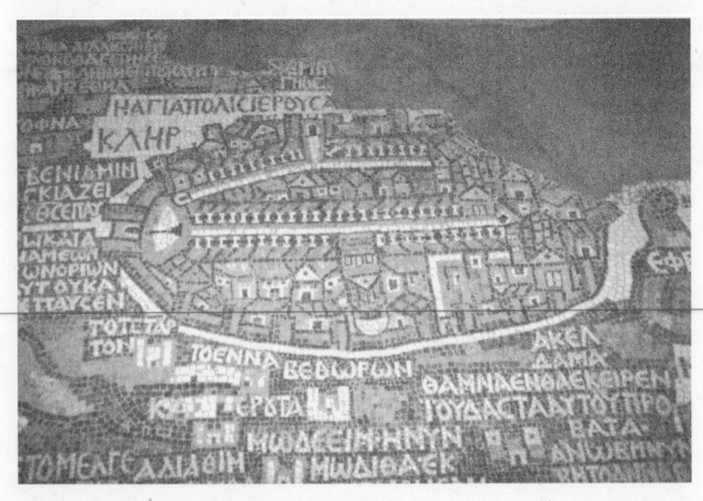

Figure 5. The Madaba Map

be gained from examining the Madaba Map, a mosaic designed in the sixth century for the floor of a church in Madaba, Jordan. The artist has depicted a bird's eye view of the whole Levant, with Jerusalem depicted at the centre of a Land which spreads across the River Jordan.

This was also a time of relative peace. The eastern borders of the empire were generally secure. If anything, a greater threat to stability came from within Palestine's own borders, when there was the great Samaritan revolt in AD 529. On a slightly different note, panic was caused in Jerusalem back in May 351 when a strange *parhelion* effect on the midday sun caused the sunlight to appear in the shape of a cross. Jerusalem is frequently prone to flurries of apocalyptic excitement. Could this be the sign of Christ's imminent return? Many people thought so, and Cyril recounts how they flocked into the churches for the next few days.

But perhaps the most significant upheaval during this period came a few years later during the brief reign of Julian the Apostate (361–3). This was the emperor who resumed the persecution of the Church. In a provocative move, deliberately designed to set back the Constantinian developments in Jerusalem, he gave orders for the Jewish Temple to be rebuilt.

The Temple Mount had deliberately been left in ruins by Constantine. Thereby a striking contrast was created with the hill five hundred metres to the west on which there now rose up the splendid construction of the Holy Sepulchre. Eusebius had noticed this, seeing it as a contrast between the old and new Jerusalems (*Life of Constantine*, 3.33). So a palpable tension was built into the very fabric of the city, a tension which can be sensed to this day. Worse still, Constantine's edicts had only allowed Jewish visitors to enter Jerusalem once a year, on the anniversary of the destruction of the Temple. To be sure, this was an improvement on the total ban which had been imposed by

Hadrian back in 135. Nevertheless it was a sign of the natural tensions between two now distinct religions, each of which would like to lay claim to Jerusalem. Although it was eventually repealed by the Empress Eudocia in 438, it would leave a lasting legacy within the city for centuries to come.

Julian saw an opportunity to overturn all this. Throughout the empire Christians woke up to find that the halcyon days of Christian emperors had disappeared almost as quickly as they had come. As far as we can tell, work was indeed begun on the rebuilding of the Temple. Then, as now, this would inevitably cause quite a stir among the local populace. Then Julian was killed in battle, and it was all brought to a halt. He was succeeded by a series of pro-Christian emperors. Looking back on it, we can see that the Byzantine era had now finally come to stay. For the next 250 years the province of Palestine would experience a welcome measure of political peace and stability.

Jews and Christians side by side

Estimates vary as to what percentage of the population would have called itself Christian in this period. There were still no doubt large pockets of ancient paganism, and we are being naïve if we dress up Jerusalem in glowing robes of sanctity. Jerome complained on one occasion that the city was just as full of 'prostitutes, actors, soldiers, mimes and buffoons' as anywhere else (*Ep.* 58.4). Similarly, Gregory of Nyssa doubted that God's grace was more abundant here; instead 'cheating, adultery, theft, idolatry, poisoning, quarrels and murder are everyday occurrences' (*Ep.* 2.10). Probably the majority of the city's population, however, was Christian by the year 400 (and would remain so until the 1920s). There were also a significant number of Christians in the rest of the Holy Land, especially in Caesarea and other major towns. The remains of impressive churches can also be found in the five or six major cities built in the Negev desert to the south by the Nabataeans.

Galilee, however, from the second century onwards, was predominantly Jewish. So during the Byzantine period it is estimated that some fifteen new synagogues were built in the Galilee region. In the period before Constantine, Eusebius had listed only three villages in Palestine as a whole which were predominantly Christian, only one in Galilee (*Onom.* 26.13; 108.1; 112.14). Yet it is fairly clear, during this earlier period at least, that there were small Christian communities in Nazareth and Capernaum (see e.g. Eusebius, *EH,* 1.7.14). When we move into the fourth century, however, the evidence is less clear. In fact, Epiphanius claimed that Christians were not allowed to live in Nazareth, Capernaum, Tiberias or Sepphoris (*Against Heresies* 30.11). This may well be an exaggeration, designed to increase his readers' respect for Count Joseph, a converted Jew who had sought Constantine's permission to build churches in Galilee in the face of Jewish opposition. Even so, it certainly reveals just how small was the Christian presence in Galilee, the very place where Jesus had conducted the chief part of his ministry.

In contrast, the area just to the south of Galilee, in and around Cyril's Scythopolis (modern Bethshean), was predominantly Christian. Nevertheless, during this period some five or six synagogues were built in the region. These include the remarkable ones at Rehov and Beth Alpha. The mosaics of these various synagogues reveal the continuing importance for the Jewish people of the Temple and bear witness to the hope, which continued throughout this period, that Jerusalem might once again be in Jewish hands. It was a hope which would resurface quite powerfully when at last the Christian rule over the Land showed signs of weakening.

Jerusalem and the wider world

Meanwhile Jerusalem continued to play a major part in the wider Christian world. From this time onwards maps of the world frequently placed Jerusalem at the very centre. This would continue into the medieval period (as, for example, in the 'Mappa Mundi' in England's Hereford cathedral). It was a concept first made popular by Bishop Cyril of Jerusalem, who spoke of Golgotha being the navel or 'the very centre of the earth' (*Cat.* 13.28); after all, had not the Psalmist spoken of God working his 'salvation in the *midst* of the earth' (Psalm 74:12)? So Jerusalem was not just back on the map; it had come to occupy centre stage in the Christian world. And what went on in Jerusalem (not least its colourful Christian liturgies) would be of real interest to many far away who themselves were never able to visit it.

Not surprisingly, then, the city's bishopric was raised to the level of a patriarchate in the 450s. This was during the episcopacy of Bishop Juvenal, who thereby joined the bishops of Rome, Alexandria, Antioch and Constantinople as one of the five leading bishops, overseeing the historic centres of ancient Christendom. This was at the time of the great 'Monophysite' controversy which split the Church in the East (see further below in chapters 7 and 9). It was during this period too that the Empress Eudocia was living in Jerusalem, commissioning lavish buildings which included a church in honour of St Stephen (now in the grounds of the Ecole Biblique, just north of the Damascus Gate). Then, a hundred years later the Emperor Justinian would leave his mark on the city, building the Nea church 500 metres to the south of the Holy Sepulchre.

Meanwhile, just a few miles away to the east, the Judean desert was becoming the home for hundreds of monks attracted from all over the empire by the prospect of a life of prayer within walking distance of Bethlehem and

Jerusalem, the so-called 'cities of the Incarnation'. We now pick up their story. But first, the place itself.

THE FLOWERING OF THE DESERT

Starting out from Jerusalem, driving west towards Jericho or south through Sinai to Eilat, we come face to face with the desert. This landscape has always held a strong fascination for dreamers, wanderers and searchers after God. Deserts and cities seem the exact opposite of one another, but the remarkable thing about the desert in Israel is that it is so near to the city. You can stand on a hill at the eastern edge of Jerusalem, looking westwards over this busy, energetic urban sprawl. Turn around and the view is stunningly different. Miles of brown, rocky, arid wilderness, the Dead Sea lying in the middle distance, and the hills of Transjordan stretching away into the pale horizon.

The 'Judean desert' is the strip of land sloping down from the hills on which Jerusalem, Bethlehem and Hebron are situated, and the Dead Sea, including the southern part of the Jordan valley. If 'desert' suggests mile upon mile of graceful sand dunes, then think again. This is actually mountainous country, riven with deep valleys cut into the rock, stony, hard and unforgiving. Some rain does fall here, enough for the Bedouin to graze their sheep during the winter. Rainfall normally varies between 100 and 300 mm per year, becoming drier towards the Dead Sea to the east. When this rain falls and gathers, flash floods can come roaring down the gullies with great force and suddenness, sweeping away everything in their path, including roads. Erosion caused by these floods leaves an indelible mark on the landscape, with sand and rock scoured by thousands of small valleys and creeks. The only other source of water in the Judean desert are the natural springs, of which there are only three, at Jericho, at Ain Feshka, further south, and at Ein Gedi near the western shore of the Dead Sea. In the winter months, a thin shade of green covers much of the landscape, but this vegetation is soon burned off by the searing heat as spring and summer roll on.

For those who've never seen it before, it is a quite stunning landscape. Hill after hill of barren ochre rock, sand and dust, fantastic chasms gouged out of the hillsides, all of it stretching for mile after mile, at a glance all monotonously the same, but on closer inspection full of intriguing variety. Apart from the occasional Bedouin tents huddled together in the barrenness, some sheep tracks, the occasional sheepfold, and traces left by those who have tried to live there, here is a landscape not crafted by human hands, where in fact humankind seems insignificant and irrelevant.

The desert fathers

Taking the old road from Jerusalem down to Jericho, the same one taken by the Samaritan in Jesus' parable, you can, if you look closely enough, see traces of a lost way of life. Looking up into the cliffs beside the path, you see countless caves. Look closer and it is possible to see, at the entrance to some of these caves, small stone walls, not covering the whole entrance, but enough to provide some protection for anyone inside. These walls provide a tiny visual clue to a huge movement, now mostly vanished from the area, but which once drew the admiration and fascination of people across the Byzantine world. It was, and still is, a controversial movement. Whatever we make of it, it undoubtedly had a deep impact on society in both eastern and western Europe, kept Christianity and literary culture alive during the Dark Ages, and shaped the minds of vast numbers of people through the medieval period and beyond. It was the movement known as Monasticism.

These stone walls, or entrances which are carved into doorways, are often a sign that the caves were used at some point as 'cells', or small dwellings, by Christians who lived in the area. It is hard to imagine it now, but, travelling through the Judean desert at some point in the fifth century AD, it would have been hard to go far without coming across a monk, or a monastery or both. The Judean desert is not a large area, roughly forty miles from north to south and fifteen miles east to west, but at the height of the movement in the fifth and sixth centuries AD, the region was swarming with monks. It is estimated that there were around seventy separate monasteries in the area, some of which contained just a handful, the largest of which contained around four hundred monks. Cave after cave in this moon-like landscape was used as a cell for privacy and for silent meditation and prayer. In the words of Athanasius, the great Christian controversialist of the fourth century, 'The Christians are spread everywhere, and at length, even the desert is filled with monks.'

The desert life

These 'desert fathers', as they became known, lived in a variety of ways. Some lived in what was known as a 'laura', after a Greek word meaning a lane. This took its cue from the pattern adopted by Antony (c. 250–356), the most famous of the early monks in Egypt. A group of individual recluses would live in their own cells in a common area (often scattered alongside a footpath or lane leading to their main building, hence the name). They would come together for worship at weekends. Some lauras were built into the side of cliffs, with cells hollowed out of caves in seemingly impossible locations, accessed by dizzy and complicated systems of ladders and hewn-out walkways. A monk with vertigo was in for a particularly unpleasant time.

Others lived in 'coenobia', after the Greek words for 'common life' (*koinos bios*), after the pattern of another of the early monks, Pachomius (d. 346). Here they would live a shared life of prayer, work, and eating together. Monks would live in cells in the monastery, which was normally a square fortified building which often looked like a fort or estate.

Some monasteries, especially here in Judea, were a combination of the two types, with a central communal area for young, newly recruited members, and separate cells scattered around the vicinity. Anchorites would live in their cells on dried bread, water and dates during the week. At weekends they would bring the baskets and ropes they had woven to the central community to be taken off to be sold in the market, receive Holy Communion, take a hot meal and stock up on supplies for the following week.

In both types, laura and coenobium, all monks had a cell. Cells were frequently divided into two rooms, and some even had a small plot of cultivated land which grew vegetables. The cell might contain a reed mat, a sheepskin to keep the monk warm during the long cold desert nights, an oil lamp, and a vessel to hold food and water. In the cell, the monk would pray for long hours, meditating on a text of Scripture which had been memorized or recently read in the common worship of the community. There, or perhaps just outside in the sun, he might work, often weaving mats, sandals or baskets, just as Antony had done, work deliberately chosen so that it would leave the mind free for prayer and contemplation of God.

An old monk described the foundation of their life to a younger disciple as 'meditation, reading the Psalms and manual work'. Many were illiterate, so were dependent on memorizing passages of Scripture read in church. A visitor wandering among the monks would often hear the other-worldly wail of the 'synaxis', the common recitation of the Bible, designed to impress the words and meaning of the Scriptures into their hearts and minds. This could continue long into the night. Besides this there was also the practice of 'meditation', a more solitary musing upon Scripture, where a few verses at a time would be repeated out loud.

The Psalms in particular were chanted, using the words as the prayer of the monks' own hearts to God.

Each group of monks would have an 'Abba', or father, for the monastic life took the model of apprenticeship very seriously. Junior monks were to learn the lifelong habits of prayer, overcoming temptation and living the spiritual life through imitation and listening to the wisdom of the Abba, an experienced master.

The daily routine consisted of a round of work, prayer, reading and sleep. Work could mean agricultural labour, cultivating a small patch of carefully irrigated desert soil to provide food for the community, or it could mean the kind of weaving mentioned above. Work provided discipline. It provided for the basic needs of the community, by producing items which could be sold for the relief of the poor. It also gave unexpected opportunities for evangelism. One group of monks made baskets with three handles instead of the customary two. These would then be sold at the local market. On being asked why the baskets had three handles, the monks would reply: 'It is because our God is three-in-one. Let me tell you about him ...'

Food was sparse, but adequate. Monks would deliberately eat less than would satisfy them, although the quality was sometimes better than peasants could expect. The staple diet was water, and a kind of dry bread called *paxamatia* which was specially baked so that it would keep indefinitely. This could then be moistened, and salt added for taste when it was time for it to be eaten. Soup, olives, lentils and dates are mentioned in the stories of the monks; figs and grapes were luxuries, and wine, though not at all common, was not banned.

The monks themselves became something of a tourist attraction. Travellers would visit the monasteries, asking for wisdom from the Abba, marvelling at the many miracles which were said to take place around them. Some saw this movement as a fulfilment of the prophecies of

Isaiah 35, where 'the desert and the parched land will be glad; the wilderness will rejoice and blossom'. It is still possible to see why, when the monasteries today represent a small oasis of vegetation in the barrenness around. Many of these pilgrims wrote down stories of the monks, which were subsequently assembled together into collections of tales. The most famous of these were the *Sayings of the Fathers,* a collection of quotations, short stories and anecdotes from the lives of these remarkable people. These stories offer marvellous and sometimes barely credible accounts of the monks and their feats of asceticism and endurance. It was felt that the monks' devotion to God gave them a concentration of spiritual power. Miracle stories are liberally sprinkled in these collections, and the admiring visitors looked on the ascetics with awe and wonder, ascribing to them not just miraculous feats, but even the survival of the human race:

> Many of them have stopped the flow of rivers and crossed the Nile dry-shod. They have slain wild beasts. They have performed cures, miracles and acts of power like those which the holy prophets and apostles worked ... Indeed it is clear to all who dwell there that through them, the world is kept in being, and that through them too human life is preserved and honoured by God.

The monks of Judea

Although the movement began in the Nile valley in Egypt, it wasn't long before monks began to gather in the desert east of Jerusalem. The desert landscape, conveniently sited right next door to the great 'holy places' of Christendom, proved hard to resist for Christians of the Byzantine period. The monks could remain in their cells and monasteries, but then at the time of the great festivals of Christmas, Easter, Ascension and Pentecost, they could walk up over the hill into Jerusalem or Bethlehem to join the crowds worshipping and celebrating there. Most of the Judean monasteries were built on the western edge of the desert, far enough into the wilderness to feel the isolation and silence they craved, yet near enough to Jerusalem and Bethlehem for occasional visits.

Judean monasticism emerged in the fourth and early fifth centuries, when a number of key figures established monastic communities in the area. Men such as Chariton, Euthymius, Sabas and Theodosius all came to Jerusalem on pilgrimage and stayed to form monasteries in the area, some of which survive to this day. The movement came to a sudden end when the Arabs swept across Palestine in 614 before its eventual fall in 638. In some present-day monasteries, the monks will show you the bones of monks killed in these attacks over thirteen hundred years ago.

Living monasteries can still be seen in the desert east of Jerusalem. The easiest one to visit is probably St George's Choziba, built into a cliff just off the road from Jerusalem to Jericho; it was founded originally in the fifth century (most of the present buildings are from much later). Here can be seen some impressively precipitous cave-cells high up in the rock face, complete with dangling baskets to lift supplies, and dizzying ladders for the use of the monks who remain there. Part of its vision from the beginning was to provide hospitality to pilgrims on the way up to Jerusalem, and it continues that tradition today.

One of the largest monasteries in the area is the Great Laura of Mar Saba, further to the south. Here in AD 478, Sabas fixed a rope down which he could climb into an unused cave (the cave is still identifiable across the valley from the main monastery buildings today). Water was only accessible a mile and a half away, and food was provided by nearby Arabs. After five solitary years of attention to God alone through prayer and meditation, Sabas felt God calling him to welcome others and a community of monks began to grow around him. The monastery is still an impressive piece of architecture, clinging to the side of the sheer Kidron valley as it winds its way to the Dead Sea. The monastery church still displays the remarkably preserved body of St Sabas himself, who died in AD 532.

WHY THE DESERT?

This, of course, is the big question. It is hard for us to imagine five years of voluntarily imposed solitude. Perhaps the nearest we can get is to read the accounts of the western hostages in Lebanon in the 1980s with their graphic accounts of the profound psychological and spiritual effects of such long periods of being alone. Yet they were not there by choice. Why did so many people voluntarily leave comfortable lives in the cities, towns and villages of the Roman Empire to choose this stark, uninviting, dangerous life?

As might be expected in such a diverse and spontaneous movement, there are a whole host of reasons. Some sound strange to our ears. Many Christians felt that since the empire had turned Christian (beginning with Constantine's conversion and then by official decree in the reign of the Emperor Theodosius in the 380s), the demons had been driven out of the cities into the wilderness. It was therefore the task of those committed to the cause of God to go out to do battle with them there. For others this was a way of seeking salvation by abandoning the evils of 'civilization' for the silence of the desert. But no monk dreamed that by leaving the city he had left temptation behind. In fact their experience was the opposite. In the extreme silence and emptiness of the desert, things came sharply into focus. It was no longer possible to drown out the deepest cries of the heart, the secret longings and desires, the hidden self-centredness which creeps into all of life, the inattention to God which can be so easily excused in a busy life. It was perhaps this sense that the desert enabled them to face up to who they were and what God had called them to be, that drew them to such an inhospitable and barren setting. For them it became the place of testing.

A simpler answer to our question of motivation might be that they did it in imitation of Jesus. Jesus had gone into the desert to fast and be tested for forty days (the Greek word for temptation and testing is the same). Besides this, we are often told that he retired to deserted places at regular intervals during his ministry. Mark 1:35 tells us that 'very early in the morning, while it was still dark, Jesus got up, left the house and went off to a solitary place, where he prayed'. Similar verses are dotted around the Gospels. It seems that Jesus moved fairly regularly between the towns and villages, and solitary places, especially the desert.

The theme of the battle with Satan, central to Jesus' temptation in the wilderness, is a regular theme of the monks. The desert, and in particular, the cell, was the place where the monk was faced constantly with temptations of greed, anger, lust and self-will. It was the place where he could stand against the wiles of the devil, and engage him in combat. The monk could leave behind possessions by leaving the city for the desert, but the fight to leave behind the desire for possessions was only just beginning.

Asceticism and self-denial were not ends in themselves, but means to the end of a life free from slavery to possessions, from overwhelming desires for anything less than God himself. One story relates how a monk was plagued with sexual thoughts when he remembered his wife, who presumably had died before he left for the desert. Some over-eager monks laid all kinds of extreme rules of fasting and self-inflicted pain on him, so that he became too weak to stand. A wise brother visiting from another monastery gave him different advice: 'give all this up, take a little food at the proper time, say a few prayers, and give your anxiety over to the Lord. Truly our body is like a cloak. If you take care of it, it lasts, but if you neglect it, it is damaged.' We are then told the conclusion of the story: 'The brother listened, and acted in this way, and in a few days, the warfare ceased.'

Breaking records of self-denial for its own sake was not what really mattered. As one monk put it: 'many have injured their bodies without discernment and have gone away from us having achieved nothing. Our mouths smell bad through fasting, we know the Scriptures by heart, we recite all the Psalms of David, but we have not that which God seeks: charity and humility.' At their best, what mattered to the monks was God, serving and worshipping him, and everything else came a long way behind.

Alien ways

There is another side to this movement, which should caution us against becoming too romantic about it. By any measure, some of the monks were very odd indeed. At times they seem to shade into lunacy. We hear stories of monks standing up for years on end, only eating cabbage leaves during Lent, piling chains around themselves, sitting on pillars, letting their hair grow as long as possible. Occasionally their competitiveness led them to try to outdo one another in feats of self-denial. In some stories, there are strong hints of a frenetic theology of justification by works, as if their acceptance by God was somehow dependent upon their extreme dedication and self-denial. Some of the monks seem to hope that enduring suffering on earth will somehow cancel out any punishment to be visited upon their sins at the last judgement. We might question their fixation upon Jesus' temptation in the wilderness at the expense of his more public ministry. Perhaps most strikingly, they exhibit a distaste for the body and sometimes a horror of any physical pleasure at all that is hard to reconcile with a God who 'richly provides us with everything for our enjoyment' (1 Timothy 6:17). This hatred of the flesh, the sharp separation of the life of the soul from the body, owes more to the pervasive Greek philosophy of the time than it does to the Bible.

Despite all this, however, and being fully aware of the need to be discerning as we read these stories, there is still something compelling about them. Although sometimes misguided, sometimes lacking a clear grasp that the guilt of sin has already been dealt with on the cross, they still challenge complacency and the shallow level of spiritual life at which so many of us live today. They have left an indelible mark on the history, architecture and idea of the Holy Land. The lessons we might learn from them will be explored in a later chapter.

Chapter 7

ARRIVALS AND RETURNS: FROM THE SEVENTH CENTURY TO TODAY

History moves on. What a contrast there is between the Holy Land today and what it would have been like in AD 600! A Christian visiting around that time would have encountered a land marked by churches, long used to Christian rule, and inhabited by a large number of fellow believers. Despite the six intervening centuries, there was an evident sense of continuity with the time of the Gospels, and Christian visitors might be forgiven if they went round in a kind of Christian cocoon.

But today the visit is so much more complex. It's not just that Tom and Sarah, in their quest for the steps of Jesus, have to wade back through the alien cultural layer of the Byzantines. They have to cope with all that has happened since – especially the arrival of Islam, the Crusades, and the rise of Zionism. Each of these, together with many other historical events, has altered the landscape and the cultural dynamics of the country in profound ways. So this chapter, which rounds off our historical survey, is designed to bring them up to speed with some of what has gone on in this long period going back nearly fourteen hundred years.

Our focus is deliberately on the earlier part of that period. We do this for several reasons. For a start, in contrast to other eras in the history of the Holy Land, the period from 1200 to 1800 was comparatively uneventful. Then, too, what has happened since 1800 stares you more obviously in the face, so it will be touched on in the next chapter when we look at the 'Land and its People' today. Yet it is also because in the Holy Land we must never presume that more distant history can be dismissed.

On the contrary, people living in the Land are strongly affected to this day by what happened centuries ago. Collective memories reach back far into the past and the retelling of that history forges the consciousness of the people. The Persian invasion in 614, the arrival of Islam in 638 and the era of the Crusades – these may seem quite irrelevant to us, but in fact each of them continues to have a profound effect on the way Christians think and act in the Land today. If modern visitors are ever to understand what makes the Holy Land tick, they are going to have to look at that history. So we consider each of these three major episodes in turn.

THE PERSIAN INVASION (614)

This is an event which often gets overlooked. It is easily eclipsed by what happened next – the arrival of Islam. At the time, however, far greater shockwaves were caused within the Holy Land by the invasion of the Sassanid Persians. In the summer of 614 Jerusalem was besieged and then stormed by the armies of Chosroës II. A massacre ensued, the holy cross was seized, and many local Christians were deported to Damascus – including the patriarch Zachariah. As it turned out, the Persian occupation of Jerusalem was short-lived – in 628 the Byzantine emperor Heraclius would regain control and return the holy cross to the city. Yet it was a key episode in the history of the Holy Land. It signalled that Byzantine control in the region was weakening. For the Christian Holy Land the writing was on the wall.

Jewish and Christian responses

Not surprisingly, as news of the impending invasion spread, there was rejoicing in some quarters of the resident Jewish population. As in the days of the Babylonian exile, hopes were kindled that their currently 'polluted' Land would be restored to them – again through the agency of an eastern king. It is unlikely that they joined forces with the invading armies. Yet some of their number may have returned to Jerusalem to offer sacrifices and to celebrate the feast of Tabernacles, symbolizing their hope that the Christian occupation of the city might now come to an end. And in some apocalyptic writings, probably dating from this period, they expressed their hope that the age of deliverance had at last dawned. The full-scale development and appropriation of the Christian Holy Land since the fourth century had come to dispossess the Jews of what they still deemed to be their inheritance. Though long buried, Jewish hopes for the Land were evidently far from dead, and they now came flooding back once more to the surface.

Meanwhile the Christians mourned. The loss of the city, which had become so dear to them, was a devastating shock – far worse in its theological ramifications than the earlier sack of Rome in 410. This was the Jerusalem of Christ and the Bible! Now it was the turn of the Christians, not the Jews, to turn to the biblical book of Lamentations; like Jeremiah of old, they wept for Zion. Strategos, a monk at the monastery of Mar Saba, deliberately set his account of the *Capture of Jerusalem* against the background of the Old Testament. The deportation of Zachariah, being led away over the Mount of Olives and uncertain whether he would see Zion again, was similar both to the fleeing of David from the city (2 Samuel 15) and to the deportation of the Israelites in the sixth century BC. Once in Damascus the Christian exiles used the Psalms to weep for Zion 'in a strange land'.

Meanwhile Sophronius, the companion of the travelling monk John Moschus and who later succeeded Zachariah as patriarch of Jerusalem, lamented for the city in graphic terms – as though it was the 'heavenly city' of Jerusalem, the celestial city of God on earth. In an earlier period of the Church's life Christians would almost certainly have distanced themselves from such intense displays of affection for Jerusalem. They would have seen such devotion as characteristically more 'Jewish' than Christian. Now, with the loss of the city, it became clear just how much Christians too had come to love this place. Jerusalem had got under their skin.

Perhaps the most significant legacy of the invasion, however, was simply its brutality. Many monks met their deaths – for example, at the monastery of Mar Theodosius, just south-east of Jerusalem, where their skulls are still preserved in the charnel house. Many churches were desecrated or severely damaged. The one major building which was spared this fate was the Church of the Nativity in Bethlehem. There was something about the Magi depicted in the mosaic on its facade, complete with their Persian-styled headgear, which obviously touched a chord in the hearts of the would-be attackers. But for Christians it was a devastating blow – the end of an era. For them the Holy Land would never be the same again. And another shock lay just around the corner.

THE ARRIVAL OF ISLAM (638–1099)

The arrival of the Muslim cavalry in 638, in terms of damage to buildings or loss of life, was mild by comparison. There had been a major battle at the Yarmuk river in August 636. Yet when the Muslim forces arrived at the walls of Jerusalem during the Christmas period in 638, there was only a brief siege before the city surrendered. And there was the hope that this invasion too would be short-lived. The patriarch Sophronius, who had seen the Persians leave the city, believed the 'godless Saracens' would similarly soon be driven away. God might be disciplining the Jerusalem Christians for their sins but the Byzantine emperor would soon come to rescue the city and to vindicate God's cause.

Changes in Jerusalem

But that did not prevent Sophronius from having to surrender the city to the conquering Caliph Omar. He did so, dressed in his full patriarchal regalia. He invited Omar to pray in the Holy Sepulchre, but Omar declined on the grounds that, if his followers learned that the caliph had prayed in the church, they would certainly convert it into a mosque. Instead he prayed just outside. Sure enough, the place is now marked by a small 'Mosque of Omar'. The church of the Holy Sepulchre was left untouched. And Sophronius died not long afterwards.

The most famous buildings from this early Islamic period are those on the Temple Mount (or in Arabic, the *Haram Esh-Sharif*). The Byzantine Christians had deliberately kept this vast space within their city in a state of ruins – as an abiding testimony to the truth of Jesus' solemn words concerning the Temple's imminent destruction. Indeed, in the famous Madaba Map the Temple Mount is omitted altogether (see above, figure 5, p. 122). Now it provided the perfect place for the adherents of this new religion to mark the city with their own buildings.

The 'Dome of the Rock' was located over the highest rock in the area. It was completed in 691 by the Umayyad Caliph Abd al-Malik. Its design consciously borrowed from recent Byzantine architecture and indeed Byzantine Christians were employed in its construction. Ironically it is the only 'Byzantine' building as such to have survived in Jerusalem. In all probability Caliph Omar had earlier built a small house of prayer near this holy *sakhra* ('rock'). Now it would be marked for the future by this beautiful octagonal structure.

Islam, then as now, was respectful of the biblical tradition. So it was appropriate to be building in this location which was associated with both Abraham and Jesus. Yet the Dome of the Rock was also clearly intended as a powerful symbolic statement of the conquest of Islam over both Judaism and Christianity. For Jews this was the rock where Abraham had been called to sacrifice Isaac. It had also lain underneath the area of the Holy of Holies in their former Temple. Now it was all appropriated by Islam. Meanwhile for Christians the message was clear. There might be many splendid Christian churches in the area (which often impressed Muslim visitors) but this building would eclipse them all. In particular, its location on the opposite hill to the church of the Holy Sepulchre made a powerful statement. Ever since the time of Eusebius (*Life of Constantine* 3.33 in AD 337), Christians had intimated that their church, built opposite the ruined Temple Mount, was a symbol of the triumph of Christian faith over Judaism. Now the Dome of the Rock returned the compliment: Islam was superior to Christianity.

So the tension between the three monotheistic religions came to be written quite clearly into the architecture of the city – into its very stones and structure. And in case this was not clear, an inscription was in due course placed around the Dome of the Rock which urged Christians as the 'People of the Book' to see Jesus only as an 'apostle', to deny the Trinity, and to be clear that God did not have 'a son'.

The other building, on the southern edge of the Temple Mount, was what came to be known as the Al Aqsa mosque. An early Muslim tradition speaks of Muhammad's 'night-journey' in which the prophet was believed to have gone up from Mecca into heaven via Jerusalem – or, at least as it says in the Qur'an, from 'the furthermost sanctuary'

(*Sura* 17.1). This 'furthermost sanctuary' eventually came to be identified with Jerusalem and with this mosque in particular.

Even before the identification was made, however, Jerusalem clearly was recognized as important within Islam. The earliest direction for prayer (the *qibla*) was not Mecca, but Jerusalem (*Sura* 2.136ff) – no doubt reflecting the early influence of both Judaism and Christianity on Muhammad's teaching. In the early years of Islamic administration Jerusalem was also the place where government officials were to take their oaths of office. Jerusalem was simply too important, both in religious and political terms, to be bypassed. After Mecca and Medina it would come to be the third most important city within the Islamic faith, protected and embellished by successive Islamic dynasties – Umayyad (661–750), Abbasid (750–954) and Fatimid (975–1171). To this day Muslims know it simply as *'al-Quds'* ('the Holy').

The Land under Muslim rule

So Jerusalem was now under Muslim rule. Constantinople might stand for another eight hundred years, but in the Holy Land the Byzantine era had finally come to an end. At first it might seem like another passing phase. Yet by the end of the seventh century, when it became clear that Islam was here to stay, some Christians began to see these events in apocalyptic terms. One writer (now known as Pseudo-Methodius) saw the arrival of the Arabs in Jerusalem as signifying the 'last days' of the 'Antichrist' and longed for a Messiah-like figure, the 'King of the Greeks', to rescue the city and the 'promised land', thereby inaugurating a millennial peace. Christians now found themselves in a similar position to the Jews, longing for a restoration of Jerusalem – though, of course, they understood that restoration in quite different ways.

Even so, there was no pressure on the Christian community to leave Jerusalem or the Holy Land. Recent archaeology shows that there was little disruption in the culture, and churches continued to be built. Indeed, some of the best Byzantine artwork dates to this early Arab period – perhaps testifying to better governmental administration and lower taxes. Because the depiction of human faces was offensive to the Muslims, deliberate desecration of church mosaics and icons was not uncommon; but these were soon replaced with something more acceptable. And Christians, such as the famous monk from Mar Saba, John of Damascus (657–749), could still recite a list of all the churches marking the scenes of the Gospels. Writing from his tiny, dark cell to defend the Christian use of icons, he went on the offensive, seeing the Gospel sites as themselves being like icons. They were receptacles of divine energy, pointing to the continuing presence of God on earth.

In John's famous work, the *Fount of Knowledge*, he offered a critique of Islam. But he still saw it very much as a form of Christian heresy, and there were certainly many points of similarity between Muslim religious practice and that of Byzantine Christians; for example, when they prayed, both frequently practised fasting and prostration. Others, however, were beginning to see the contrast in sharper terms. Inevitably there were occasional tensions with the Muslims. But a *modus vivendi* was established, which in many ways has continued to this day.

The variety of Christian churches

Some reckon that in fact Christians continued to be the majority of the population within Palestine for several centuries. By this date there were several different Christian churches represented in the city. Back in the second century, the first Gentile church would presumably have been Greek-speaking. During and after the fourth century, however, we begin to witness the arrival in Jerusalem of various other nationalities: Syrians, Armenians, Egyptians, Georgians, and Latins (such as Jerome) for whom Greek was no longer the mother tongue.

In the fifth century matters became more complex (see further below in chapter 9, at figure 9, p. 204). No longer was it just a matter of different language-groups using different liturgies. The great Monophysite controversy following the Council of Chalcedon in 451 split the Church of the East. The 'Orthodox' believed that Christ had two distinct natures – one human, the other divine. The so-called 'Monophysites' (Greek for 'one nature'), who claimed to be equally 'orthodox', insisted he had only one nature – a divine one. After much hesitation, Jerusalem's Bishop Juvenal eventually sided with the Orthodox, but for many others in the Middle East the Monophysite theology prevailed. The church in Alexandria adopted it, leading to the formation of what is now the Coptic Church. So too did the Syrians. Some suggest that the Monophysites were influenced by a growing antipathy to Byzantine rule based in Constantinople. This might then explain why many Monophysites would later respond positively to the prospect of an alternative form of rule from Arabia and were won over to Islam – especially, for example, in Syria.

So from this period onwards there would be numerous sub-groupings in Jerusalem, some Orthodox, some Monophysite. With the arrival of Islam in the seventh century, things became more complex still. It is unclear just what proportion of the indigenous population converted to Islam in those first decades under Islamic rule. It might have been quite considerable, though the fact that Palestine was more pro-Byzantium probably meant the percentage was less than elsewhere. Of the many Christians who retained their faith, however, the majority gradually adopted the new Arabic language and adjusted to the realities of Muslim rule. Manuscripts survive of the ninth-century translation of the Gospels into Arabic by a man called Stephen of Ramlah. Hence the phenomenon of Arab Christianity, a phenomenon about which many today are quite ignorant. It is too easily assumed that the speaking of Arabic is a sure sign of Islamic faith.

In fact, Arab Christians have probably constituted between 10 and 20 per cent of the population in the Holy Land from the tenth century until recent times. And they may also, with some degree of confidence, posit that their ancestors were in the Holy Land long before the arrival of the Muslims – though those ancestors probably did not speak Arabic, but Syriac (Aramaic) or Greek. Nevertheless Greek remained the official language of their church hierarchy in Jerusalem. The Arab-speaking Christians did not establish a breakaway church but instead continued as members of their previous churches – the majority of them Greek Orthodox.

At this stage, the Latin-speaking Church was not strongly represented. We do, however, have the accounts of several visitors to Palestine from the West during this period: for example, Epiphanius the Monk, St Willibald, and Bernard the Monk. So pilgrimage was still an important possibility for adventurous individuals, who returned no doubt with fascinating tales of how things were done in the eastern Church.

THE LEGACY OF THE CRUSADES (1099–1800)

In the eleventh century, as we know too well, all this changed. The story of Christian involvement in the Holy Land was to enter its darkest phase – the era of the Crusades, launched by Pope Urban II in 1095 when he called on Christians to liberate the Holy Places. This is not the place to recount the history of the Crusades in detail. Instead we focus briefly on the lasting legacy it left in the Holy Land.

Reasons and results

Scholars have given various explanations as to how and why the Crusades came into being, including political issues in Europe and the western Church's need for a new focus. Others wonder if, for example, the Crusades were a response to the Great Schism of 1054 between the eastern and western churches – a subtle way of proving that western Christians were the true Church. Or were they a long-delayed reprisal against the Muslims for their conquest of Spain and southern France? – an 'object lesson' to eastern Christians that they should have resisted the rise of Islam long before?

There were several genuine triggers within the Holy Land itself. One was the capture of Jerusalem in 1071 by the Seljuk Turks, who prevented the continuing stream of pilgrims from visiting the city (though the Fatimids actually regained control of the city early in 1099). Another was the desecration and almost total destruction of the church of the Holy Sepulchre back in 1009. Having stood intact for nearly seven hundred years, this central church within Christendom was brought crashing to the ground on the orders of the Fatimid Caliph Hakim. The delicate peace between Christian and Muslim in the Holy Land was now visibly in tatters and stories would soon be circulating about the inappropriateness of the holy sites of Christendom being vulnerable to the attacks of the 'infidel'.

Recent surveys suggest that more of the original tomb may have survived than has commonly been supposed. Yet the Byzantine treasury could not afford anything like a thorough rebuilding. The new church sponsored by the Emperor Constantine Monomachus (1042–8) was just a shadow of its former self. The rotunda above the tomb was reconstructed, but the former basilica to the east of the tomb was lost forever. Instead the new church was built in what previously had been the courtyard.

This was the church that the Crusaders would eventually reach and enter with tears on 15 July 1099. Having just massacred the entire Muslim population they now entered the church singing the *Te Deum*. That day marked the beginning of the Latin kingdom in Jerusalem, which would last for nearly ninety years. The first king, Baldwin I (1100–18), and his successors would bring to Palestine a previously unknown level of effective administration, based on the feudal system. Numerous castles and abbeys were built, many of which can still be seen. Yet that day of bloodshed in 1099 continues to have its ramifications in the Middle East today.

The aftermath

For, ever since, profound questions have been raised concerning a theology of 'holy sites' which could leave in its wake so great a trail of destruction and havoc – the use of the 'holy' to justify the 'unholy'. Modern Muslim residents in the Middle East, for example, are prone to see any western interest in the Holy Land (of whatever kind and from whatever source) as marking a similar Crusading mentality.

Yet Christians too have their questions. For the eastern Church this was a time when they experienced enormous suffering at the hands of western 'Christians', who seemed unable or unwilling to make any distinction between eastern Christians and Muslims. Both suffered the full weight of Crusading atrocity. To put it mildly, considerable damage was done to the delicate *status quo* which the eastern Church had been building up for centuries with the Muslim authorities.

Meanwhile, within the western Church, it is no coincidence that the Reformation churches reacted against the excesses of medieval pilgrimage and interest in relics. For they were conscious not just of some of the superstition and false religious motivation which could attach itself to these practices. They also knew from their own not-too-distant history what could be the calamitous end-result of such thinking – if pushed to extremes.

For the reformers Gospel history was important, but when people started fighting over possession of the 'holy places' of the Gospels, things had clearly gone too far. True holiness was an attitude of heart and a pattern of life, irrespective of place, and God's true presence could be found wherever Christ's word and sacraments were duly administered. Surely there were other, better ways of believing in the Incarnation and responding to its truth? Could you not have a high doctrine of Christ without being forced to an elevated view of the places where his feet had trodden? Hence the rediscovery in the Reformation period of New Testament themes such as the universal nature of Christian worship and the power of the Spirit to make Christ present – dependent not on location but on faith. John Milton spoke for many in his description of the paradise of fools:

> *Here pilgrims roam, that stray'd so far to seek*
> *In Golgotha him dead, who lives in heav'n.*
> (PARADISE LOST 3. 476–7)

The theology of Cyril of Jerusalem back in the fourth century, when he elevated the 'holy places' of the Gospel in honour of Christ, may have been a natural development in his own day. But now, in the light of the Crusades, it could be seen to contain within it a dangerous seed – at least if it fell into the wrong soil.

Cyril had in addition boosted the concept of Jerusalem as a 'holy city'. This had further inspired the Crusaders, who longed to reach Jerusalem and who burst into songs of joy when they first caught a glimpse of the city on 7 July 1099 from the hill of Nabi Samwil – subsequently also known as Mountjoy for that reason. After the Crusades this concept too would come to be questioned: look at the unholy conflict that results when two religions compete for a city which they both consider 'holy'. Was not the focus of the New Testament instead on the heavenly 'New Jerusalem'? Paradoxically, the Crusaders did have a strong emphasis on the heavenly Jerusalem. Think, for example, of the famous hymn *O quanta qualia* by Abelard (1079–1142), with its celebration of the Sabbath rest in the 'true Jerusalem'; or of the popular hymn 'Jerusalem the golden', based on a hymn of Bernard of Clairvaux (1090–1153). So this New Testament emphasis had not been forgotten. It was just that they saw no contradiction in emphasizing simultaneously both the earthly and the heavenly Jerusalems. Indeed, the heavenly city gave new meaning to its earthly counterpart. So this same Bernard would encourage his hearers to go on the Second Crusade and would help to establish the new order of the Knights Templars.

Looking back on the Crusades and the reformers' reactions we sense the conflict between two quite different strands within the Christian faith. One keeps a steady focus on the spiritual nature of the faith, the other sees no harm in giving due attention to the historical and geographical roots of the faith. Both are legitimate, both probably necessary. The question is: how do you hold these together appropriately? In some ways the whole history of Christian attitudes to the Holy Land before and since could be written in terms of the tension between these emphases and the swing of the pendulum between them.

After the Crusades

The Latin Kingdom effectively came to an end with the crushing defeat of the Crusaders by the Ayyubid leader Saladin at the Horns of Hattin (just west of Tiberias) on 4 July 1187. Some Crusaders, however, remained in the area until

1291 when the Mamluks captured their stronghold in Acre. The Holy Land would then remain under Muslim rule (the Mamluks and then from 1517 the Ottomans) until the twentieth century. The magnificent walls of the present Old City were built during this period by Suleiman the Magnificent, who ruled the Ottoman Empire from 1520 to 1566.

Despite the savage treatment meted out by the Crusaders, Saladin and subsequent Muslim leaders allowed the various Christian communities to continue living in the Land. These would have been the 'Byzantine' communities, with only a few Latin Catholics in their number. Before the Crusades there had been a steady trickle of Christian pilgrims from the West (mainly Italians and Franks), and quite a few never returned. But it would take some time before the effects of the Crusades were forgotten, allowing western Christians to establish their presence once more. In due course, however, the various Catholic orders began to establish themselves; one of them, the Franciscans, returned as early as 1335 and would gain the role of being the 'custodians of the Holy Land', responsible for the preservation of a number of the traditional sites.

It is to this period that we owe, for example, the concept of the 'Via Dolorosa' (the 'Way of the Cross'). Ever since Cyril's day in the fourth century, Christians had re-enacted Jesus' movements from Gethsemane to Golgotha in different ways. In the fourteenth century, however, the Franciscans devised a commemorative route which initially began and ended in the Holy Sepulchre. Some two centuries later it was modified, not least at the request of western pilgrims who had become familiar with a fourteen-stationed version back in their home churches. Not for the last time, Jerusalem had to adapt for its foreign visitors – who wanted the reality on the ground to match their previous imagination.

By and large, however, these were the quietest centuries in the turbulent history of the Holy Land. Islamic rule

1. Arab men walk the streets of modern Bethlehem.

2. Orthodox Jewish men gather around a stone tomb on the Mount of Olives.

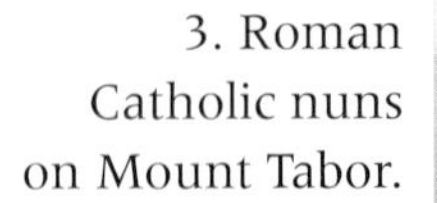

3. Roman Catholic nuns on Mount Tabor.

4. Palestinian Christian boy scouts celebrate Easter Sunday with a procession of bagpipes through the narrow streets of the Old City.

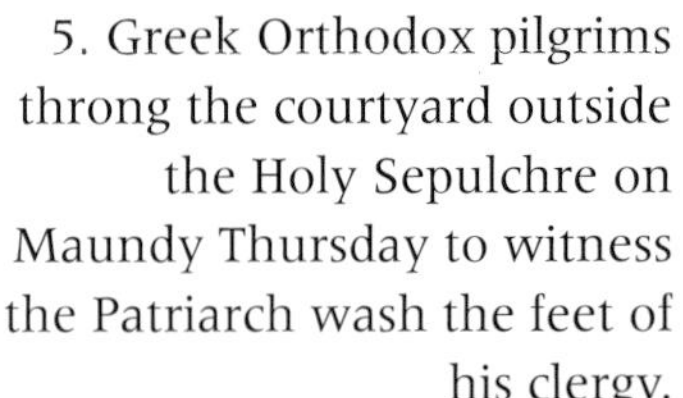

5. Greek Orthodox pilgrims throng the courtyard outside the Holy Sepulchre on Maundy Thursday to witness the Patriarch wash the feet of his clergy.

6. Greek Orthodox pilgrims prepare for the ceremony of the Holy Fire on Easter Eve in Jerusalem.

7. St George's Monastery, in the Wadi Qelt, beside the road from Jerusalem to Jericho.

8. Desert monks still inhabit cells perched in the most inaccessible of sites in desert cliffs.

9. First century tombs at Bethphage (see 'The Pilgrims' Tale (2)').

10. The hill frequented by Jesus: the Mount of Olives, seen here from the Old City, is the location for Jesus' triumphal entry on Palm Sunday, Gethsemane (bottom right) and the Ascension (traditionally on its summit).

11. The Holy City? Jerusalem from the Mount of Olives.

12. *Dominus Flevit* – a poignant stop on the Palm Sunday walk (see 'The Pilgrims' Tale (2)').

13. A group of pilgrims enter the Old City by St Stephen's Gate.

14. St Anne's – the finest example of a Crusader church in Jerusalem, later used as an Islamic school. Located near the Pool of Bethesda, and built on the traditional site of the home of the parents of Mary, mother of Jesus.

15. Walking in his steps: the first-century Temple steps are one of the few sites in present-day Jerusalem where we can confidently say that 'Jesus walked here'.

16. The model of first-century Jerusalem in the grounds of the Holy Land Hotel shows Herod's Palace (foreground), where Jesus was probably tried, and how the Temple (right of centre at far edge) dominated the city.

17. Inside the church of the Holy Sepulchre: the edicule built in 1810 over the traditional burial-place of Jesus.

18. The Garden Tomb: a quieter place to reflect on the death and Resurrection of Jesus.

showed no signs of weakening, and the disastrous effects of the Crusades were quite enough to cause the western Church not to get involved again in any significant way – once bitten, twice shy. In the sixteenth and seventeenth centuries the Roman Church succeeded in drawing some of the eastern Christians into communion with the see of Rome, thus creating the so-called 'Uniate' church (the Greek Catholics, the Syrian Catholics etc.), but otherwise the Christian community remained comparatively unchanged. The eastern churches continued to value their presence in Jerusalem, and Arab Christians continued to live as a respected minority within the country. Occasionally disputes broke out between them – as when the Ethiopians were exiled to the roof of the Holy Sepulchre in the seventeenth century – but their respective rights were quite carefully monitored by the Islamic authorities. With hindsight, knowing the rapid changes that have overtaken the Land in the last two hundred years, this long aftermath of the Crusades might well be seen as the 'calm before the storm'.

THE MODERN ERA (1800 TO TODAY)

Western interest in the Levant had, of course, never entirely disappeared. Throughout the previous centuries there was a quiet but unbroken stream of pilgrims (mainly Catholic) who came to the Land. But the area began to arouse interest – in political and then religious terms – after the military campaigns of Napoleon in 1799. He had been trying to forge a route through to India. Perhaps the West could once again be reconnected to its eastern roots? Then between 1830 and 1840 the Egyptian Ibrahim Pasha gained control over Palestine and Syria. As well as being a sign that Turkish rule was evidently weakening, this had the effect of making travel safer in the area. The time was ripe for the rediscovery of the Holy Land – especially among Protestants.

During the next hundred years, numerous Protestant denominations would establish their presence in Jerusalem in some way. Having a *pied à terre* in the city somehow legitimated the right of the denomination to exist elsewhere in the world. It was also the era for a spate of European and American visitors, who left an abundance of written material reflecting their visits. Some of the more famous include:

- the scholar Edward Robinson (in 1838), who denied the authenticity of almost every traditional site, including the Holy Sepulchre, and who discovered 'Robinson's Arch'
- the missionary James Barclay (from 1851 to 1854) who also was one of the first Christians to be allowed on to the Temple Mount, and who discovered 'Barclay's Gate'
- the Pre-Raphaelite artist William Holman Hunt (visiting four times between 1854 and 1892)
- the author Mark Twain, whose fairly scathing reflections were published in *Innocents Abroad* (1869)
- the military Charles Warren (1867), who wrote various books for the Palestine Exploration Fund on the archaeology of the Temple and Jerusalem
- the Scottish lithographer David Roberts (1842), whose paintings have become justly famous
- George Adam Smith, the Scottish writer of the superb *Historical Geography of the Holy Land* (1894)
- T.E. Lawrence (1914–15) who wrote up *The Wilderness of Zin* as a recent survey of southern Palestine.

Three different strands

One prime motivation for visiting the Holy Land was the modern, up-and-coming science of archaeology. Fascinating opportunities now opened themselves up to people who wished to investigate the archaeological and historical background of the Bible. Various publications began to be produced (such as the English *Palestine Exploration Quarterly*) with news of recent discoveries, and numerous archaeological excavations were carried out, both in Jerusalem and elsewhere – led by men such as Warren, Conder, Schick and Wilson.

This was also the period which saw the beginning of the quest for the historical Jesus. This was an attempt to get behind what were seen as the later accretions of Christian orthodoxy. For others it was all part of a general movement, influenced by Romanticism, attempting to get in touch with the more human aspect of Jesus. Either way, it meant that the Holy Land was a rich quarry to be mined, bringing forth new insights with which to understand the ancient scriptures.

Side by side with this Protestant interest in history and archaeology, there continued as before the more sacramental approach of Catholic and Orthodox pilgrims. One of the most fascinating accounts of such a pilgrimage is Stephen Graham's description of a Russian pilgrimage to Jerusalem in 1912 – just a few years before the Russian revolution brought such pilgrimages to an abrupt halt. In the previous decades there had been a vast influx of pilgrims from Russia. For them, as for other Orthodox believers, pilgrimage was often thought of as an ideal means of preparing for death. So to this day elderly Greek Cypriots, for example, will come to Jerusalem to buy and to anoint the shroud in which they hope soon to be buried.

A third strand within nineteenth-century interest in the Holy Land is quite different again. Arising solely within Protestant circles, it was the belief that the Holy Land (and in particular, the Jewish people) were still to play an important part within God's purposes, because of various statements and prophecies found in the Bible. A common expectation was that the Jewish people would be restored to their homeland.

This early Christian form of what might now be called Zionism can trace its roots to the writings of Frances Kett and Thomas Brightman in the late sixteenth century. Yet it only began to develop apace in the early years of the nineteenth century. Christian missionary work among Jewish people appeared on the agenda of various European denominations, and many missionaries actually came out to the Holy Land to live and work among the small Jewish population. The Anglican Church, for example, founded a new bishopric in Jerusalem in collaboration with the Lutheran Church, the first bishop being a converted Jew named Solomon Alexander.

There had probably been a small Jewish community within the city for quite some time, but this gradually increased. It was a leading Jew of his day, Moses Montefiore, the first Englishman allowed to buy land in Jerusalem (in 1858), who encouraged Jerusalem residents to live outside the cramped Old City walls. Among the western missionaries, high hopes were expressed about Jewish conversions to Christ in Jerusalem, but the reality on the ground was not always so promising. Some missionaries worked among eastern Christians, trying to bring them into the fold of their western denominations. Such activity was not unnaturally seen as 'sheep-stealing' by the local hierarchy and was not appreciated. Yet it explains, for example, the existence of Palestinian Arabs who are now not Greek Orthodox or Catholic but Anglicans or Lutherans.

Another way in which the evangelistic concern for Jewish people could be redirected was by developing theological and prophetic schemes whereby Jewish conversions to their Messiah were either not necessary (because God has 'two covenants' – one for Jews, one for Gentiles) or else the prerogative of God alone; God himself would accomplish his purposes towards his ancient people in his own time and way. Such theologies naturally continue to this day.

So within nineteenth-century Christian faith and practice there were at least three quite different approaches to the Holy Land: those inspired by issues of history and archaeology, those living in the imaginative world of pilgrimage and piety, and those inspired by scriptural prophecies concerning Israel. It was a heady brew of different perspectives, all being inspired by the Bible but in different ways. For some the Bible was a thing of the past, for others a signpost to the future; for some there was faith without much concern for history, for others there was history but with little room for faith. The important debates as to how we put all these together would continue down to the present day, and the stage for those debates would continue to be that small strip of land at the east of the Mediterranean.

The twentieth century: key events and modern questions

So the scene is set for the tumultuous events of the twentieth century, each of which has further coloured the complex mosaic of life in the Holy Land:

- the end of over three hundred years of Ottoman rule in 1917 and the era of the British Mandate (1917 to 1948)
- the steady influx to the Land of Jewish people awakened by the call of Herzl's political Zionism (articulated at the Basel conference in 1897), or responding to the horrific challenges of European anti-Semitism and the Holocaust
- the inevitable clashes between Jews and Arabs leading up to the proposed UN partition of Palestine in 1947
- the wars between Jews and Arabs of 1948, 1967 and 1973

- the changing face of the Land in the light of modern technology and the different political aspirations of its various communities
- the mass increase in tourism resulting from international air travel
- the significant work of Israeli and other archaeologists in unearthing more of the biblical past
- the attempted peace negotiations of the 1990s as the hard issues were faced of the Israeli need for security and the Palestinian desire for a national identity.

The impact of these events will be considered in the next chapter. But for now, as we look back over two thousand years of history in Part Two, it is sufficient to stress that any Christian visiting the Holy Land today must do so with humility, in the light of all that has gone before. We are the latest participants in a historical process that has been developing for two millennia. Tom and Sarah arrive to find a Holy Land that has not been sealed since biblical times in a time-warp capsule and kept pristine for their cameras. Instead, it is a Land marked forever by the intervening history – both ancient and modern.

THE PILGRIMS' TALE (3)

Roger stood waving his umbrella, trying to catch the attention of the group. He said it was time to move on, as the Muslims would soon be coming off the Dome of the Rock after Friday prayers, and they would get caught in the rush. Tom and Sarah gathered their thoughts and took a few hurried pictures as they prepared to leave behind the tear-shaped church of Dominus Flevit. They found themselves back on the tarmac path down the Mount of Olives. Ahead of them, they could see the fantastic bright golden domes of the Russian Orthodox church of St Mary Magdalene, like an upside-down bunch of garlic cloves clustered tightly together. The path straightened until it ran into a busier cross-road. They found themselves stopping in a small paved area beside the path, with Tony about to speak.

In a moment we will be in the olive groves of Gethsemane, but we stop here because it's quieter – further away from the noise of the buses.

A lot has happened since Jesus wept over the city on Palm Sunday. He has entered the city, demonstrated his authority over the Temple, cleared out its traders and used it as a forum for his teaching. He has sat with his disciples on the Mount of Olives, warning them of the Temple's imminent destruction. Over the hill in Bethany a woman has, strangely, anointed him for burial. And now late on the Thursday evening, coming up the Kidron valley with his disciples after the 'last supper' in the Upper City, a Passover with a difference, he has come here to Gethsemane.

In some ways Gethsemane is the crunch-point in the Gospel story, where everything comes together and where we are taken to the very heart of the matter. This is the 'hour' for which Jesus has been preparing, but also the moment when the forces of evil begin to be unleashed – the 'hour when darkness reigns'. Here as in the Transfiguration, Peter, James and John gain a unique view of Jesus alone at prayer and talking with God as his Father, 'Abba'. Here, as at the outset of his ministry, we see Jesus experiencing a time of testing and 'temptation', but resolving to go God's way. Here, at the foot of the Mount of Olives, we see the reality of Jesus' task – in stark contrast to the task which the crowds so enthusiastically expected him to carry out when they came over the top of the Mount. And, above all, it is here that we begin to see what had really been going on just now at the Last Supper, and what would be happening the next day, at the crucifixion.

Note three things in particular: First, Jesus' decision. Jesus' deciding to wait here in Gethsemane speaks volumes about how he saw his task. Many wanted him to storm the city and establish the Kingdom of God by the power of the sword. On the other hand, he could so easily have retreated over the brow of the Mount, had a bed for the night in Bethany and in due course set up a monastic community in the desert – like the people at Qumran. Both were real and very attractive temptations – popular acclaim or peaceful retirement. Jesus did neither. He resolutely decided to wait here – as a sitting target. Yes, the secluded garden enclosure was a convenient place to pray (especially when the rest of the hillside was covered with Galileans camped out for the night), but it was also a convenient spot for Jesus to be arrested 'on the quiet' – without too many others knowing about it. Why had Jesus set himself up like this? Why did he decide to wait?

And, please note, he waited a long time. His disciples, who were fishermen and quite used to being up all night, could not keep themselves awake. Three times he came back and found them sleeping. We are talking here about a long wait of several hours – perhaps till around two o'clock in the morning – almost certainly caused by the chief priests having to make some last-minute decisions and preparations before they could risk coming to arrest him. Why did Jesus wait? In short, because he had decided to go through with his mission, even if it broke him apart. Almost every ounce of his being would have urged him to flee over the hilltop, but he waited ... and waited. Why? Because there was no other way to fulfil what he had come to do.

Note, secondly, Jesus' dread. This is no play-acting, no easy parlour-game. 'His sweat', we read, 'was like drops of blood' (Luke 22:44). His soul 'was overwhelmed with sorrow to the point of death' (Matthew 26:38). Other martyrs have faced their death more calmly than this. What explains Jesus' dread? Yes, there was the natural recoiling from the physical and verbal abuse that would come his way in the next twenty-four hours. But to describe all this, Jesus used the imagery of a 'cup' (Luke 22:42; cf. Mark 10:38) which he had to drink. Jesus was picking up the imagery of the Old Testament prophets who depicted God's judgement as being like a cup which the guilty had to drink, a cup of God's wrath at the evil in the world. Now Jesus had to drink that cup of divine judgement. The cup which his Father was presenting to him was a cup which would cause him to be separated from his Father. Jesus' dread was of this extra spiritual reality behind the physical suffering – the dread of entering willingly into the very judgement of God. Or, to put it another way, he might be the King of a new Kingdom, but this Kingdom would only be established through the death of the innocent King. It was not a pleasant prospect if you yourself were that King, that unique Son of the Father.

We too perhaps recoil from these ideas. Was this really what God wanted Jesus to go through? Yet Gethsemane reveals there was no other way. If there had been, we can be sure Jesus would have seized it with both hands. After all, that's what he was praying for – an alternative route, a 'let-out' from this living hell. 'Father, if you are willing, take this cup away from me; yet not my will, but yours be done' (Luke 22:42). But nothing came. This was the Father's 'will'. Here in Gethsemane we see Jesus and his Father straining together towards the cross. Here we are taken to the heart of the crucifixion. Any ideas that the crucifixion was either unnecessary or had nothing to do with sin and judgement are denied by the very olive-trees of Gethsemane. So Jesus accepted the cup from the only person who could make it bearable – his Father.

Thirdly, Jesus' desire. At one level Jesus' desire was for the cup to pass from him. Yet more deeply he longed for God's will to be done. And through it all he desired that others, you and I, would benefit from what he did. He had given his disciples the 'cup' at the Last Supper, eagerly desiring that soon, when he had established the Kingdom and himself drunk the 'cup' of God's wrath, they would be able to drink it and find it to be the 'cup of salvation'. 'Drink this, all of you,' he had said, 'for this is my blood of the new covenant which is shed for you and for many, for the forgiveness of sins' (Matthew 26:27–8). That's what we do, Sunday by Sunday throughout the world, finding that, through what Jesus did, God's judgement is turned to mercy.

So Jesus desires today that we should recognize our need of what he did and then receive it with open hands. Perhaps it was the thought of us that somehow held him here in Gethsemane. Perhaps he knew the joy there would be among his followers for centuries to come. Isaiah had predicted: 'though it was the Lord's will to cause him to suffer, he will see his offspring ... after the suffering of his soul he will see the light of life and be satisfied' (Isaiah 53:10–11). As we go now to Gethsemane, to see the ancient olives, to be quiet inside the church, and to see the rock which since very early times Christians have marked as the place where Jesus agonized in prayer, let's be people who bring Jesus joy – people who are eternally grateful for what he did for us here, when he waited ... and waited.

The group was sombre now and moved at a slow pace as they turned into a small gate in a wall beside the road, and found themselves in a square symmetrical garden with ancient, gnarled olive trees surrounded by carefully arranged flowers. The garden was already full of people. They went along the path skirting the edge of the garden and followed the crowds into a church at the far side.

On walking inside, the effect was dramatic. The deep purple windows allowed only a dark sepulchral light through, lending a note of intense sadness and gravity to the scene. People shuffled around, speaking in hushed voices, as Tom and Sarah stood looking towards the focus of the building, an exposed rock upon which Jesus was said to have prayed in Gethsemane.

Tony's words had sunk deep into Tom's mind. They had drifted around as he walked about the church, but now they slowly settled into a steady clarity. As they went back out into the garden, he tried to imagine Jesus looking back up the hill towards the safety of the desert and then turning to face the city again. Something lodged firmly in his mind – a kind of resolution, almost a decision.

'Sarah, you know what you were saying back at the airport?'

'No – I can't remember. Remind me.'

'You said you thought that maybe God wanted me to come here for a reason. I don't know whether he did or not, but if he did, I think I'm working out what it might be. I was thinking about Jesus in the garden back there. I'd never thought of it like that – that he could just have walked back up the hill and escaped. You know, it feels a bit like that for me. Maybe you haven't been in this Christian thing long enough to know this feeling that you're drifting, going through the motions, but it does happen. It just struck me that I could walk away too. I could walk out on God. It's a real live option.'

Sarah looked a little shocked. 'You're not losing your faith, are you?'

'No, I'm not. Anyway, I don't think you "lose" faith; you just stop making it the centre of your life. Maybe I've just realized I don't want that. I don't want it to be something I do half-heartedly. Being here just makes that feel impossible, if you know what I mean. It's like I've either got to go back over the hill and give it all up, or I've got to get on with what God has in mind for me.'

'What do you think that is?' asked Sarah.

'I've no idea. In some ways it doesn't matter what it is. Maybe even Jesus didn't quite know what would happen. But it's as though I'm needing to decide what really matters to me in life.'

By now, they had left the garden and were at the bottom of the hill. They stood by a busy Jerusalem road, passing through the floor of the Kidron valley. They dodged the cars, ran up a little rise to the right, turned off the main road up the other side of the valley and approached a large gate in the city walls. Roger slipped alongside them.

'This is St Stephen's Gate,' he said. 'This is where we go into the Old City.' Then he caught Tom's eye and leaned over, a bit too close for comfort, adding, 'Are you all right, Tom?'

'Yes, I'm fine, just thinking a bit,' replied Tom, preferring to keep his thoughts to himself and Sarah. They passed through the tall, castellated structure and proceeded down a narrow street, between high untidy buildings on either side. Some young Israeli soldiers stood beside the path, machine guns slung over their shoulders, talking loudly. Sarah noticed three Palestinian teenagers approaching. One kicked a stone aggressively as he passed by, just missing one of the soldiers. The soldier swung round and stared threateningly at the perpetrator, and Sarah felt herself tighten with fear as he laid a hand on his gun; but the tense moment passed, and she was able to walk on by herself.

As they proceeded, Tony talked. He pointed out a beautifully simple, unadorned church called St Anne's. It was built, he said, by the Crusaders, and was an eloquent reminder of that troubled period of Christian involvement in the Land. He said they were walking down the Via Dolorosa, the route used by medieval pilgrims to re-enact the last walk of Jesus to the cross. They passed under a half-arch, which he referred to as the 'Ecce Homo' arch. He said it had something to do with the Roman emperor Hadrian's rebuilding of the city in the second century.

By this stage, Sarah was hopelessly confused. In five minutes they had moved from the time of Jesus, to the present day, back to the Middle Ages, and then back into the Roman Empire. Quite apart from struggling to understand the details, she felt the weight of history buried beneath her feet in the layers of earth, stones and debris which held the secrets of the past. She was just another layer of history, another pair of feet to walk in this place after the millions of others who had gone before – before and after the feet of Jesus himself. Just as when she had watched the Greek pilgrim singing, she felt she was just a small part of something far bigger than she had ever imagined.

They twisted and turned around the tiny streets of the Old City. Stalls and shops, vibrant with colour and light, were set into the walls on either side. Traders tried their hardest to entice them inside these Aladdin's caves of carpets, pottery and food. Tom couldn't help noticing the gaudy, soulful portraits of Jesus with long flowing brown locks in which he was either carrying a lamb, pointing to a flaming heart on his breast, or holding out his hands like a traffic policeman. By now he was more amused than angry at these, and nudged Sarah as they passed, to make sure she saw them.

'One of those would look great on my mantelpiece!' she grinned, thinking of the delicate taste and pastel shades of her flat in London.

'No pilgrim should be without one,' he agreed. They caught each other's eye and laughed. Eventually the group funnelled through a small archway into another courtyard, square this time, packed with people. Black-garbed Orthodox priests with square pillbox hats mingled with American tourists with baseball caps and cameras. A small man wearing a red fez stood in the corner beside a large two-arched doorway in the far corner of the courtyard. One of the doorways was solidly bricked in, the other one opened into a darkened church beyond.

'This is it,' whispered Tom.

'This is what?' replied Sarah.

'The Holy Sepulchre. I've seen pictures of it in the guide-book. It's where they reckon Jesus died, and where his tomb was.'

'Doesn't look much like it now,' said Sarah with a distinct note of dismay in her voice.

They entered the archway and found themselves inside the church. It took a little while before their eyes adjusted after the brightness of the sunlight outside. Intense-looking pilgrims scurried everywhere. In the background they could hear the intoning of a Latin hymn echoing out of some distant corner of the building. The stone walls and pillars looked old and tired, apart from a bright, stylized mosaic on the wall opposite depicting Jesus being brought down from the cross. A few women were kneeling beside a large reddish slab of stone before them, which Roger told them was the stone on which Jesus' dead body was said to have been anointed. They turned to the right, and made their way around a semi-circular walkway inside the dark, echoing building. Then they descended some steps, which in the dim light made them feel as if they were going down into the bowels of the earth. At the bottom, they stood together with the group in what looked like a large hollowed-out cave. Tony quietened them, and began. This time his voice was slightly hushed, drawing them closer towards him as a group, to be less distracted by the other visitors who came and went. He was obviously quite excited, and wanted the group to share in what he felt.

We are now standing in a cistern carved out several centuries before Christ. This general area was later quarried for its stone, possibly causing this cistern to be opened to the elements. At the same time, almost above our heads the quarriers came across a cracked block of stone which they left untouched. This rock, standing some four metres above ground level, is now the traditional site of Golgotha or Calvary. If this tradition is correct, then the natural rock above us is the continuation of the rock of Golgotha, and we are surrounded by the very stone which witnessed the crucifixion of the Rock of Ages. Just think of that.

Tom looked across the group at Sarah, who was clearly doing just that. Her face, as well as those of most of the group, looked lost in thought. He noticed a few quivering lips and faces trying to fight back tears as Tony went on.

In Jesus' day, so it is argued, this area would have been outside Jerusalem's north-western wall by some fifty metres. We cannot be sure if this was a regular site for Roman executions, though the name ('the place of a skull') seems to suggest this. It would certainly have been clearly visible to those entering the city by the 'Gennath', or Garden Gate, some sixty metres to the south-east.

Within fifteen years of the crucifixion, however, this area was brought within the city walls. Any tombs here would have been ritually cleansed, and houses built within the vicinity. Then in AD *135, when building his new pagan city, the emperor Hadrian used this area for building a forum and a temple dedicated to Aphrodite. Probably he was quite unaware of the site's significance for the small Jewish–Christian community in the city – it was just a convenient spot near the centre of his new city and on quite high ground. But no wonder the Christians were quick to ask Constantine in AD 325 for permission to clear the site!*

When they did so, they found several tombs (one of which they were convinced was Jesus'), as well as the mound of rock above us which was soon identified as Golgotha. The whole area was then covered with a vast basilica going eastwards from the tomb. This cistern here also comes into the story, with later tradition suggesting that this was where Queen Helena found some pieces of the 'true cross' – hence the chapel above us is dedicated to St Helena.

Meanwhile, just a few metres to the north of us here, and again well below the floor level of the Constantinian buildings, a stone was found in 1971. On it was a graffito of a ship with some letters scratched on it, which were later deciphered as Latin for 'Lord, we have come'. There are lots of questions about this, but just conceivably it might have been left by a western pilgrim visiting the site at the time when the foundations of Constantine's church were being laid. If so, then we can sense some of the excitement that people felt on discovering after a gap of nearly three hundred years these places associated with the two central events in Christian faith – the crucifixion and the Resurrection of Jesus. 'Lord, we have come!'

And we too have now come. There is a sense in which every Christian believer throughout the world has been to the cross, has died with Christ, and so is connected to this event in Jerusalem. But there is nothing quite like coming to visit that spot for oneself – to see the place where your Christian life began.

Tony paused briefly as a small group of middle-aged French Catholics squeezed down the steps into the chapel where they stood, looked around noisily, realized they were stumbling into the quiet meditation of the group, and left, outnumbered and a little embarrassed.

We left the story with Jesus being arrested in Gethsemane and taken back into the Upper City for his trial before Caiaphas. Early the next morning he is brought before Pilate and now finds himself outside the city once more – but this time outside its western wall. It has all happened so fast. He is no longer a free man. He is on the way to his execution, his 'Via Dolorosa'. He has been condemned to be crucified.

Crucifixion was acknowledged to be the most barbaric form of death, with victims slowly dying of suffocation, unable to pull themselves up sufficiently to breathe. It was reserved only for slaves and political rebels, and was not to be mentioned in polite Roman society. For the Jews it was doubly degrading. In their scriptures they understood anyone hanging 'on a tree' to be under God's curse; they were also keenly sensitive to the fact that victims were left to hang naked (alluded to tactfully by the Gospel writers when they talk of lots being cast for Jesus' clothes).

But Luke shows Jesus, even at this time of acute suffering, thinking not of himself but of others. 'Father, forgive them,' he prays for those crucifying him, 'for they know not what they do' (Luke 23:34). And on the way to Calvary he thinks not of his own plight but of that awaiting the city: 'Daughters of Jerusalem, do not weep for me; weep for yourselves and your children' (v. 38). Thinking not of himself but of the city he loved, Jesus foretold that there would be a devastating disaster. If Jerusalem continued with its present policy, it too was on its own Via Dolorosa.

So Jesus was lumped together with the likes of Barabbas, arrested for insurrection (v. 19) and the two brigands crucified with him. Yet as Luke insists in his narrative, Jesus was in fact quite innocent of this charge of being a political rebel against Rome (the Roman centurion calls him a 'righteous man': v. 47). Instead Jesus is suffering on a trumped-up charge as though he were a political zealot – even though this was precisely what he had himself denounced! If so, we see here an extra dimension to the love of Jesus, dying as one of his people, taking up their cause and their cross, facing and bearing the very judgement of which he himself had warned them.

Yet, as we know, even if this were not enough, there was far more to the cross than this. There is the irony of it all. People mock him for claiming to be the Messiah and the 'King of the Jews' (vv. 35, 38), but so he was – he was doing the very thing which, if only they knew it, they needed their Messiah and King to do for them. And note too the irony of his promise to the man crucified with him: 'Today you will be with me in Paradise' (v. 43). Extraordinary words of confidence and authority from someone himself about to die, seemingly with nothing to offer!

Above all, however, there is Jesus' incredible achievement, symbolized by the Temple curtain (over on the other side of the city) being torn in two at that very hour (v. 45). The Gospel writers record this to indicate their conviction that through Jesus' death a new way into God's presence had been forged. At last an effective sacrifice had been offered. Divine judgement has been met by divine forgiveness, brought about through none other than divine self-sacrifice.

So on the cross, we are dealing not just with a man dying for his own cause, nor just with the true Messiah dying for his own people, but also with the Son of God dying for the whole world. It operates on all these levels. And the cross is also the work of the Creator God, going to the depths to reveal his love for us, coming to where we are, bound up in sin and death, in order to rescue us.

It is an incredible story, which we know well. And the New Testament writers never cease to be amazed at what Jesus has done for us here at Calvary: it is an example of self-giving love, but so much more than that as well. Jesus on the cross is the 'Lamb of God' who 'bears the sins of the world', 'slain before the foundation of the world'; 'the righteous one dying for the unrighteous'; 'the atoning sacrifice for our sins'.

But perhaps for our purposes today, St Paul sums it up best when he personalizes it and speaks of the 'Son of God who loved me and gave himself for me' (Galatians 2:20). Here was a man caught by the vision of Jesus crucified, who knew this great act of love had been done not just for everyone in general, but also uniquely for him. I sometimes wonder if, on some of his visits to Jerusalem, Paul didn't sneak over here to this area now brought within the city wall, just to contemplate what had happened here. Be that as it may, the cross was the centre of Paul's life, the place where he was forgiven, the place where he received for himself the love of the Father. It can be the same for us too.

Let's keep a moment of quiet and then perhaps one or two would like to lead us in short prayers of thanks for what Christ has done for each one of us – quite possibly within just a few yards of where we are now standing.

Sarah stared at the cold rock jutting out from the sides of the cistern walls. The thought that these rocks had heard Jesus' cries of pain, the racking sobs of his mother and the disciples, the biting laughter of the crowd, pierced her like a sword. She felt her own eyes brimming with tears as the scene floated vividly before her mind. Of course, she had sung about Jesus' death, and had thanked God for what it meant to her, many times during the past year. Yet now, being here, it sank into parts of her heart which it had never quite touched before.

After the song, they climbed back up the stairway, past pillars dotted with hundreds of small carved crosses, which Roger told them had been etched by obscure medieval pilgrims centuries before, back on to the semi-circular walkway. Retracing some of their steps towards the entrance to the building, they were directed up more stairs to a raised chapel, dark and hushed by the presence of whispering pilgrims. In particular, a young Palestinian woman caught Sarah's eye. She was kneeling, with a very small baby in her arms, to one side of the chapel, eyes closed, one hand raised in prayer. Against the far wall stood a riot of colour, silver plate, icons and life-size pictures of people. From the low ceiling hung a tangle of lamps, shedding a dim light into the sombre atmosphere. It slowly dawned on Sarah that she was standing on the rock of Calvary. The initial shock gave way to a profound disappointment as she compared what she felt was a gaudy, elaborate display to the 'green hill far away' of her imagination. She had pictured a rounded hill, with three crosses against a darkening sky. Instead she found a small cramped room, a jumble of unnatural-looking images of Jesus, Mary and some disciples, and a musty smell.

They stood quietly for a minute or two. Sarah looked across at Tom, who seemed lost in contemplation. He looked as if he was far more affected by the place than she was. Funny that, she thought. He was the cynic, she was meant to be the spiritual one. Tom stepped forward, and she saw him kneel down to put his hand through a small opening in order to touch the rock of Calvary. He stepped back alongside Sarah, and glanced in embarrassed fashion at her.

'I suppose I shouldn't have done that. It's a bit superstitious, isn't it, touching the rock like that? It just seemed … the right thing to do, somehow. You know how you always hear about Jesus dying on the cross for you. I just wanted to convince myself it was real – it really happened in a real place.'

They walked back down the steps, and went on anticlockwise around the church, again using the semi-circular walkway. They paused at a pillar which Tony told them was part of the original Constantinian church. He explained how the rest of the fourth-century church would have stretched away behind them to the east, and how the bit they now stood in, which had been built by the Crusaders, would instead in Constantine's day have been open to the sky – a gardened courtyard in front of Jesus' tomb.

Tom slipped away from the group and ran ahead, as decently as he could in a church, to see if he could get inside some first-century tombs that Tony said were worth a look at the far end. He couldn't get near them. Apparently the Greek ambassador was being given a special tour and swarms of visitors were lining up to stoop inside the famous *kokhim* tombs in the Syrian chapel. 'Don't worry, we'll come back early tomorrow morning,' Tony said, making light of it. 'But they are worth seeing. They do give you a good idea of what Jewish tombs in the time of Jesus might have looked like. They're also pretty good evidence that this area was outside the city wall at the time of the crucifixion – they wouldn't have allowed tombs inside the city. You'll just have to use your imagination.'

With that, he led the group forward into a domed area, at the centre of which stood a large square edifice that seemed to be held together by scaffolding. Tom thought it looked like a retired spaceship. This, Tony explained, was the 'edicule', marking the spot of the tomb of Christ. They shuffled to a halt as some black-garbed clerics walked by. Then Tony began again. It was the climax of the tour within the Holy Sepulchre, and the group could sense this was a moment their guide had been waiting for.

So we stand now outside the traditional tomb of Jesus. The present structure over the tomb (known as the 'edicule' or 'little house') only goes back to the early nineteenth century. Few people think it is attractive, and it is in imminent danger of falling down – hence the iron girders placed round it during the time of the British Mandate.

But perhaps we can go back in time in our mind's eye, and sense the excitement of those Byzantine excavators when they cleared away the pagan temple and found 'contrary to their wildest dreams' a tomb still intact after nearly three hundred years. It was an amazing moment, which Eusebius describes as itself a kind of Resurrection: just as Jesus had returned to life after three days, so now his tomb had been restored to light after nearly three hundred years!

Of course, some of us might have been tempted to leave the tomb exactly as it was. They wanted to do something better, however.

The one who had been buried in shame was now to be proclaimed as the King of Kings. So they cut it free from the surrounding cliff face, allowing people to walk around it, and built a small 'house' structure over it. A large dome, similar to the present one, was built over the whole area, while in front of the tomb there was that courtyard, open to the sky.

And that's how it remained for nearly seven hundred years until the caliph Hakim ordered the destruction of the church in 1008. Then there was a disastrous fire in 1808. So understandably people imagined that none of the original rock could possibly have survived. Recent tests, however, suggest that more of the original may be there than was formerly supposed.

So, despite its appearance, there is the distinct possibility that this was indeed the place where Jesus was raised from the dead.

Whether or not it is, this remains the place where for nearly seventeen hundred years Christians have come to remember the events of that first Easter Day. The women came to the tomb and found the stone rolled away; they saw the body had gone, though the garments mysteriously remained. They rejoiced when they met the Risen Jesus, and they then spread the message that death had been conquered, and that this Jesus was the unique Saviour of us all.

So we join ranks with Christians down the ages in proclaiming the Resurrection in this place, known in the eastern Church appropriately as the Church of the Resurrection. Every Easter, Christians converge here for the ceremony of the Holy Fire. On Holy Saturday the church is filled to capacity, each person with their special Easter candles. The Greek patriarch goes into the tomb around midday and then suddenly a flame can be seen inside the edicule. It is passed out through the two holes in the side of the antechamber. Within moments the bells are ringing and the church is alight with hundreds of candles. It would cause most fire officers a heart attack, and it's not good if you suffer from claustrophobia! But for them, as for us, it is a powerful expression of Christian faith and hope in the Resurrection of

Christ. 'Christ is risen!' they proclaim; and we respond, 'He is risen indeed! Alleluia!'

'Christ is risen!'

'He is risen indeed! Alleluia!'

Tom turned to Sarah, and whispered, with some animation in his voice, 'I've just realized; I've never before been in a church with an empty tomb.'

Part Three

THE CONTEMPORARY SCENE

Christians in the Land Today

Chapter 8

THE LAND AND ITS PEOPLE

At long last you have arrived. You are now in the very Land of the Bible. This may be a culmination of many years of secret hoping that one day you would be there. In Parts One and Two we looked at some of the issues to think through when preparing to visit the Land – questions of Christian theology, key points in history. Join us now as we enter the Land together.

But don't make the mistake that many Christian visitors make. With their interest in biblical sites – finding the spot where this or that happened – they too often keep their eyes, as it were, 'on the ground'. They travel round in air-conditioned buses, cocooned from the reality of the world outside their window. They then muster their strength for visiting the next holy site, so this too can be ticked off on their place-packed itinerary. Instead we need to look up, gaining a sense of the Land as a whole, and to look outwards, meeting the people and beginning to sense their situation. This is not a theme park, laid out expressly for our enjoyment. It is a real place, a real home to real people.

So in this chapter we introduce you first to the physical contours of the land and then to the peoples who now live there, highlighting some of their recent history and conflicting agendas. In chapter 9 we focus on the indigenous Christian community with all its struggles and hopes. In chapter 10 we go back out to the desert in order to make sense of all that we have learnt, and to be renewed for our Christian life and service – wherever that might be. Finally in the Appendices we draw all this together by giving you some brief tips on how best to approach your visit and the biblical places in the Land.

APPRECIATING THE LAND

As we approach the Land we begin by hearing the way the Old Testament describes it: 'the land of promise'; the 'land flowing with milk and honey, the most beautiful of all lands'; a land that is 'good', 'beautiful', 'delightful', 'pleasant' and 'desirable' (Ezekiel 20:6; Deuteronomy 8:7; Psalm 106:24; Jeremiah 3:19 etc.). Unlike Egypt its water came not from a great river, but 'from heaven' itself (Deuteronomy 11:11). Compared to the desert-filled countries round about, this land is a comparative oasis. The Israelites wandering towards it had ample opportunity to sense this. We, often flying in from the west, can easily miss it – though a satellite picture would make it plain! So be on the lookout for signs of its fertility and enjoy some of its rich produce.

Having said that, in a land where there is little rain between May and October, water remains a precious commodity and a source of worry and disputes, a cause for prayer and thanks. And much of the ground, especially in the hill country, is thick with rocks. In an old Jewish fable God sent two storks with two large sacks of stones to be distributed over the inhabited world, but one of the bags – half of the world's rocks – burst over the land of Israel! Hence the three-thousand-year-old terraces developed on the hillsides to increase vegetation; hence too the aptness of Jesus' parable about four different types of soil.

This strip of land is indeed an amazing phenomenon. Yet it is also so tiny. Crammed into the eighty miles (maximum) between the Mediterranean and the hills of Transjordan, the country has a total length of only 150 miles 'from Dan to Beersheva' (that common biblical way of describing the length of the Land from north to south). You will need to get used to how close things are to each other – Bethlehem is just seven miles from Jerusalem, and you can walk from Nazareth to Jerusalem in just four days (or do it by bus in under three hours!).

Enjoying the differences – of geography and history

Yet in this small space there is such variety. And each distinct region is laden with biblical history. Try to visit as many of these regions as possible:

- The **coastal plain**, dominated by modern Tel Aviv, but with biblical sites such as Joppa and Caesarea Maritima. Until Herod the Great built the mammoth harbour at Caesarea there were few natural harbours on this coastline. The Israelites were not great sea-lovers – this area was lived in chiefly by the Phoenicians – and they spoke in some awe of the sea and those who travelled on it (see e.g. Psalm 107:23–4).
- The **foothills** (or *Shephelah*, rolling hills) that come down towards the coastal plain and to within twelve miles of the coast. Here the Israelites frequently had to fight their enemies in defence of their territory further to the east – think of Samson and David against the Philistines.
- The **hill-country** in the centre of the Land, with its mountainous backbone running some ninety miles from north to south. This small area, slightly off the main coastal road and outwardly insignificant, lies at

the heart of the biblical narrative. It includes the ancient sites mentioned in the 'patriarchal' narratives in Genesis – Bethel (to the north) and Bethlehem and Hebron (to the south). It was frequented by key biblical figures such as Abraham, Joshua, Samuel and David. But remember here too Samaria, the Northern Kingdom of 'Israel' (scene of prophets such as Elijah, Elisha, Hosea and Amos) and which later became the land of the Jews' enemies, the Samaritans.

- **Jerusalem** itself, in and around which was acted out the central drama of salvation. No visit can exclude the Mount of Olives, frequented by Jesus and the perfect place to consider the importance of Jerusalem and to reflect on the significance of Jesus. But don't miss out on other places nearby which feature in the biblical story: Anathoth (birthplace of Jeremiah), Gibeah (home of Saul) and Ein Karem (possibly the birthplace of John the Baptist in the 'hill-country of Judea': Luke 1:39).
- The **plain of Jezreel** (or the Esdraelon valley), flanked to the west by Mount Carmel and the modern port of Haifa, and to the east by the rounded hill of Mount Tabor and the hills of Gilboa. This was a 'bread-basket' in the ancient world and the scene of many battles: think of Deborah against Sisera, Gideon against the Midianites; remember the deaths of Saul and Jonathan fighting against the hording Philistines, and of King Josiah against Pharaoh Necho at the battle of Megiddo. But overlooking the plain too were the hills of Nazareth, into which a young boy could climb for a good view before starting out on his public ministry.
- The **Galilee**, centring on the lake, but including the steep hills to the north-west and reaching up to the Golan Heights on the east. Isaiah had sensed the international role of this 'Galilee of the Gentiles' (Isaiah 9:1). It becomes the central focus of Jesus' ministry,

which was based in Capernaum on the north-western shore of the lake, but reaching out to the surrounding villages of Chorazin, Bethsaida, Magdala and the Plain of Genessaret. Though there is no explicit evidence that Jesus visited the two pagan cities of Tiberias and Hippos which were also on the lake, his working in this area necessarily entailed his coming into contact with Gentiles. The barren expanse of the Golan Hills, overlooking the lake, were a key resource for prayer, but when he wanted a quality period alone with his disciples he took them further north towards Mount Hermon and the area of Caesarea Philippi.

- The **Jordan rift valley**, now divided in two by the international border between Israel and the Hashemite kingdom of Jordan. In just a hundred miles the waters of the Jordan flow down from Mount Hermon (9,200 feet above sea level) to the Dead Sea (1,300 feet below sea level), the bottom of which is a further 1,300 feet below that! Here we can remember the stories of Joshua and Elijah, the ministry of John the Baptist, and Jesus' encounters with Zacchaeus and Bartimaeus in Jericho. As you travel further south along the Dead Sea, you encounter Qumran (the place of the Dead Sea Scrolls), the springs of Ein Gedi (where David hid from Saul) and the area associated in biblical memory with the cities of Sodom and Gomorrah.
- The **Judean desert**, going down to the Dead Sea and then extending into the Negev and eventually to Eilat on the Gulf of Aqaba. This expanse of desert was where Israel was 'tested for forty years'. So not surprisingly, as God prepared the ground for the New Covenant, people were called by John back into the desert and Jesus went there too. It is the place of testing, of self-examination, and of renewal in the service of the true God, as we shall see in chapter 10.

For Christian visitors, there is no doubt that Jerusalem and Galilee are the two most essential places to visit. Opinions differ, however, as to which is best to visit first. If you are following closely the ministry of Jesus, then obviously it makes good thematic sense to start in Galilee and then follow him 'on the way' up to the city. Many, however, especially those on a short stay, prefer to do it the other way round. Jerusalem is a busy city and makes many demands on the visitor, so a few days in Galilee can allow some of the dust to settle. In Appendix II we outline an itinerary which we have used several times. The visit to Jerusalem comes before the time in Galilee, but also after an extended time in the desert. You might like to try something similar – it works really well.

The bridge between the continents

But before going on to meet the people of the Land it is worth taking note just how the Land's relationship to its neighbouring countries affects both its geography and history. For, when set in a wider context, the Land can be seen as a 'land-bridge' between continents.

In geographical terms this is best sensed in the remarkable phenomenon of the Judean desert in the fourteen miles between Jerusalem and Jericho. As will be seen from figure 6 (p. 185), no less than four major features of world geology converge in this small area – the East African rift valley, the Egyptian Sahara, the 'Syrian steppe' country, and the Mediterranean fertile belt. In other words, here you see coming together north and south, east and west! Geologically it is indeed the meeting point of Africa and Asia.

But the same can be sensed when you see the Land as a comparative oasis in the desert of the Near East. With inhospitable desert to its east, it was inevitable that throughout history this narrow strip would also be the

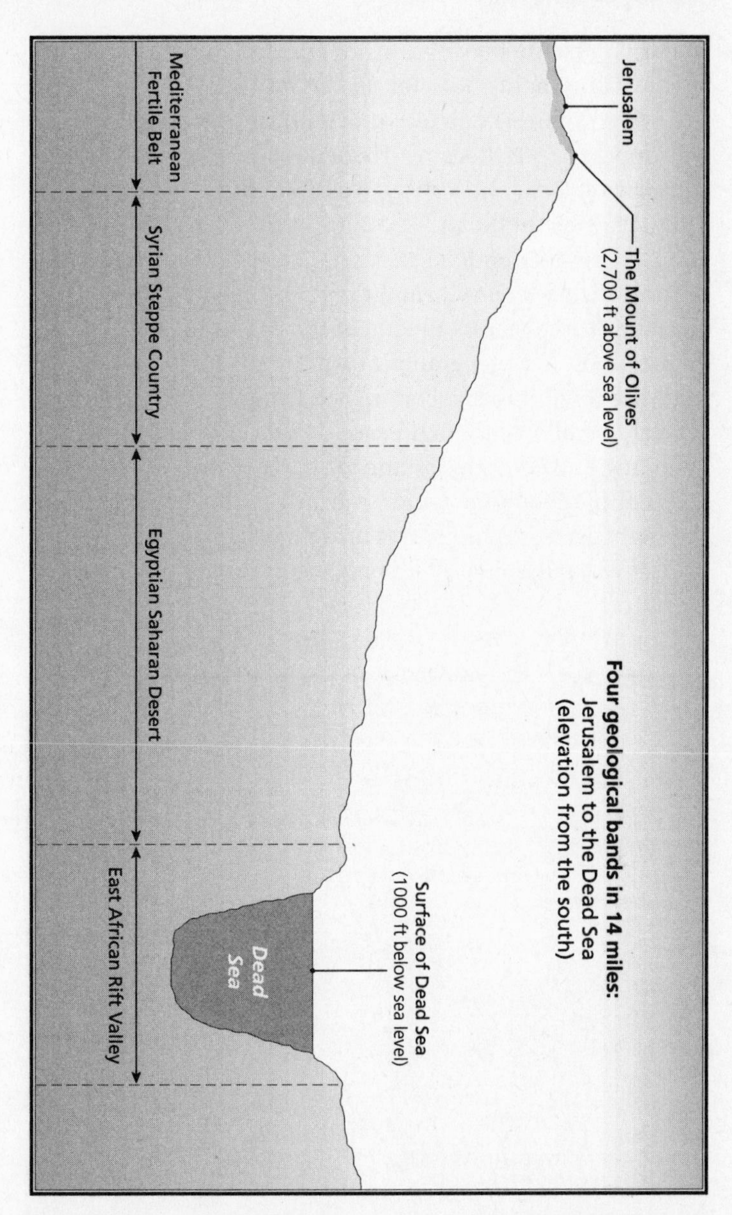

Figure 6. Four geological bands in 14 miles: Jerusalem to the Dead Sea (elevation from the south)

major land route between Africa and Asia. In ancient times this was the main route for all the traffic flowing between the two main centres of civilization – Egypt and Mesopotamia. It became the equivalent of an ancient motorway. That motorway was known as the *Via Maris* (the 'Way of the Sea'). It came up the coastal plain and then crossed inland on its way towards Damascus, first cutting through the Carmel range of hills and then going through Jezreel across the top of the Sea of Galilee.

Inevitably this geographical feature of the Land brought with it a tough history. For anyone living in this area would scarcely be allowed much peace – especially when the surrounding powers were jostling for position or simply needed some of the food that could be grown in this fertile area. So when the Israelites tried to set up an independent state in this area, it was rather like a bird building its nest in the middle of

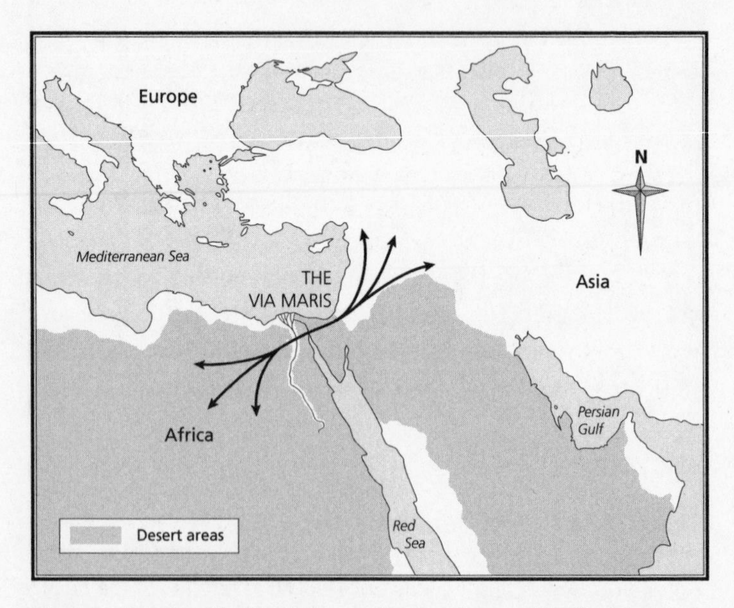

Figure 7. The land-bridge between the continents (the Via Maris*)*

a road junction – it would not make for a quiet life! Not surprisingly, then, the hill of Megiddo which defended a vital pass on the *Via Maris* became the scene of numerous battles between the great powers; it would pass into biblical imagery as the obvious scene for the ultimate battle between good and evil – Armageddon (Revelation 16:16). You are entering a land of tension and bloodshed, fought over through the centuries – in part, simply because of its prime location at the crossroads between two continents.

Having said that, there was a sense in which Jerusalem itself and the Land at the heart of Israel's life was slightly to one side of the main road. To get there, you needed to make a conscious detour. This means that Galilee tended to be more cosmopolitan and international than Jerusalem and the hill-country to the south. Jerusalem was not a major trading centre, more of a religious backwater. To this day, many who live near the Mediterranean find little need to go up to Jerusalem.

So Jesus' choice of Galilee as an initial base for his ministry was significant. Yes, he would have to go up in due course to the religious city of Jerusalem, but for now he would be found in Capernaum – a small fishing village perhaps, but located on the main highway which linked together the continents of the world. In other words, it was a brilliant place for a preacher with a message that would ultimately capture the world; a neat springboard for a gospel designed for 'all nations' (Matthew 28:19). As he himself said, 'do not put your light under your bed, but rather where it can be seen' (Luke 8:16).

MEETING THE PEOPLE

This land, however, is far from being a mere museum, full of beautiful exhibits but void of humanity. No, it is home today to over nine million people. Despite what some claimed in the nineteenth century, this never was a 'land without a people'. If the Land comes to mean a lot to you on your first visit, imagine what it might mean for those who live here.

Hopefully after a few days you will become better equipped to recognize some of the different groups represented here. In addition to the various expatriate communities and small minorities such as the Druze, there are in fact some 4.8 million Jews and 4.1 million Arabs within the post-1967 borders of 'Israel' – two historic peoples side by side. Let's look briefly at each in turn.

The Jewish people

Since the fall of Jerusalem in AD 70 there has almost certainly been a continuous, but small, presence of Jews within the Land. By the fourth century they were the predominant group within the Galilee region, with key rabbinic centres located in Sepphoris and Tiberias. Under Muslim rule their numbers dwindled, but the city of Safat, perched high up in the hills and visible from Lake Galilee on a clear day, became a key centre for Jewish life and for the study and practice of the Kabbalah, a form of Jewish mysticism in the Middle Ages.

By the early nineteenth century a steady trickle of Jewish people came to Jerusalem, many inspired by a religious attachment to this historic land and city. Towards the end of the century, in response to the twin threats of Jewish persecution in Russia and assimilation in Europe, political Zionism began to develop, with Theodore Herzl articulating the desire for a Jewish homeland. Initially, other countries such as Uganda or Argentina were suggested as suitable places. But the Land of Israel (in Hebrew *Eretz Israel*) quickly came to the fore as the natural and obvious place to implement this ideal. To this day, even if they are not motivated by a strong theology of the future or a nostalgia for the past, Jewish people have a strong emotional attachment to the Land. It has become vitally important for them.

And many began to settle. In 1880 Jewish residents were a tiny number among the three hundred thousand Muslim and Christian inhabitants in the region. But by the time of the Balfour Declaration in 1917, when the British government declared its written support for the 'establishment in Palestine of a national home for the Jewish people', there were already around 60,000 Jewish residents in the land (about 10 per cent of the overall population). Many of them were working in agriculture to make the land more productive.

The 1920s saw significant and violent clashes between the expanding Jewish population and the Arabs. The British, who had been given responsibility for Palestine under what was known as the British Mandate, came under increasing pressure as their ambiguous position towards both groups became increasingly apparent. They also had to handle the vast number of Jewish immigrants seeking refuge from the horrors of Hitler's anti-Jewish policies. Eventually Britain sought to resign the Mandate, forcing the United Nations to attempt a solution. They suggested a partition of the Mandated Territory (giving 56 per cent to the Jews and 44 per cent to the Arabs), but this unsatisfactory solution was unlikely to be accepted by those on the ground; it gave way to the fierce fighting of May 1948, when Israel announced the establishment of an independent state. When the fighting was over, Israel had gained substantially more than what had been proposed in the partition plan (see figure 8, p. 190). It was an odd-shaped territory with a narrow corridor going up from the coastal plain through the foothills to Jerusalem. The Jordanians controlled the surrounding area (known as the 'West Bank' of the river Jordan), the Egyptians ruled the Gaza Strip, and the Syrians the Golan Heights to the north-east of Galilee. All these three areas (together with Sinai for a while) then came under Israeli rule after the Six-Day War in June 1967.

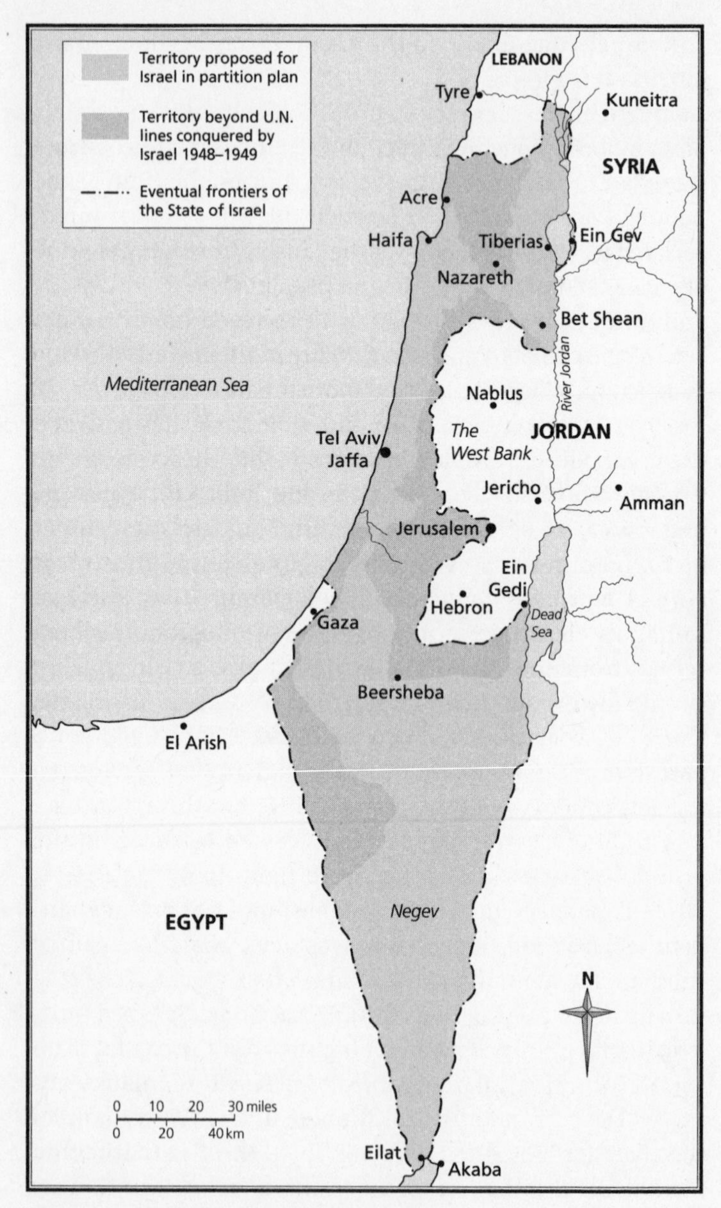

Figure 8. The United Nations Partition Plan (1947) and the eventual frontiers of Israel (1949–67)

It is, of course, a painful history, viewed from many different angles and leaving thousands of broken lives on both sides of the conflict. It is a tale of mutual fear, insecurity and injustice. No visitor to the Land can be so cocooned as to bypass this reality of very recent history which profoundly affects everyone resident in the Land today. Nor should they. We do well to try to understand it. We need sensitivity, a preparedness to listen to both sides, and caution in our judgements. Despite its frequent press coverage, western visitors can still be surprisingly confused or unaware about this history. 'Why is it called the "West Bank"?' they frequently ask. It is not the purpose of the book to take this complex matter further, but there are numerous books which do cover the issue in more detail (see Appendix IV, 'For Further Reading').

For now our point is simply to highlight the number of Jewish people for whom the Land is home and to mention the many different backgrounds from which they come. Throughout the world there are some eighteen million Jews, of whom just under 20 per cent now live in Israel. The major ethnic division is between the majority *Ashkenazy* Jews (who chiefly come from Europe and America) and the *Sephardi* Jews (whose origins are in North Africa and elsewhere and who in appearance and customs are more similar to the Arabic community). Those who have made *aliyah*, who have 'gone up' to the Land of their forefathers, have come from a wide variety of countries – most recently from Ethiopia and the former Soviet Union. These recent arrivals have helped to keep the population growing and, despite the resultant upheavals, have been generally welcomed into Israeli society. All new residents are required to learn Hebrew (the official language of Israel, refashioned from the ancient language by Weismann in the late nineteenth century), but on the streets you can often now hear Russian being spoken as well – in addition to Yiddish, the colloquial language of the Jews in Europe.

In religious terms, many modern Israelis are quite secular in outlook, indeed atheistic, but the three main categories of Judaism (Orthodox, Conservative and Reformed) are all represented here. Among the latter group, there are also the 'Ultra-Orthodox', many of whom can be found in the neighbourhood of Mea Shearim in Jerusalem. A visit can be an eye-opening part of your tour, giving you an appreciation of this significant minority within Israeli society. Traditions established in Europe several hundred years ago are preserved, with strict rules about dress and Sabbath observance. Paradoxically, such Ultra-Orthodox Jews are frequently non-Zionist, being opposed to the political state of Israel on the religious grounds that only the Messiah himself can establish such a state – the 'restoration of Zion' will take place in God's own time. They and others, however, still find it significant to be observing Torah in the very Land of Israel – for many commandments within the Hebrew Bible do relate in some way to this particular Land. There is an important 'triangle' within the Scriptures between God, his people and this Land. So they find it religiously appropriate to be in *Eretz Israel;* they just have hesitations about giving theological backing to the contemporary political state.

So, there are religious non-Zionists and non-religious Zionists and many shades in between! To an outsider it can all be very confusing. In general terms it is fair to say that the early pioneers of the Zionist movement were quite secular and not motivated by strongly religious concerns. Since 1967, however, with the unification of Jerusalem and the possibility of settling in the heartland of the biblical Land, there has been a significant increase in the number of religious Zionists – those who believe the modern state of Israel is God's intention for them and an outworking of the promises contained within the Hebrew Bible.

Such people will tend to be on the 'right wing' of the Israeli political spectrum, generally reluctant to compromise too much on issues of negotiation with the Arab community. There are, however, some 'left-wing' religious Jews who see peacemaking as a biblical commandment, even if it means some loss of the Land which (in their eyes) is still theirs by biblical mandate. Meanwhile, secular Jews display a wide variety of opinions on the vital issue of Jew–Arab relations, though for them the issues are strictly political. God and the Hebrew Bible are not involved in working out the right solution to the modern problem. It is rather a pragmatic question of ensuring Israel's long-term security and the right to exist peaceably in this part of the Middle East. Nevertheless, as a result of proportional representation, the small religious groupings can exert a disproportionate influence on policy within Israel's political system. So religion and politics can rarely be separated in Israel today.

From this brief survey you will sense that modern Israel is far from being a uniform society. You may find a wide variety of viewpoints and practices among the Israelis you meet. Returning to the Land has not automatically led to a new cohesive Judaism; rather it has exposed the many cultural and now political differences. So be careful not to stereotype or pigeonhole. You might initially have expected this particular state to be different from others, supposing that it would be held together by a united, cohesive set of shared religious values and beliefs. But that uniformity has largely broken down, not only through centuries of varying practice but more particularly as modern Jews have faced the issue of their identity and come to different conclusions.

In particular, the spectre of the Holocaust can never be forgotten. This caused belief in the providential God of their fathers to be severely shaken, giving birth to an agnosticism and atheism unparalleled within Jewish society. Secular western values became attractive. Many Jews outside Israel have pursued a personal policy of assimilation into their surrounding society. Those resident in Israel still, by the nature of things, wish to preserve their distinctiveness. But the question still presses: what, then, makes a person a Jew? Is it to be defined by religious belief, by adherence to a certain number of traditional customs, by political commitment to the state of Israel, or simply by birth (a Jew being simply a person born to a Jewish mother)? Not surprisingly, this is a much-debated question within Israel today.

Christian visitors to the Land today need to be sensitive to all these issues of religious background and political hope. They need too to be aware how their own beliefs about God and his purposes for the world might appear to someone looking on from a Jewish perspective. And we cannot escape the fact that all encounters between Jews and Christians are inevitably coloured by the history of such encounters going back through the last two thousand years. There have been some sorry and sad episodes in that history, many of which bring little credit to the followers of the Jewish Jesus. But the question still presses at the end of the day: what do we make of Jesus of Nazareth? And what does it mean to walk in his steps?

The Arab community

But no visitor to Israel today can escape the fact that another people lives in the Land as well. From 1948 onwards there were at least one hundred and fifty thousand Arabs within the borders of Israel; they were given Israeli citizenship and so are known as 'Israeli Arabs'. In your visit you are most likely to meet them when in Galilee. But since 1967, with Israel's conquest over East Jerusalem and the West Bank (i.e. west of the River Jordan), the number of Arabs within the borders of 'Israel' has quadrupled. Unless you try very hard (which, we suggest, is not a good idea), your visit will inevitably bring you into contact with this large segment of the population – who in their own preferred self-designation should be thought of as 'Palestinian Arabs'.

Unlike their fellow Arabs who were living within Israel between 1948 and 1967 (the Israeli Arabs), the 'Palestinian Arabs' do not hold Israeli passports, and consider themselves to be living in occupied territory. Israeli Arabs might sometimes have the same feeling, but by and large they have settled into living as a minority within Israel. Not so the Palestinian Arabs living in Jerusalem and the West Bank. These, together with many Palestinian Arab refugees scattered into neighbouring countries, as well as the many who have emigrated to other parts of the world, have for years hankered after an independent Palestinian state of some kind. They long for international recognition as a people with historical roots in this Land who are yet distinct from the Jewish people; the Jews have their own state of Israel recognized by the United Nations, why not the Palestinians? There's the issue: two peoples each claiming a historical (and for many, a religious) right to the same narrow strip of land.

But there is immediately a profound irony at this point. Consider where the majorities of these two people live: the Jewish Israelis on the coastal plain, the Palestinian Arabs in the hill-country further to the east. In biblical times the predominant pattern was exactly the reverse. The ancient Israelites were strongest in the hill-country, but seldom held sway over the coastal plain, which instead remained a stronghold for the Phoenicians and the Philistines. Hence the struggles over this central part of the biblical land. Using the ancient biblical terminology, Israelis will refer to this as the hill-country of 'Judea and Samaria'. Palestinians and others still refer to it as the 'West Bank'. This is where the issue becomes acute.

Even the terminology reinforces the paradox. For, although there is no historic link whatsoever between them, the 'Palestinians' have adopted a name which is etymologically derived from the 'Philistines'. They are simply claiming to be inhabitants of this Land which since before Roman times has gone by the name of 'Palestina'. Jews in the time of Jesus and indeed until modern times might have been happy to use this term, but increasingly it has become the non-Jewish way of referring to this strip of land. In political discussions it becomes clear that choice of words is all-important. But so too is a reading of the biblical narratives which is sensitive to how ancient words can take on new, unintended meanings for modern readers!

Palestinian identity is sometimes charged with being a new idea. After all, a hundred years ago, when this area was still part of the large Levant administered by the Ottoman Turks in Istanbul, the Arabic communities in the region were not especially pursuing 'Palestinianism'. This was before the days of the modern drive for nationhood, and they were all part of a region and a pan-Arabic culture which stretched way beyond the little River Jordan. But with the subdivision of that area into constituent nations, it was natural for those resident in 'Palestine' to seek a similar national destiny. The evident rise of Jewish national aspirations only served to spur their own. To be sure, many Arabs came into the area in the seventy years prior to 1948 (just as, of course, many Jews were arriving too), but the vast majority of today's 'Palestinians' can trace back their family origins to the Land through many generations – some at least to the era of the Crusades, others even further back. Even if individual family claims are inevitably open to question, there is no denying that in general terms there have been Arabs resident in 'Palestine' since the Islamic conquest of 638. So we are talking about long-established roots. But do those ancient *roots* give them modern *rights*?

Most Palestinians would see the last hundred years as a sorry saga – defeated militarily and wrong-footed politically. Tensions inevitably rose before and during the British Mandate as more Jews returned and bought up more of the

Land. Two different cultures, belonging as it were to two different time-zones, were now face to face with each other. The British might support the Jews through the Balfour Declaration, but what about their promises during the First World War to help win for the Arabs their national independence? For the Arabs the UN partition plan of 1947, even if it now looks different with hindsight, at the time seemed scarcely fair. Why should the Jews, who (according to some estimates) only occupied 7 per cent of the Land, now be told by New York they could have 56 per cent?

The war of 1948 was then, as they call it, 'the disaster' (*an-Nakba*); it resulted in the destruction of four hundred and fifteen villages, and some seven hundred and fifty thousand refugees. Many of the refugees were housed in makeshift camps established in Lebanon and Jordan, and also within the West Bank itself near Jericho and Bethlehem. The war of 1967 was similarly disastrous, resulting in a further three hundred thousand refugees and the 'occupation' of the West Bank and the annexation of East Jerusalem. This meant that almost a million Arabs were now under Israeli rule. Might seemed to be right. Although Israel's gains were denounced by the United Nations (Resolution 242 of November 1967), the international community responded little and increasingly turned against the terrorist activities of the Palestinian Liberation Organization. Meanwhile in the occupied territories daily injustices had to be borne, many of which continue to this day: the difficulty of getting permits to build, to dig wells, or to travel, the difficulties of remaining a resident of Jerusalem or, if not a resident, of gaining access to the city.

The Camp David accords of 1979 settled some important disputes between Israel and Egypt but failed to address the Palestinian issue. Only with the *Intifada* (the almost spontaneous 'uprising' of 1987) did the tide seem to turn, as western TV viewers saw Israeli troops beating tiny stone-throwing children. The David who in 1967 had heroically defeated Goliath was now turning against a new generation of Davids. The pressure of holding down a whole people was becoming too great for Israelis and new ways had to be found. The Oslo accords of the early 1990s, leading to the famous handshake on the White House lawn between Yitzhak Rabin and Yasser Arafat in 1993, paved the way for the return of some pockets of land to Palestinian self-rule. The PLO renounced terrorism and recognized the right of Israel to exist within secure borders; in return they now have some autonomy over the Gaza Strip and 11 per cent of the West Bank (including Jericho and Bethlehem). But is that all they are going to get? The ongoing violent scenes reveal how deep the tensions are, and how irreconcilable the two national agendas.

Ultimately the Palestinians long for a state of their own, but full independence is extremely unlikely given the Israeli desire for security. How can these twin desires – security for Israelis and justice for Palestinians – be reconciled? The Arab seeks his due; the Jew fears his elimination. Many Palestinians, and some left-wing Israelis, hope for what they call a 'two-state solution', with the two separate national identities being recognized but with open borders between them. Perhaps there could even be a federal arrangement of some kind including Jordan? But a key issue centres on Jerusalem: could this city, special to so many on religious grounds, ever be shared politically? Could two nations share it as their capital? Could it be given a unique status of some kind, and recognized as an international city? But for most Jews there is no doubt that this is for them the 'eternal capital' of their nation, and there is comparatively little room for compromise.

Another key issue on the ground concerns the Jewish settlements in the West Bank and around Jerusalem. The population of this 'occupied' territory is still 85 per cent Arab. The number of Jewish residents, however, has continued to rise steadily since 1967 with the building of numerous settlements in these areas. These settlements have caused incredible friction. Left-wing Israelis oppose the settlement programme, knowing it is a major stumbling-block towards a lasting peace. Meanwhile Palestinians, not unreasonably, resent the presence in their midst of these Jewish enclaves. As more and more link-roads are built across their land in order to allow safe passage to the Israeli residents, they are gradually witnessing this area of their 'Palestine' being divided up into tiny 'townships' or 'bantustans'. The 'settlers' might, in their eyes at least, be better called '*un*settlers'.

For many Israelis, however, control over the West Bank is seen as vital for their security. Israel before 1967 was in certain places only ten miles wide and Jerusalem could only be reached from the west. So security is a vital issue. So too is religion and history. After all, this is the centre of the biblical Land. Some would therefore see the Old Testament as giving them a historical right to its ownership – still others, a divine right. Issues of justice or security too quickly get entangled with issues about the meaning of the Bible. Does the promise to Abraham, that his descendants would 'inherit the Land', give modern Israelis the divinely sanctioned title deeds to this same Land today? Many Jews think so; and many Christians support them.

Maybe now we begin to sense why Christians need to think through their interpretation of the Bible. Sitting at home in our armchairs, some of these issues might appear rather academic, but how people read the Bible will have a knock-on effect on the ground here in the West Bank. Are the biblical promises still valid? Even if at any period in history the Jews have not 'possessed' the Land, have they still technically 'owned' it in God's sight? How is the Old Testament to be read by Christians in the light of the New? Some of our preliminary answers to these questions can be found above in chapter 3. These are questions that Christians cannot evade.

Nor should they avoid meeting the Palestinians and seeing how things look from their perspective. A whole new outlook on the Bible can emerge as we read the Psalms celebrating Zion and Israel, or as we sense how biblical passages (e.g. the book of Joshua) have been used to justify recent political actions. We also gain a whole new perspective on history, as we sense the keenly felt perspective of the East – that westerners are still Crusaders at heart and that Palestinians have been paying the price for western guilt after the Holocaust.

Conclusion

So it is vitally important on your visit that you meet some of the local Arab community – just as it is important to meet the local Jewish community. You need to hear both sides. In recent years, however, the majority of tours have given visitors little opportunity to go far inside the West Bank. Few people these days get to see the central hill-country of the Bible, with its important sites such as Nablus, Shechem, Mount Gerizim, Samaria and Hebron. But it is well worth a try – not just to see these places and the terraced landscape familiar from one's picture-Bibles, but also to meet the people.

It is possible, for example, to go on visitors' tours of some of the Jewish settlements and to hear lectures on their vision for the Land; *kibbutzim* too are worth a visit. But try too to see some Arabic culture and to sense their way of life. A visit to a refugee camp or to an orphanage can be an eye-opening experience. But it may just be a matter of talking to people on the street. And if ever you get a chance to visit an Arabic village, take it. For you will soon discover that some of their ancient traditions bring you back in an uncanny way to the culture of the Bible. If you want to imagine your way back into the biblical period, to think what it might have felt like to live in the times of Amos or Jesus, the nearest modern equivalent is to be found not among the Jewish population of Israel but among its Arab population. This too is another irony. It only serves to underline the shared cultural history and the considerable proximity between Jews and Arabs – both come from a common Semitic background and are, as it were, first cousins. But sometimes, as we know too well, close relatives clash violently. Remember Jacob and Esau. Can they share the inheritance, or will it get torn apart in the desire for exclusive possession?

So no visit to the Land is complete without meeting the people and taking on board their recent history. Yes, it makes for a less comfortable visit. But it is important not to go round in a 'biblical haze', concentrating so much on biblical events and places that you miss the contemporary situation right under your nose. It is a beautiful land, teeming with variety and highly photogenic. But it is more than a quarry for your picture postcards. It is home to many, and a place of deep pain and fervent hopes. Christian visitors, tuned to the heart of Christ, will sense his love for all – not least for those who live in the Land of his birth. And the people, not just the places, will provoke them to prayer and to action.

Chapter 9

THE LIVING STONES

There are others you must meet too – the local Christians. One of the great ironies – and sadnesses – of modern tourism to the Holy Land is that many Christian visitors rarely make contact with their fellow Christians who actually live here. Again the focus tends to be on places, not people.

Prior to their departure very few first-time visitors have a clear picture in their mind on this score. One of the authors, when a young child, imagined that people living in Israel lived on some kind of heavenly dwelling above the earth! Many adults have other ideas which are only a little more connected to reality. Some imagine the place to be full of Christians. Others presume the opposite: because it is 'Israel', then surely everyone is Jewish and not Christian? Some have heard of the existence of Jewish Christians; most have never heard of the Palestinian Christians. The idea that anyone could be an 'Arab Christian' seems to them to be a contradiction in terms. Surely all Arabs are Muslims?

It comes as a surprise to many to discover that the overwhelming majority of Christians in the Land today are Arabs. The total Christian population within the post-1967 borders of 'Israel' is currently estimated at around a hundred and twenty thousand. Of these only three thousand and five hundred or so are Jewish Israelis (i.e. they are Jewish Christians or Messianic believers). The vast majority are Arab Christians, the remainder being expatriate Christians of one kind or another. The number of Messianic believers has been gradually increasing in recent years, but the number of Arab Christians has been steadily decreasing – as significant numbers have left the country with its many problems and sought a better life somewhere else. In the 1922 census Christians made up 11 per cent of the non-Jewish population of Palestine; today that figure has dropped to under 5 per cent. And within Jerusalem itself the Christian population has dropped from forty-five thousand in 1947 to under ten thousand today. The number of Palestinian Christians now living abroad is now just under half a million, with a greater number of them living in Melbourne than in Jerusalem!

This haemorrhaging of the Christian community is a very real concern. William Dalrymple in his excellent book *From the Holy Mountain* has highlighted the plight of all the Christian churches throughout the Near East, asking what things will look like within a generation. This was the part of the world where Christianity was born, but will it survive? And if this is true of the Near East as a whole, it is particularly the case within Israel/Palestine – the place where it all began. In a visit in 1992, the Archbishop of Canterbury feared the prospect that the Holy Land (and Jerusalem in particular) might become an 'empty theme park', a kind of unreal Disneyland – where visitors found the places of Christ but none of his people.

So this chapter will outline for you the Christians of the Holy Land, its indigenous Church. Again it is a complex story, but intended to whet your appetite to meet some of these people who share in your faith, and to help you to be able more quickly to distinguish between the various

Christian groups. Where have they come from and what are their concerns for the future? The Psalmist said that the 'holy ones in the Land' were 'all his delight' (Psalm 16:3). This is the Land of the Holy One, but also the Land of the Holy Ones – people made holy through their faith in him. They should be our delight too. Or, as people frequently say (alluding to the imagery used in 1 Peter 2:5), we need to ensure we don't just come to visit archaeological 'stones' and physical places. We must come to meet the 'living stones'.

THE HISTORIC CHURCHES

The 'indigenous Church' is a simplified term for what in reality is a very complex mixture of various Christian congregations. All of these are represented in Jerusalem and many can be found elsewhere in the country. In your travels outside Jerusalem you are most likely to meet Christians in towns such as Nazareth and Bethlehem, where local Christians can constitute up to half of the total population. There is also a significant number of Christians in various villages in the hills of Galilee and in West Bank towns such as Ramallah. However, the full variety of the Christian communities can best be sensed when you are in Jerusalem. During your stay in the city, why not try to worship with them on a Sunday morning or arrange to meet them for an evening? Spend time in the Old City beginning to recognize some of the different groups that are present.

Nowhere else in the world can compare with Jerusalem for the bewildering variety of Christian communities to be found within a mile or so of each other. When you think about it, this is inevitable. Jerusalem has an undeniable place in Christian history as the city in which the gospel message was first proclaimed. So vast numbers of Christian denominations have found it important to maintain within Jerusalem a representative Christian congregation.

This process, which is especially apparent in the last one hundred and fifty years, with the arrival of various western Christian groupings, can also be observed among those ancient Christian communities which have been in Jerusalem for centuries. It is not simply a practical issue of wishing to have a 'branch office' in Jerusalem that can welcome any pilgrims who visit, making them feel 'at home'. Somehow the presence within Jerusalem of such a congregation lends a certain authenticity to the denomination's claim to be a true church of Christ. Without such a presence, on the other hand, a denomination might well feel more vulnerable concerning its apostolic credentials.

As a result, there are within Jerusalem not only the historic Christian denominations (Eastern Orthodox, Oriental Orthodox, Eastern-rite Catholics, Latin-rite Catholics) but also the Anglicans and various Protestant churches (Lutheran, Baptist, Presbyterian, Reformed, and others such as the International Alliance Church, the Nazarenes, Mennonites, Pentecostals, Assemblies of God etc.). Then too there are also a significant number of Messianic–Jewish congregations. However, such Protestant groups, including the Anglicans, constitute perhaps only 5 per cent of the total Christian population. The vast majority of Jerusalem's Christians belong to what may helpfully be termed the 'historic' churches.

The split over Chalcedon

Figure 9 (overleaf) gives you at a glance an overview of these historic churches and how they relate to one another. At first it looks hideously complicated, but a few key historical pointers can begin to make sense of it. In the first four centuries of its life, the Church in general experienced a strong bond of unity across the Roman Empire and indeed beyond its borders. Strenuous efforts were made to secure the unity of the 'worldwide' Church in the face of many

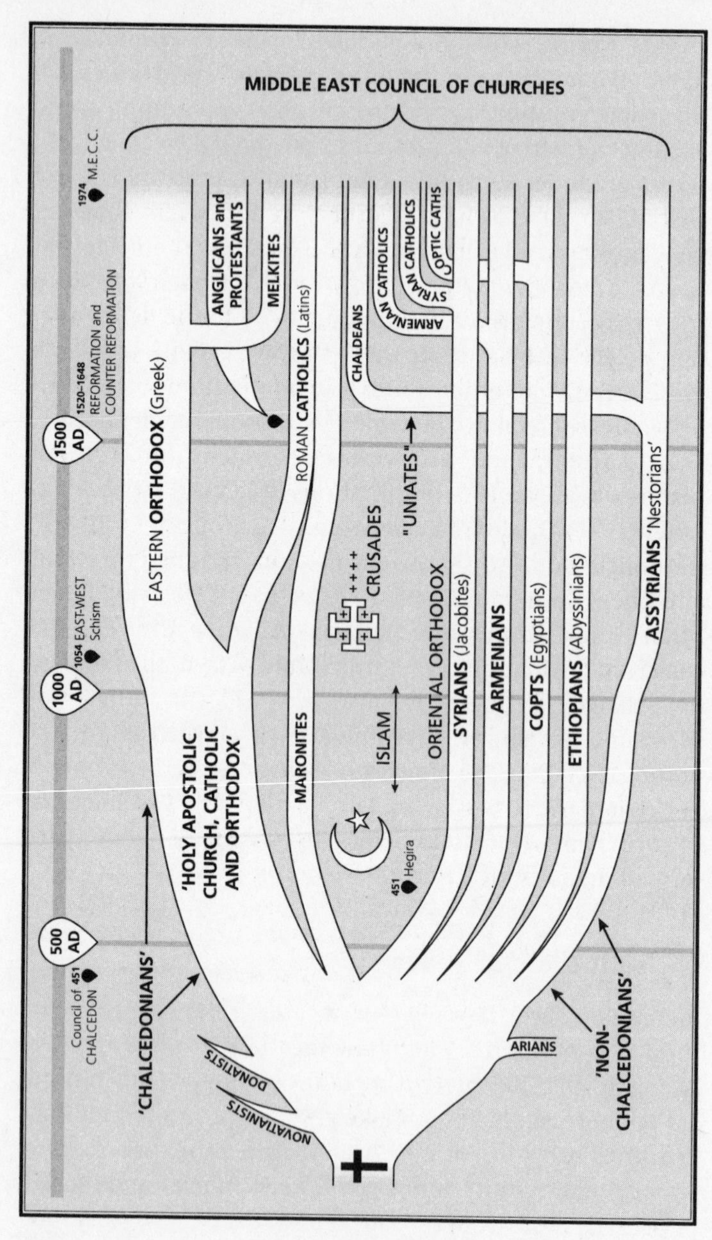

Figure 9. Overview of the development of historic churches

diverse movements, ideas and attacks. 'Catholic' (meaning 'across the whole') was the adjective used to describe this amazing phenomenon of an institution held together 'across the whole' of the world – from Britain to Mesopotamia.

As we saw in chapter 7, however, a significant minority (known as the 'Monophysites') were unable to go along with the decisions of the Council of Chalcedon in the year 451. This brought into existence a new set of churches. To this day their followers still claim the title 'orthodox', though the Chalcedonian churches beg to disagree. These Monophysites then are the 'Oriental Orthodox' or 'non-Chalcedonian' churches.

In the Holy Sepulchre, for instance, you will find Syrians, Armenians, Copts and Ethiopians. All of these belong in this category. They are fiercely loyal to their different national traditions and languages. The Syrians will proudly tell you that they still use in their liturgy the Aramaic language of Jesus. Go to their church of St Mark in the Old City and ask them to read you the Gospel reading for the day. The Armenians will tell you that they were the first nation to be converted *en masse* to Christianity in the early years of the fourth century. Go to their cathedral of St James and walk around the Armenian quarter of the city. For visitors it may seem like another world, but for them this is their home. They will also draw attention to the horrific genocide of 1915–17 at the hands of the Turks, when it is estimated that around a million Armenians were killed. This is often forgotten in the West; they too, like the Jews, experienced a concerted attack within the twentieth century on their right to exist as a separate people. So for them their community in Jerusalem plays a large and vital role in the continuance of their faith and national identity.

These groups do not therefore see themselves as 'Arabs'. They see themselves as continuing the Christian traditions which were already in place *before* the arrival of the Arabs in the seventh century. You are unlikely to meet them elsewhere in the Land apart from in Jerusalem. The same is not true, however, for the Chalcedonian churches, who make up the majority of Arab Christians today. So the Arab Christians, whom you will meet throughout Israel/Palestine, essentially owe their origins to those *Greek* Orthodox Christians who went over to speaking Arabic as their mother tongue for everyday purposes (see above, chapter 7). They continue to use Greek as their liturgical language. A good place to experience this is in the 'parish church' of St James (Mar Yacoub); if you stand in the courtyard outside the Holy Sepulchre, facing the main doors, the entrance to Mar Yacoub is on the left. On Sunday morning local Palestinian Arab Christians will arrive for their service conducted in Greek.

Eastern and western Christians

With the Great Schism of 1054, the eastern and western halves of Christendom began more visibly to go their separate ways, again marked by the language difference between Greek and Latin. Within the eastern half of the empire only a group called the Maronites (now most populous in Lebanon) kept in communion with Rome, rather than with Constantinople.

The growth in numbers of Roman (or 'Latin') Catholics who came to reside in the area after the Crusades then complicated things somewhat. As you will see from the diagram, there were people in most of the other 'denominations' who gradually sought communion not with the Patriarch in Constantinople, but with the Pope in Rome. The Oriental Orthodox churches which did this became known as 'Uniate' churches ('in union' with Rome). The Greek Orthodox who did this became known as 'Melkites' (originally a pejorative term used against the Byzantines who were the 'king's people' and had gone along with the emperor at Chalcedon). It is simplest, however, to think of this latter group as 'Greek Catholics' – that is, their liturgy and theology are Greek, but they are in communion with Rome. There are a number of such communities up and down the Land, but your best opportunity to meet them is if you go to their church just 120 yards to the north-east of the Jaffa Gate. There you will find a church filled with beautiful modern icons and a warm-hearted liturgy, marked by impressive singing.

That was basically the situation until the nineteenth century when various Protestant denominations began to establish a presence in the city. In general these churches were staffed by, and catered for, expatriate Christians living in the Land. But in the early days quite a number of the local Arab Christians were persuaded to become Anglicans or Lutherans. Such 'sheep-stealing' was not appreciated by the Greek and Roman authorities, but it explains the existence of Arab Christians who are now Anglican.

For those from Britain it can be quite an eye-opening experience to go to a church and hear the Anglican liturgy in Arabic, to listen to well-known Anglican hymns set to Arabic words and even, in some cases, to attend a service in Arabic based on the 1662 Book of Common Prayer! Try to visit St George's Cathedral in Jerusalem at 9.30 on a Sunday morning, or drop into Christ Church, Nazareth – just sixty yards to the west of the main entrance to the Basilica of the Annunciation. For nearly thirty years now the Anglican Bishop in Jerusalem has been an Arab Christian. The bishop elected in 1998 came from Nazareth, so technically he is an Israeli Arab who is also (in his own description) a Palestinian Christian. This gives him, as he jests, four overlapping identities – one better than the Trinity!

Relationships between the churches are much better than any detractors might suggest. Obviously there have been numerous disputes through the centuries and sometimes it takes time for fences to be mended. One of the dangers of 'holy places' is that they tend to be jealously guarded and positions become entrenched. But external pressures (sometimes in the face of Islam, more recently in response to Israelis) have brought them together in new ways, resulting for example in the promulgation of various statements concerning their views about Jerusalem. When in Jerusalem, Jesus prayed that his followers would be one (John 17:11). How good it would be if Jerusalem, despite its bearing the scars of Christian history, became the place where that unity was regained.

The issues they face

These Arabic-speaking Christians live with a whole array of important issues and tensions on a daily basis. There is a strong temptation to emigrate. If they choose to stay in their homeland, they face dwindling numbers, practical struggles, political stress and religious conflict.

On the one hand, for the last thirteen hundred years there has been the issue of being a minority within the majority Muslim population. Generally a *modus vivendi* has been reached and relationships are good. 'Conversions' between the two communities are now exceedingly rare. Tensions, however, can arise for Arab Christians in the political arena as they assess on different matters where their primary loyalty resides – is it with their Arab identity or their Christian one? And in recent years, as they look around to developments in other Arab nations, there will always be a fear about the rise of an exclusivist Islamic 'fundamentalism'. In general terms, the Christian minority has tended to include a higher proportion of the well-educated. This goes some way to explaining why many of them have been tempted to emigrate, being more socially mobile and closer in their mindsets to western values.

On the other hand, Arab Christians also have to relate to the Jewish State of Israel. This makes demands on them at a political level, as they contend with the perceived injustices experienced by their people, who long for greater freedom.

It also affects them at a religious level. For these are Christians for whom the Bible is important as the ground of their faith. Yet many western Christians use the Bible to justify the modern policies of Israel. So to their Muslim fellow-Arabs, they can look like unwitting collaborators with Israel. 'After all, is it not *your* Holy Book which is being used against us Palestinians? Whose side are you on?'

Truly here they are caught in a painful place, located ambiguously somewhere between the two other religious groupings who are contesting for political power. As in other walks of life, those in the middle may sometimes have a role to play when it comes to reconciliation, but they can often get torn apart in the process – frequently being judged by one side as being implicitly on the side of the other. And when they speak out for justice and liberation, they turn to a book where the primary motif for liberation is the liberation from Egypt of the *Israelites*.

This begins to raise the deep questions in the Middle East: who are truly God's people today? How exactly should this Bible be read? What does it mean for a Palestinian to walk in the steps of Jesus the Jew? In his own day Jesus had to walk through a political minefield, with people from all shades of the spectrum hoping he would join their cause. What would Jesus say and do today? With his love of outsiders and his conviction that Israel's hope was being fulfilled in him, he might well have questioned extreme claims for Jewish nationalism. But his stance towards the occupying Roman forces suggests he would equally have questioned any violent means of solving a dispute over land. Jesus' example offers an extremely tough middle ground, hard to maintain but a path to freedom.

THE MESSIANIC BELIEVERS

No account of the local Christian community would be fully complete, however, without mentioning the small number of Jewish Christians – or, as they would prefer to be called, 'Messianic Jews'. A handful of Jewish believers in Jesus may have been present ever since the return of Jewish people to the Land got under way in the nineteenth century. Certainly the early Christian mission agencies had the goal of increasing this number. But there was little response. It is only since 1948 and especially since 1967 that there has grown up a recognizable number of such Jews who accept Jesus as the Jewish Messiah.

There has been much speculation as to how many such believers there are within the Israeli community. However, the recent publication by Skjott (*Facts and Myths about the Messianic Congregations in Israel*) gives us at last the results of a fairly comprehensive survey. It now looks as though there are over fifty congregations scattered throughout the Land, of which nearly twenty are in Jerusalem. There has been a significant increase in the last ten years, not least resulting from the arrival of Jews from Russia, many of whom were already believers and some of whom have come to a new faith since their arrival. So although worship in these congregations is normally in Hebrew, a second common language is not English, but Russian! The overall number of Jewish believers may now therefore be approaching four thousand and set to increase. This is obviously a small number when compared to the number of Israelis (4.8 million) and indeed the number of Arab Christians (one hundred and twenty thousand), but it means that they are now no longer a group that, for whatever reason, can be politely ignored.

So if you are visiting the Land, why not try to meet up with some of them? Many meet for worship on Saturdays (Jewish *Shabbat*) – as does, for example, the Hebrew congregation which meets on the premises of Christ Church (inside the Jaffa Gate). They are an integral part of God's people in the Land – yet more of the 'living stones'.

After all, the vision of St Paul for the Church was that it should always be made up of Jews and Gentiles. If in Galatians he warned Jewish believers not to dismiss Gentile believers, in Romans the boot was on the other foot: Gentile believers should not be arrogant towards, or dismissive of, Jewish believers. Salvation has come to them through Jesus, who was a Jew and a 'servant of the circumcised' (Romans 15:8; cf. 9:5). In Romans 11:17 he develops his famous imagery of the vine (representing Israel or perhaps, better, Jesus who as Messiah embodies Israel), pointing out that Gentile Christians have been grafted in to this vine by grace. They should look forward to more Jews ('the natural branches') being re-ingrafted through the ongoing work of the gospel. So Christians should rejoice that, worldwide, more Jewish people have come to faith in Jesus the Messiah during the last twenty years than, so they say, in the previous two thousand (there are now an estimated two hundred and fifty thousand Jewish believers worldwide). The Church must never forget its Jewish roots and should always be a place in which both Jew and non-Jew can find God's grace through Messiah Jesus.

The issues they face

If you meet some Jewish believers in Israel today, you will meet people who are keenly aware of their identity and who are trying, often in difficult circumstances, to forge creative ways of being loyal both to their Jewish identity and their faith in Jesus. And they often find themselves as the 'odd one out'. Thus they sometimes feel dismissed by their fellow Jews (for example, they are the only Jews who do not have an automatic right to make *aliyah* to Israel). On the other hand, their fellow Christians often treat them as though they were an embarrassment – either because they believe all Christians should act like Gentiles, or because the existence of Messianic believers undercuts their own preference to focus on dialogue with Jewish people, not evangelism.

Messianic believers are indeed often highly committed to the task of evangelism to their own people, often at considerable personal cost. They face a hard task and their resolve to bear witness to Jesus in authentic ways should earn our respect and call forth our prayerful support. This desire for authenticity causes them in general terms to be quite wary of the mainstream Gentile Christian tradition, believing that many things may have passed into the bloodstream of the Church which might be merely 'Gentile'. If there had been more Jewish believers in the period after the New Testament, they will argue, then perhaps liturgical and doctrinal developments would have turned out very different. So Messianic believers find themselves wanting to return to the Bible in order to uncover an authentic 'biblical' approach to matters of faith and order and are cautious about arguments from tradition.

In part, of course, this all stems from the general Jewish wariness of Christianity, with its history of opposition to Judaism. In embracing 'Christian' faith, Messianic believers are perceived to be crossing enemy lines. Can they be both Jewish and Christian? Often, they sense, the Church has unwittingly conspired with the synagogue to say 'no, you cannot'. But they see this as wrong, and are eager to maintain their Jewishness even as they practise belief in Jesus. Hence their desire to develop Jewish styles of worship, hence their attitude towards Torah and their hesitancy to use the symbol of the cross – a painful symbol within Jewish memory. They call Jesus by his Hebrew name, Yeshua, and prefer themselves to be known not as Jewish Christians, but as Messianic Jews. For many of them the very word 'Christian' has too many Gentile overtones; 'Messianic' is another way of saying the same thing! But it raises the question of which is their primary identity. Which should be the noun and which the adjective? Are they Jews who are Messianic, or Christians who are Jewish? Or, as they might insist, both?!

Once again it is hard to be caught in the middle. As for the Palestinian Christians, so for the Messianic believers, it is hard to be pulled in two directions at the same time. Can you be authentically Arab and Christian? Can you be authentically Jewish and Messianic? And even if you see no tension, those around you will see otherwise, trying to insist that your national or ethnic identity must take precedence.

In both groups this can lead to the phenomenon of 'compensation'. This is where Christian believers, in order to be tolerated by the national majority (non-Christian Jews or Muslim Palestinians) and in order to offset the fact that they belong to a religious minority, compensate for this in the political realm by becoming ardently pro-Israel or pro-Palestinian. You can see this to some extent in the Palestinian Christian community, where some of the best advocates for Palestinian rights come from the Christians among them. You can see it in the Messianic community, with some of the believers taking a strongly 'nationalist' line on issues relating to sharing land or making peace with the Palestinians. Although there are quite a number on the left wing of the political spectrum, many Messianic believers move instead towards the right wing of Israeli politics, taking a tough stand on the Palestinian issue. And, of course, if they have come from a secular Jewish background, their new-found faith in the Bible means that they will begin to see Israel's right to the whole of the biblical Land as part of God's fulfilment of his good purposes towards Israel. This then undergirds their politics with a potent theological base.

When all this is then combined with a keen sense that Messianic believers are playing a central role within the worldwide Christian community and that they are at the vanguard of God's purposes which are gradually unveiling in the Middle East, you have a heady brew of ideas. Christians visiting from the West may find themselves with a deep sympathy for, and identification with, this significant part of the body of Christ; but they may also be slightly uneasy at the theological and political positions that can be generated in this environment. After all, once you are convinced that God is doing a new thing through you as a key player, there is a danger of a necessary measure of control being lost. And the desire to develop a theological tradition which is independent from that of mainstream Christianity, while understandable, is also not without its dangers. Against all this, however, there are also real, encouraging signs of growing theological maturity within the movement, as they develop an authentic Jewish witness to their Messiah.

Reconciliation between Jew and Arab

The above description, however, should help you as a visitor to understand why there is still comparatively little meeting between Palestinian Christians and Messianic believers. There is some significant collaboration in the Galilee region among the Israeli Arabs, but not so much in the Jerusalem area.

In principle, the return of Jews to the Land and the emergence of Messianic believers within their number should make possible in our day and in Jerusalem the fulfilment of the New Testament's great vision: that Christ through the cross can make 'out of the two, one new humanity' (Ephesians 2:15). He can bring 'peace' to the great division that exists between Jew and non-Jew, and which threatened to rip apart the earliest Church. But there is a long way to go.

At the moment both Messianic Jews and Palestinian Christians might be forgiven for thinking that they currently have enough struggles trying to establish and preserve their own identities without having to make conciliatory noises to a group 'on the other side'. For in political terms that is what they currently are – members of the opposing party. They are part of a much wider conflict of two nationalisms fighting over a common land. So it is hard for the two groups, in the light of their political situations, to be seen to be making common cause.

As in any conflict, with wars in the recent past and ongoing tensions and atrocities, there are hurts on both sides. Each Christian will have a tale to tell and a need to forgive. Some will be prone to generalize about 'all Palestinians' or 'all Israelis' and find it hard to see how a member of that community can be a fellow Christian. Opponents can easily be 'demonized' and dehumanized in one's imagination. Moreover, because of the above-mentioned factor of compensation, it is highly probable that the Christians will in any case find themselves taking political positions which are at the opposite extreme to one another, rather than neatly meeting in the middle.

Nevertheless there is some important work of reconciliation going on between Palestinian and Israeli believers (see for example Munayer, *Seeking and Pursuing Peace*). Often this will involve shared trips into the desert on smelly camels – a good way to discover a shared humanity before ever getting around to discussing religion or politics! Meetings have also taken place where the hard, divisive theological issues relating to the Land have been discussed. One of the authors has been involved in editing the papers from this ongoing process (Walker, Wood and Loden, *The Bible and the Land*), which will be of interest to those wanting to take the matter further.

But, even as a visitor, you too can play an important role. Meet your fellow believers in the Land. Make yourself better informed about the issues facing them. Be quick to listen and slow to pass judgement. Reflect on what you hear and be known as a peacemaker. On occasions you may be able to say a 'word in season' or explain to one side how things might look to people on the other side of the divide. But often it will be wise to be quiet, and instead to hold these people in your prayers. 'Blessed are the peacemakers'; 'seek peace and pursue it' (Matthew 5:9; Psalm 34:14).

OTHER CHRISTIAN GROUPS

Finally a brief word should be said about the various expatriate Christian groups living and working in the Land. Since the middle years of the nineteenth century a significant number of overseas Christians have stayed here for various lengths of time. Many continue to come out under the auspices of mission agencies (such as CMS, CMJ, Bible Lands Society, World Vision etc.). They come to work in the local congregations or guesthouses, or in the medical or humanitarian institutions of the Land, where their labours are much appreciated.

Since 1967 several other Christian groups have come to Jerusalem with an expressly Christian Zionist agenda. Often influenced by dispensational approaches to the Bible, they believe not only that the return of the Jews to the Land of Israel is within God's providence, but that it is the beginning of a series of prophetic fulfilments in this region. God will act out in literal terms the things predicted in the Bible, especially in the Old Testament. Any suggestions that these may have been fulfilled in Christ (albeit in not quite such literal ways, but truly and really nonetheless) are firmly rejected. Key verses, used in support, are Luke 21:24 and Romans 11:25. These are interpreted to mean that, when the 'time of the Gentiles' is over, Jerusalem will no longer be 'trampled on' by Gentiles and God will work in such a way that 'all Israel will be saved'. The return of Jerusalem to Jewish control in 1967 is therefore for Christian Zionists fraught with significance: the prophetic clock is now ticking.

Various scenarios are therefore projected: some are preparing, for example, for the building of a new 'third' Temple, which somehow will replace the Muslim Dome of the Rock. Others, despite their professed love for them, predict that the Jewish people will go through a period of significant tribulation before Christ returns to inaugurate his millennial reign. Some suggest we are currently seeing the fulfilment of Ezekiel 37–8, with the return to the Land being the prelude to a divine act in which he will bring new life to the 'valley of dry bones'. All sorts of schemes are proposed. Undergirding most of them, however, is the firm belief (shared by others who would disassociate themselves from other aspects of Christian Zionism) that God is fulfilling a distinctive purpose towards the Jewish people, a purpose which is different from what he intends for Gentiles. This includes a divine right to the Land of Israel, promised to Abraham, and frequently a belief that Jewish evangelism is unnecessary since God himself will accomplish this mysteriously by his own act.

Some Christian Zionists will go even further, suggesting that God's distinctive purpose for Jewish people means that they have a separate 'track' of salvation. This is known as 'two-covenant theology' because it suggests that God relates to the Jews and non-Jews under two different covenants – Gentiles approach God through Jesus, Jews through Torah. It was espoused by Martin Buber in the 1940s and has grown in popularity since then as Christian–Jewish dialogue has developed, combined with an increasing theological relativism concerning the claims of any one religion.

But at this point, many would beg to differ, believing that this is precisely the opposite of what Paul outlines in Romans, when he insists that God shows 'no partiality' towards Jew or Gentile but treats them identically in accordance with the gospel of Jesus, the Messiah of Israel. To argue that the gospel is not for Jews would be for Paul deeply anti-Semitic, and a complete failure to see how Jesus really is the 'goal of the Law' or the 'climax of the covenant' (Romans 10:4). Paul's conviction that Jewish people are still 'beloved because of the patriarchs' (11:28) indicates an election of privilege but not necessarily an election of status; Paul still labours for their salvation (9:3). They may be 'Israel' 'after the flesh', but the Old Testament emphasis on a remnant proves that 'not all Israelites are Israel' (9:6).

Some of those who oppose the two-covenant theology most strongly are Messianic believers. As stressed above, they firmly believe in the task of Jewish evangelism. The alternative theology undercuts this directly. They also sometimes wish that the vast sums of Christian money, given in support of Israel through Christian Zionists, might instead be used to further the cause of the gospel within the nation of Israel today. A two-covenant theology may make good sense politically if the West wishes to show its solidarity with Israel and to assuage its sense of guilt for the past. It may make sense for those who espouse religious relativism. But it will hardly square with the New Testament conviction that Jesus is the true centre and fulfilment of the story of Israel, and that the gospel is for all – both Jew and Gentile. In the terminology of Jesus' parable of the prodigal son, Israel may indeed be the Church's 'older brother', but he too needs to be brought into the party.

Again during your travels, it would be good to meet and talk with some of these expatriate groups and to discuss their views on Israel in the Bible and how they see the future working out.

CONCLUSION

From this survey you will sense that a visit to the Land does indeed raise all kinds of theological questions. It may be that after your visit you will return to Part One again to see how we have begun to tackle some of these points. But there are also numerous books which can take you further, some of which are listed in Appendix IV.

You will also sense that Jerusalem is a city which attracts all kinds of religious beliefs, some of them quite bizarre. Almost every shade of Christian tradition and opinion can be found here. There is also a documented mental illness known as 'Jerusalem syndrome', with Israeli specialists trained to take care of people who lose touch with reality while they are there. It is not unheard of to meet a modern-day Messiah over breakfast!

For what brings people here from all over the world is not just the city's religious history; it is also a sense that this is a city with a future. It is indeed a numinous city, a city whose life is religion, a city perhaps with a unique destiny. So it can be quite an exacting place for Christians to visit. If they dare to break out from their own circle, they will soon meet believers who hold very different opinions from their own! And, although many find the atmosphere exhilarating, many find it too intense – even oppressive. It causes them to wonder if perhaps the city is still affected in some way by the great cosmic battle which once took place here – when 'the rulers of this age' and the 'powers of darkness' revealed their worst but were defeated by the love and power of the cross. Why has the 'city of peace' known so little peace? Why is it so hard here to uphold the name of Christ? In some mysterious way does a cloud still hang over it from that awesome day, never to be forgotten?

So in your visit to the Land of the Bible, but especially in Jerusalem, you will need some spiritual discernment. Be determined that through your own visit the name of Christ will be honoured more, not less. Pray that your own faith in him will be deepened, not distorted or disillusioned. You will be challenged by lots of things. You will be stretched as you reach out in Christian love to other believers, and as you learn from them, even if eventually you beg to differ. You may come away with a new vision of the importance of Christian unity and yet its difficulty. Indeed, as soon as you lift up your eyes from issues of biblical archaeology and history and begin to see the issues facing the 'living stones' in the Land today, you will almost certainly be moved to 'pray for the peace of Jerusalem' and for the cause of Christ in his home country. How hard it is here for his followers to 'walk in his steps', but how important that there should be many who try to do so.

Chapter 10

DISCIPLES IN THE DESERT

A student was once asked at the end of a course on nuclear physics whether he was still confused. He replied, 'Oh yes, but at a much deeper level.' A tour of the Holy Land can make you feel much the same. Jerusalem in particular can be a bewildering and exhausting place. So it is no accident that as this book draws to a close, we return to the desert, the place for reflection, for quietness, and for listening to the voice of God.

If you have the opportunity to schedule some time in the desert on your trip, it is well worth the effort. On visits to the Holy Land, the authors have sometimes taken groups into the desert to find space to sit alone, even if just for an hour or two. They are encouraged to leave behind cameras, pens, gadgets, take nothing with them but a Bible, and experience the stillness there. Even such a short exposure to the desert is often a profoundly moving experience. Many say it was the most memorable episode in their whole visit to the Holy Land. 'Breathtaking', 'challenging', 'disturbing' are words often heard in reaction. The stark beauty, the simple emptiness, where few plants grow, where there are no buildings, no sound, no company, is so remarkably different from our normal experience that it shocks us.

It would be a shame if a visit to the Holy Land left us with photos and memories, but unchanged inside. All through this book, we have tried to show how a visit to the land of the Bible can renew and refocus faith in the God of Jesus Christ. The biblical sites can help us in all kinds of ways, but are often busy, noisy and crowded. The desert can add an extra dimension to a tour by giving space for God to speak to us afresh.

The desert experience can seem very far from the life of the contemporary Christian. The stories of the desert fathers seem so strange to us – prophets in the wilderness listening for the voice of God, Jesus tempted by the devil, and the desert fathers and mothers, those bizarre, alien figures whose whole way of life seems so odd, so at variance with our busy, active, energetic lives. What are we to make of them? To be sure, some of their theology and quite a lot of their behaviour are hardly to be imitated today. But were they still on to something? This chapter tries to explore what to expect and what might be learnt from a few hours spent in the desert landscape, and from those who spent many years there in the past.

THE DESERT IN THE BIBLE

Although it's easy to miss it, the desert plays a significant role in the Bible, albeit a decidedly ambiguous one. On the one hand, it is a place of desolation and emptiness, of the absence of God. It is of course the location of Israel's wilderness wanderings, forty years' travel towards the promised land, where safety and home seemed far away, if it existed at all. Here the people repeatedly grumbled at Moses and at God for not providing clean water (Exodus 15:22–5; 17:1–4) and good food (Exodus 16:1–3). It was the place where the people of Israel tested God, where God's anger burned against them (see e.g. Psalm 95), yet it was also the place where Israel's own identity was tested – their calling to be God's faithful people.

Later, the dryness of the desert reflects the Psalmists' thirst for a God who feels far away. The punishment for those who trust in human powers and refuse to trust in God is to 'dwell in the parched places of the desert, in a salt land where no one lives' (Jeremiah 17:6). The desert is the place of temptation for the Psalmist (e.g. Psalm 95:8), and of course, in a replay of Israel's desert journey, for Jesus himself. Finally, the desolation of the desert will be overcome in the last days: the prophets predict the flowering of the dry rocks and empty wastes as a sign of God's redemption of Israel (e.g. Isaiah 35).

Yet at the same time, these wilderness lands play another role in Scripture. They are the place where, time and time again, characters within the biblical story meet with God, and hear his word for the nation. Moses meets with God in the burning bush in 'the far side of the desert' (Exodus 3:1). The people of Israel discover God's trustworthiness as they are led through the wilderness on their way to the promised land. Here, God gives Israel the law at Sinai, outlining his will for his rescued people. Jacob wrestles with God, alone in the desert, in the defining moment of his life (Genesis 32). At critical points of his prophetic career, Elijah meets with God there, finding his needs provided for in danger (1 Kings 17) and being lifted out of despair (1 Kings 19).

In the New Testament, after the voice of God has been silent in Israel for generations, John the Baptist emerges out of the desert with God's announcement of the coming King. As Luke puts it, 'the word of God came to John son of Zechariah *in the desert*' (Luke 3:2 – see also the prophecy in Isaiah 40:3). And then of course in the archetypal desert experience, Jesus himself is led into the wilderness to face the great enemy. At his baptism, Jesus has just been addressed by the voice from heaven as 'my Son whom I love, with whom I am well pleased'. After the people of Israel had been rescued from Pharaoh at the Red Sea, their identity and calling were immediately put to the test in the desert. In exactly the same way, Jesus is also immediately put to the test. 'If you are the Son of God …' taunts Satan. Is he? Will he remain faithful, and seek God's Kingdom in God's way? Or will he fail in his test of forty days in the desert, as the Israelites had done in their forty years?

The desert is the place of struggle, the place of temptation, where the demons within and without are confronted, yet it is also the place where God is encountered, where his voice is heard, and where people are reborn.

So the desert plays this dual role within the Bible, as a place of temptation, and a place of encounter with God. Many of today's visitors to the Holy Land see the desert as an unfortunate obstacle to be endured, an empty wilderness seen through the windows of a bus as they travel from hotel to hotel. Can we instead learn how to hear God's voice in the desert?

DISMANTLING THE OLD SELF

After a short time, the first thing that hits home is the sound of silence. If that statement strikes you as odd, then perhaps the experience is overdue. Silence does have a sound, especially when heard soon after experiencing the busyness and activism of much contemporary life. Our time is filled with many voices. The words of friends, family, the conversations of strangers, songs on radios, discussions on TV, surround us continually. Many of us are so afraid of missing an opportunity to talk that we carry mobile phones so anyone anywhere can call us at any time. And behind all this lies the background noise of computers, dripping taps, drills, washing machines, traffic, planes and people. Like a fish in water, we are so surrounded by this constant noise that we barely notice it. Some of us find noise so reassuring that our first act when walking into a silent room is to turn on the TV, put on some music, or pick up a magazine; anything to silence the silence, to fill it with sound or words.

To step into the desert is suddenly to become aware of silence, and the absence of the noise that flows around us, filling the small cracks and crannies of our consciousness. It is as if time itself stops. On his first encounter with the desert, Edward Abbey wrote:

> I became aware today of the immense silence in which I am lost. Not a silence so much as a great stillness – for there are few sounds: the creak of some bird in a juniper tree, an eddy of wind which passes and fades like a sigh, the ticking of the watch on my wrist ... A suspension of time, a continuous presence. If I look at the small device strapped to my wrist the numbers, even the sweeping second hand, seem meaningless, almost ridiculous.

Time, sound, company, all the usual boundary markers for life are removed in the desert, and it begins to be disorientating and uncomfortable. At first, the sound of silence can be a delicious relief. The desert has a stunning, barren beauty about it as well, which can be quite captivating. After a while, the novelty wears off, and there is a distinct sense of being exposed, not just to the elements, the burning sun, the hard rock, the cold of the desert nights, but also in a much more personal way. Henri Nouwen describes the desert experience of solitude and silence like this:

> In solitude, I get rid of my scaffolding: no friends to talk with, no telephone calls to make, no meetings to attend, no music to entertain, no books to distract, just me – naked, vulnerable, weak, sinful, deprived, broken – nothing. It is this nothingness that I have to face in my solitude, a nothingness so dreadful that everything in me wants to run to my friends, my work and my distractions so that I can forget my nothingness and make myself believe that I am worth something. But that is not all. As soon as I decide to stay in my solitude, confusing ideas,

> disturbing images, wild fantasies, and weird associations jump about in my mind like monkeys in a banana tree. Anger and greed begin to show their ugly faces ... The task is to persevere in my solitude, to stay in my cell until all my seductive visitors get tired of pounding on my door and leave me alone.

The desert is no theme park. In fact it is the exact opposite of the theme park. To be stripped of every distraction, every indication of status in the pecking order of normal society, every reassurance of self-worth, is a profoundly disturbing experience, and perhaps accounts for the lurid dreams, visions and imaginings which the stories of the desert fathers relate. To come face to face with ourselves, our real motives, the dark desires and secret fantasies that lurk within our own souls, is often the last thing we want to do.

We sometimes like to present a carefully sculpted image to the rest of the world. We're scared in case people see us as we really are. In the desert, this image crumbles away, as there is no one to see it. The only eyes to see us are the eyes of God, before whom there is no pretending. It is the place where, open to the gaze, and hearing the word of God, this false self is deconstructed, sometimes painfully taken apart. Those who visited the monks and wrote down their stories often spoke in awed tones about these spiritual heroes, but the best monks never saw it that way. One saying of the desert fathers was: 'Even if an angel should indeed appear to you, do not receive him, but humiliate yourself, saying "I am not worthy to see an angel, for I am a sinner".'

Any pretence to be a hero is quickly removed in the solitude and quietness. And yet the desert monks sought precisely this experience of humbling, because they knew that it was the beginning of wisdom. For the new self to be recreated in Christ, the old proud self, with its pretence, jealousy, fears and greed, had first to die.

Time spent in the deserts of the Holy Land can remind us of our need for time and space where, alone before God, we can allow his word to act as a mirror to our souls. God is of course perfectly able to speak to us in our normal busyness, yet sometimes we need to take special care to guard time away from this, to listen carefully to God's word to us. Paul reminds the Christians at Colossae that their old self has in one sense died with Christ. Yet he goes on to urge them to 'put to death whatever belongs to your earthly nature, sexual immorality, impurity, lust, evil desires and greed, which is idolatry' (Colossians 3:3–5). These, and others like them, do not belong in the life of a Christian, so they need to be brought to the surface, named, confessed and put away.

There is a great delight and a delicious relief in repentance and true self-knowledge, as the prodigal son began to find when he 'came to himself' in the 'desert' of the pigsty, and returned home to his father. The despair of being alone with himself with nothing but pigs for company was the first step towards appreciating quite how much he was loved, and experiencing the joy of forgiveness. Time in the desert can teach us the vital necessity of time alone, time when we strip away all our normal props and supports, and allow God to show us who we are, before he can show us who he is.

REBUILDING THE NEW

The desert is not just the place where false gods can be put away and the old self can die. It is also where a new person can emerge. In a saying which captures the best of the desert movement, one old man said:

> the monk's cell is like the furnace of Babylon where the three children found the Son of God, and it is like the pillar of cloud where God spoke with Moses.

The saying picks up two Old Testament stories. The first, found in Daniel 3, sees three young Jewish exiles in Babylon – Shadrach, Meshach and Abednego – refusing to bow before an idol in the shape of King Nebuchadnezzar. For their punishment they are thrown into a raging inferno. As the king gazes on, he suddenly sees a shadowy fourth figure walking with them in the fire 'looking like a son of the gods'. Christian readers of the passage have often seen this figure as representing either God himself or even as a foreshadowing of Jesus Christ. The monks were no exception. The point being made here is that in the flames, God in Christ meets with them. For the monks, as they turned their backs on the idols of their age, and walked instead into their cells, these small huts or caves became places of struggle, testing and fire. It is hard to concentrate on praying for hours, days, weeks on end. They struggled with boredom, inattention, lustful thoughts and loneliness, just as we do when we try to pray. Yet the cell slowly became a place in which despite, or perhaps through all of this, God met with them, drew close to them, and began to transform them.

The second story comes in Exodus 33 on Mount Sinai, not far from where the early Egyptian monks gathered. At a time of crisis in the Israelites' journey from Egypt to the promised land, God meets with Moses, and speaks to him 'face to face, as a man speaks with his friend' (Exodus 33:11). A pillar of cloud descends upon the tent when God is speaking with Moses, and is the sign to the rest of the people that this divine conversation is taking place. The story evokes a mixture of awe and intimacy, fear and friendship, and has often been taken as an incentive for an encounter with God. Although there remains something distinctive about Moses' (and Jesus') encounter with God, Christians are those who, 'beholding the glory of the Lord with unveiled faces, are being changed into his likeness from one degree of glory to another' (2 Corinthians 3:18).

Just as the pillar of cloud signified the place where God spoke with Moses, so the monks often found their cells to be the place where God spoke with them, where their intimacy with the majestic Living God of Jesus Christ could be established. Jesus himself had commanded his disciples to 'go to your room, close the door, and pray to your Father who is unseen. Then your Father, who sees what is done in secret, will reward you' (Matthew 6:6).

The cell, as a setting where God could meet with them and speak with them, was central to the spirituality of these people. And this is where the desert fathers' love for Scripture comes into focus. It is hard to 'concentrate on God' for hours on end. How on earth can you do it? The desert monks believed that God revealed his character primarily through the Bible, which is why it had such a prominent place in their life. So they would spend long hours memorizing it, reciting it, meditating upon it. To meditate on Scripture was to meditate on God. This was the primary means through which God spoke to them. Other voices, dreams, visions, words of encouragement from others were all subject to the voice of God in Scripture. Epiphanius, a bishop who became a monk, said that a Christian without a good knowledge of the Scriptures was in great danger, in 'a precipice and a deep abyss'. Antony himself said 'always keep God before your eyes; whatever you do, have before you the testimony of the Scriptures'. For him, having the message of the Bible constantly in mind was equivalent to being in the presence of God.

The Scriptures played a vital role within the lives of the monks. They would meditate over and over on the Bible, so that they could soak in its message and values, and begin to embody its wisdom and become the kind of people it urged Christians to be. Their desire was to allow the words of Scripture to mould them, not just into thinking differently, but into acting and reacting differently, reshaped in the image of Christ.

There is something about the quietness of deserted places which enables us to hear God in new ways. Because every other voice is taken away, it becomes possible to hear the quiet but compelling voice of God in Scripture. It is no coincidence that after years of God's silence, his voice sounded out of the desert in John the Baptist. God's word is often heard precisely at the point when someone goes alone, intent on hearing it. Jacob, Elijah, John, Jesus, all heard God speak powerfully to them when alone in the wilderness. Naturally it is not the only place where God addresses us and enables us to hear his voice. Yet we so often find it very hard to listen to God's word. We so easily run to anything else, more pleasing or immediate or less taxing on our attention than God's penetrating and disturbing voice. Without the determination to 'stay in our cell', at least for some time each day, allowing the words and ideals of Scripture to shape our expectations, our values and our unconscious reactions, we are unlikely to see much real change.

On a trip to the Holy Land, those able to spend even a few hours in the wilderness, listening to the silence and suddenly sensing the freedom from noise and distraction, can find themselves returning with a new determination and desire to listen hard for the word of God in Scripture, even in their own room at home. It is rare to find silence and solitude in today's world. Yet without it, it will be hard to hear God's word to us. With it, God will be able to transform us slowly but surely into the person he longs for us to be – the person that in our best and clearest moments we too long to be.

RETREATING AND RESPONDING

Yet wasn't all this withdrawal into the desert pure escapism? Weren't these monks who ran deeper and deeper into the desert to get away from people, escaping the Christian call to be involved in society, in acts of compassion or evangelism? Jesus sends his disciples into all the world, to preach the gospel (Mark 16:15), not to retreat into the desert to cultivate their souls. Might these monks be accused of running away from their responsibilities in mission?

Many of the monks felt the sharp edge of this issue quite keenly. We can begin to see how they tried to resolve it when we walk over the ruins of the many communities of monks who gathered in the Judean desert. The key attraction of this particular bit of desert was that it was so near to the holy places of the Gospels. They could find solitude and silence, yet they could also worship with others, and influence the wider world through the key centre of Jerusalem, with its steady stream of visitors, both important dignitaries and humble 'ordinary' Christians. This rhythm of involvement and detachment was in fact an important part of their life.

Antony, the greatest monk of them all, is a good example. He spent twenty years in the desert, then emerged 'filled with the Spirit of God' (as Athanasius puts it) to teach, counsel, heal and persuade those who flocked to him. He then moved back into the desert, but returned to help the persecuted church in Egypt. Then again, Athanasius tells us, 'when he saw himself beset by many' he set off further into the inner desert to find solitude. The dilemma is summed up in one sentence: 'Being known to be so great a man therefore, and having thus given answers to those who visited him, he returned again to the inner mountain and maintained his wonted discipline.'

The monks attracted a great deal of attention. People heard of their perceptive wisdom, their spiritual power, the remarkable things that were alleged to happen around them, and they wanted more. So Christians would flock from the cities to ask their advice, bring friends who needed healing, or simply come out of fascination to see these men and women of God. Hospitality to such visitors was highly valued among the monks. One Christian visited a solitary monk, spoke with him for some time, and while he was leaving, apologized for having disturbed his rule of silence. The monk replied, 'My rule is to refresh you and send you away in peace.'

Service of the poor was deemed of greater worth than the strictest asceticism. A Christian visitor asked one Abba, 'Here are two brothers. One of them lives a solitary life for six days a week, giving himself much pain, and the other serves the sick. Whose work does God accept with the greater favour?' The old man replied, 'Even if the one who withdraws were to hang himself up by his nostrils, he could not equal the one who serves the sick.'

This was the dilemma of the monk. They wanted to serve, to evangelize, to let their wisdom be available to the rest of the Church, to make a difference, yet they were convinced that whatever wisdom or power they had came directly from their intimacy with God. So they needed to maintain this constant rhythm of involvement with the world and withdrawal from it. Time was spent in market-places and cities, or meeting the spiritual and physical needs of those who came out to them. They took an active interest in, and influenced significantly, the theological discussions going on in the wider Church during this period, and which issued in the creeds many Christians recite today. Yet all this could not be allowed to replace the hours spent seeking God's face, meditating on Scripture, replacing self-will with the desire for God's will. When the crowds became too many, they would retreat further into the wilderness to seek the solitude and silence on which their spiritual health depended.

Jesus, it seems, felt this same tension. Luke states that 'at daybreak Jesus went out to a solitary place. The people were looking for him and when they came to where he was, *they tried to keep him from leaving them*' (Luke 4:42).

Jesus tried to go further away to seek the solitude with his heavenly Father he craved, yet the disciples pulled him back. It is the dilemma of every Christian who seeks to be faithful to God. Most of us will not come to the same solution as the desert fathers, yet something of the desert experience, seeking God in silence and solitude, is vital to spiritual fruitfulness and effectiveness.

Those who have tasted such stillness find it hard to live entirely without it. David Praill writes after years of experience of the desert: 'I am certainly no ascetic, but neither can I find spiritual ease solely in the schooling of the city. There is perhaps hope if the tension can be held creatively in my heart.' After his ordeal as a hostage in Lebanon, Terry Waite too longed for some kind of balance between the needs of people and society, and the equally pressing need to nourish the spiritual life. 'One part of me longs for the solitary life, longs to go to the desert with my books and papers and devote myself entirely to the interior journey. Another part recognizes that I must find a balance. A balance between family, solitude and community.'

Finding that balance is far from easy. For many of us, the sheer busyness of life, the pressure of phone calls, meetings, the constant availability of entertainment, ensures that we are unlikely to miss out on noise. The wilderness reminds us that we need to keep that space where God can remould us according to his Word, as we hear it and ponder it in quietness and attentiveness.

Perhaps these strange figures from the past can remind us that true Christian ministry flows from a growing intimacy with God. How easy it is to let Christian work and ministry fill our waking thoughts and keep us awake at night. God himself becomes a sideline, someone we glance at from time to time. For the monks, it was the other way round. The first priority was to seek the face of God; their ministry was the sideline, something which somehow flowed out of their communion with God.

When God is the focus of attention, everything else falls into place.

A DIFFERENT WAY OF LIFE

David Praill gives us a hint of another lesson to be learnt from the desert. 'I do not wish to idealize the desert, but it has become necessary for me to escape occasionally into wilderness so as to remind myself that the norms of so-called civilization are not the complete picture, that there is another way of being.'

The values of the desert life are completely opposed to so many of the things we hold dear. Just think of how many conversations revolve around money, how much we earn, how much things cost, how much we saved by shopping around. The desert monks were just not interested. A rich visitor to Egypt brought bags of gold with him for the monks, but was told, 'The brothers do not need it.' Determined to be generous, the rich man put the gold in a basket at the door of the church of the monastery, telling them that anyone who wanted some could take it. Nobody came. Most didn't even notice it was there. The story concludes: 'The priest said to the visitor: "God has seen your charity: go and give it to the poor." Greatly edified, the man went away.' Would that happen if a bucket of cash was left with a 'help yourself' sign on the way out of our churches today?

The signs of success in our world are a full diary, a large house, fine food, a fast car and designer clothes. In the desert, it is just about the opposite. People move on foot, or at most on a camel, hardly the fastest animal alive. John the Baptist's 'designer clothes' were a camel-hair tunic and leather belt; his food, locusts and wild honey. Our world seeks wealth, comfort, sex, power and achievement. The desert monks longed for poverty, discomfort and chastity. By our usual standards, they achieved very little. All they left behind were a few rough huts, the odd small monastery and a few stories, written down by others.

The desert reminds us that it does not have to be this way. There is an amusing story of two monks, trying to have an argument and failing miserably:

> Two old men lived together for many years and had never fought with one another. The first said to the other, 'Let us have a fight like other men do.' The other replied, 'I do not know how to fight.' The first said to him, 'Look, I will put a brick between us, and I will say it is mine, and you say, "No, it is mine", and so the fight will begin.' So they put a brick between them and the first said, 'This brick is mine,' and the other said, 'No it is mine,' and the first responded, 'If it is yours, take it and go' – so they gave it up, without being able to find an occasion for argument.

It is not hard to pick fights in our world. But imagine a world where people were so schooled in forgiveness, had so abandoned the desire for things, and were instead so devoted to the good of other people, that arguments over land, property, and rights just failed to materialize. The world of the desert reminds us of a different way, a different kingdom, a world where different values obtain. This is a world where words are seldom uttered, carefully chosen and so often carry more meaning and weight. Here the needs of the neighbour, the visitor, take precedence over the host. There is hospitality, but few possessions. Cells don't need burglar alarms, or even keys. The resources of nature are harnessed, not exploited, the barren wastes begin to flower with green. Naturally, we know this present world can never be fully like this. Often the desert monasteries weren't like this either. They had their fair share of bickering, vanity and self-seeking, like any human community. Yet these stories offer us a reminder of a different kingdom, another way of life.

To sit for a short while in one of the old cells left behind by the monks of the Judean desert is to touch on a very different way of life. Take money again. Jesus taught quite clearly that 'he who does not give up everything that he has cannot be my disciple' (Luke 14:33). Can 'ordinary' Christians today follow such extraordinary teaching? Our problem is that we have come to see a kind of bourgeois discipleship as normal, where becoming a Christian makes hardly any difference to our financial or social status. We tend to think of the full-time Christian worker, the missionary, those living in Christian communities – in other words, those who give up a lot to serve Christ – as the odd ones out, the exception. Jesus' words remind us that these latter are the 'normal' Christians. The model for Christian discipleship with which Jesus presents us is actually to give up everything to follow him. Becoming a Christian does mean giving up all claim to own anything.

With some of us, God loans our possessions and our salary back to us, to be used for his purposes and his Kingdom, but we must never forget that this is the abnormal, the exception rather than the rule. Anything we say is 'ours' is only on loan to us from God. As we look around to view our cars, home, DVD player, that favourite painting, we must remember that none of them is truly ours. We look after them not by right, but by the permission of the God to whom we belong, and we are charged to use them not for our own pleasure, but for his Kingdom. We are to lend them, be generous with them, risk them and not mind too much if they get broken or damaged in the process. After all, they are not ours anyway.

If Christians began to live these values a little more boldly than they often do, they might find evangelism a little easier. Some thieves once broke into a monk's cell, and told him mockingly that they were about to take everything that was his. 'My children, take what seems good to you' was the only response they got. Having filled their bags, they departed hurriedly, only to find the old man chasing after them, holding up a purse which they had left behind. 'Take this which you have forgotten from the cell,' he shouted after them. They were so amazed by his reaction they 'put back everything in his cell, and did penance, saying one to another, "Truly this is a man of God".' In these stories, people are converted not only by the words of the monks, but by the correspondence between their words and their radically different behaviour and values.

The life of the desert, where practically nothing of value is owned at all, is an eloquent reminder to us of 'normal' Christian discipleship, and of a radically different attitude to possessions from anything we find in our world. It also encourages us to rethink our attitude to sex, power, influence and achievement, the idols of our own day. A Church which lived just a little more dangerously, a little more like the men and women of the desert, might find more people ready to listen and take seriously the God who calls us to a new way of life which is life itself.

In the midst of a busy tour, or even a busy life, the desert can be a place where we hear God's word more clearly, dismantling the old self, rebuilding the new and enabling us to bear more effective witness to Jesus Christ, in whichever world God has called us to serve him.

THE PILGRIMS' TALE (4)

Tom's spiritual reverie was interrupted by a growing awareness of his deep need for lunch. Almost at the same time, Roger rounded off Tony's words in the church of the Holy Sepulchre with instructions for finding a restaurant not far from the church, still in the Christian quarter of the Old City.

As they stepped out into the church courtyard, the brightness of the sun took Sarah by surprise. She shielded her eyes, and felt just a little relieved to be out of the dark, faded atmosphere of the building. She too suddenly realized how tired she felt. A morning spent walking through Jerusalem, so much information to take in, and the heat of the early afternoon sun were beginning to take their toll. Tom was talking excitedly about the Holy Sepulchre. It had obviously done something for him, but she was less sure. There had been something uncluttered and elemental about the bare rock of the old quarry under the rock of Calvary, but the site of Golgotha had seemed to her just the opposite: cluttered and confused. This worried her.

They soon found themselves sitting at a table upstairs in a cool air-conditioned restaurant. After the main course, the sweet consisted of *baklava*, a sticky sweet pastry-type thing, which Tom was busily stuffing into his mouth.

'You liked that Holy Sepulchre place, didn't you?' she asked him.

'Mmmm,' he grunted between mouthfuls. 'I thought it was pretty good. You can't beat the real thing, can you? Most of the time you obviously don't know if they are the right place, but that sounded pretty convincing to me – those first-century tombs, the fact that it's been thought of as the real site for so long. It just had the feel of the real thing to me.'

'I thought you said you didn't think it mattered whether it was the real place or not?' she said.

'I don't now. In the end it doesn't matter – it's not as if the whole thing comes crashing down if you don't know exactly where it all happened. But it's still kind of reassuring to see somewhere every now and again where you can be pretty sure they've hit the spot. Helps you to realize it did happen once.'

'I suppose so. I just thought it was creepy. All those icons and lamps, and *so* dark. It should be somewhere light and airy, with bright colours and full of joy. It wasn't though. And all those denominations who fight over it all the time.'

'Probably better than having just one lot owning the whole thing and lording it over everyone else,' he replied.

The meal was soon over. The group gathered bags, cameras, guidebooks, souvenirs and hats, applied suntan cream, donned sunglasses, and like an army platoon ready to face the enemy, marched out into the mid-afternoon sun.

Before long, they emerged from the interminably confusing alleyways of the Old City through a large stone gateway into a wide open space full of traders selling brilliantly coloured fruit, clothes and sweets. This was the Damascus Gate. These were the kind of colours Sarah had hoped to see in the place of Jesus' resurrection. It seemed so much more full of life than the old church they had left behind. They walked up some steps, crossed a frantically busy road, were almost scythed in two by a wildly careering motorcycle overtaking the traffic on the inside, and to their relief, found themselves walking up a quieter road away from the city walls. Following the rest of the Holytour Pilgrimages group, they turned into an opening in a wall, by a sign marked 'The Garden Tomb'.

'Hang on, I thought we'd just been at the tomb?' asked Sarah.

'We have. This is another place they reckon it might have been. Feels different, doesn't it?' replied Tom, as they stepped inside.

They were met by a tall, tanned Englishman who welcomed them brightly. In fact the whole place felt as if they had just been miraculously transported from the Middle East to a garden in Surrey. Plants were arranged carefully in pots, the paths had been swept clean. There was even a Christian bookshop, something they had not seen in all their travels, just like the one Sarah passed on her way to work each day.

The Englishman led them along a shaded path, towards a viewing platform next to a grimy bus depot. He pointed out an unusual rock formation, which looked spookily skull-shaped. They then turned back, followed each other along a path, down some steps towards an open paved platform, where trees provided some welcome shade. On one side was a wall with a rectangular opening, and a round rolling stone beside it, which they both instantly recognized from the guidebooks. The opening had a hinged door, with the inscription '*He is not here: he is risen.*'

'This is more like it,' said Sarah, instantly more cheerful. 'This is what I had in mind. It's bright, colourful, peaceful. You can imagine the Resurrection much more easily here.'

'Yes, maybe,' added Tom a little doubtfully. He started leafing through his guidebook. 'It says here, "Unfortunately there is little possibility that this is in fact the place where Christ was buried."'

'How on earth do they know?' said Sarah. She swallowed her words as the Englishman began to explain about the site. He made out what seemed to her a good case for this being the real location of the tomb of Christ. It was all to do with the skull-shaped rock at the back of the bus station, the area being beside a busy public road, and its being definitely outside the city wall. 'There you are, it might be true,' said Sarah. Tom looked sceptical.

'But then again it might not.'

'True,' she admitted. 'Anyway, I like this place much better. It might not be real, but it *is* authentic,' she added, pleased with the pithy epigram she had just invented.

They each took turns to stoop into the tomb, and emerge into the light again. By the time Tom had come out, Roger was under the trees nearby, arranging a small table with a white cloth – a sure sign by now, they realized, that a communion service was on the way. They had to wait for a short while as a group of black American Pentecostals were holding an extended and very loud praise session in a small open-air chapel a few yards away. A large woman on the edge of the group glanced sideways as she sang and caught Sarah's eye. Something in her look of rapture and joy reminded Sarah of the Greek man on the Mount of Olives. The woman beckoned vigorously for Sarah to come over and join in. Sarah smiled back but, feeling this was not quite her style, politely declined. Eventually the Pentecostals stopped, and gave themselves to the more mundane tasks of admiring the flowers and fanning themselves in the heat. Tony stood up and asked Roger to read a passage from Luke 24 about the first Easter Sunday, and the meeting of some disciples with the risen Jesus on a road to Emmaus. When Roger sat down, Tony continued.

It's been a long day. We joined Jesus' journey as he made his way into the city on Palm Sunday. Now at the end of the day we are in a garden outside a city wall, remembering the great end to the story – the events of Easter Sunday.

We are facing an ancient tomb hewn in the rock face and, as we do so, perhaps you can imagine more easily what happened in the dawn mist on that otherwise normal Sunday. The women arrive. To their horror the rolling stone has been moved to one side. They fear the worst – that Jesus' grave has been disturbed and his body stolen. But then they are confronted by two angels who announce to them the startling news: 'He is not here; he has risen!' And so the message, at first disbelieved by his male disciples, begins to sneak out through the streets of Jerusalem. The man crucified on Friday is alive again – his tomb quite empty, as all could see!

Jesus had risen. We can sense the bewildered joy of the disciples in those first accounts. But very soon, as the jigsaw puzzle began to fall into place, and as they looked back on those previous three years and those previous three days, they became convinced that Jesus' being raised from the dead made perfect sense. 'It was impossible', they concluded, 'that death should hold him' (Acts 2:24). Death could not be the end for one who spoke the words of eternal life and who himself had the power to raise others from the dead! And so the Resurrection became the cornerstone of their message.

And it remains at the heart of the Christian faith to this day. For it reveals who Jesus is: the true Messiah, the Lord, the very Son of God himself, and the appointed Judge of humankind. It also shows God's incredible power at work in the world, and his ability in patience and love to overcome human evil with his goodness. Above all, it makes clear to individuals that death is not the end. There is life beyond the grave. Believers in Jesus can anticipate a transformed heaven and earth. Death has been overcome by life. Sin has been met with God's gracious forgiveness. Evil has been swallowed up by Victory.

And what's more, the Resurrection can affect our daily lives in the here and now. For when Jesus emerged from the tomb, God was clearly not abandoning this sad old world, but rather in the business of transforming it. So this gives us confidence that he will not discard, but rather use, everything in our lives that has been good and just and beautiful. The Resurrection makes goodness worthwhile; it makes life worth living.

This communion service gives us an opportunity to meet with this Risen Jesus. Those two disciples on their way to Emmaus later on that same first Easter Day, eventually recognized Jesus 'when he broke the bread' and gave it to them. So as we receive the bread and the wine in a moment, let us cast our mind back through today; let's bring to God anything that has come home to us in a new way; let us pray for those around us and for those who uphold the name of Jesus today in this troubled city. But above all, let us seek to meet again with this Jesus, now risen from death and alive today. He is the Risen Lord of the Church, the Lord of Creation, the one whom one day we will meet face to face. And he longs to meet with us now.

And the result? We go home, back to the place from where we set out – but this time with a sure sense of Jesus' presence. For the Emmaus disciples that meant returning to Jerusalem. For us it means the opposite – our homes and normal life are elsewhere. But wherever it is, the promise is that Jesus will travel with us on the road and that 'our hearts will burn with us' as he speaks to us through the Scriptures and as he reveals himself in 'the breaking of the bread'. May we know that presence when we leave tomorrow, knowing that Jesus is always with us. For that is precisely the message of this Garden Tomb in Jerusalem: 'He is not here; he is risen!'

After communion, Sarah and Tom sat silent for a short while. The Pentecostals had now slipped away. The sun hung low in the sky, preparing to set behind the distant noises of the city. It cast long shadows and a gentle golden light upon their faces.

Tom thought back over the day. It had been a day of tombs. His mind returned to the misty early morning by the tombs in Bethphage, where he had begun to sense his mood lift. He thought of the unexpected thrill he had felt in touching the rock of Calvary, and the ugly edicule over the tomb of Christ in the Holy Sepulchre. He gazed at the dark opening to the Garden Tomb, set sharply against the light-coloured rock of the surrounding wall. It suddenly reminded him of a graveyard near his home as a child where he and some friends often hung out, and where he had sometimes felt scared and nervous, playing among the dead. Here again, he had spent a day among tombs, but strangely it had not been a day of death, but of life.

His mind drifted back to the conversation he'd had with Sarah at Gethsemane. He had felt himself turn a corner then, and now, sitting before this open burial place, thinking over what Tony had said about the Resurrection 'making life worth living', he grasped a little more what that was. This 'Resurrection' thing was so big, so earth-shattering, that he could either build his life and his world upon it, or he had to set it to one side. Dead men just don't get up and walk again. Normally. Yet this wasn't normal. You couldn't just fit this in to your life as one of a number of things you believed, like that the world was round, or that strawberries taste better with cream. If this was true, if dead men can rise again, if there really is a whole other world on the other side of that empty tomb, waiting to be discovered, then this had to be the one most important factor in his life. The lazy, indifferent staleness of his Christianity now seemed laughable; it wasn't an option any more. This had been a day when his cynicism had begun to crumble, not before the evidence of sure locations and historical argument, but before the simple presence of the Risen Jesus Christ. He had come to Jerusalem sceptical about whether he would find Jesus there. In one sense he had been right. Jesus was not there any more than he was anywhere. In another sense he couldn't have been more wrong. Jesus had found him.

Sarah sat on a bench beside a bed of geraniums, lost in her own thoughts. It had been a day of people. In her mind, the elderly Greek pilgrim on the Mount of Olives, the young Palestinian Christian at Golgotha and the large American Pentecostal woman mingled with an image of Jesus hanging on a wooden cross in a disused quarry. She felt as if she had been plunged into a deep pool and forced to swim, made to try to make sense of this confusing place and its layers of history, faith and passion. The one thing which stood out was a sense that in that simple choice she had made a year ago to become a Christian, she had entered something far, far bigger than she had ever imagined. At the time it had felt something quite intimate, just her and God. It was still that, but she had felt strangely at one with the Greek, the Palestinian and the American Pentecostal. Having spent the day in and out of churches whose roots stretched deep into the past, she had begun to feel a small part of a huge body of people across cultures and centuries who shared the same basic faith as hers. And it all came back to the disused quarry, and what had happened there two thousand years ago. That single act was what held them together – the Greek walking the Way of the Cross, the Palestinian at the place of the cross, Sarah herself learning what it meant to belong to the people of the cross, the American praising the conqueror of death.

'It's been a good day,' she said.

'Yes, a very good day,' Tom replied, thoughtfully. 'The kind of day you remember for the rest of your life.'

'What about tomorrow?' she asked, fixing him with a note of intensity in her voice.

'What about tomorrow?' Tom replied, puzzled.

'We go home, remember?'

'Yes, of course, I'd completely forgotten.' There was an awkward silence, as he realized he needed to say something more. 'Maybe we can … keep in touch?' he added, a little nervously. She paused and looked at him.

'Yes, I'd like that. I didn't think I would when I first met you back in the airport,' Sarah laughed. 'I thought we'd be too different. Maybe we still are. But it feels like we've both come a long way today.'

The sun was dropping fast in the sky. The early evening already felt cooler, signalling the end of the day, the end of the tour. Roger was busily chasing up some stragglers in the party who had dispersed to various corners of the site. The noise of the city continued to rumble on in the background. This day spent in Jerusalem had begun to echo through the lives of these two pilgrims. In the same way, that day in Jerusalem two thousand years before, when two other pilgrims found an empty tomb, continued to echo across the earth, working its quiet enchantment in a dying world.

Appendix I

TEN TIPS FOR TRAVELLERS

THINGS TO REMEMBER BEFORE, DURING AND AFTER YOUR VISIT

Most people want to get as much as possible out of their visit. So here are some basic guidelines intended for the thoughtful Christian visitor, which you may find helpful. Not all will be suitable for your particular needs and circumstances, but implementing the ones that *are* appropriate may help to increase the value of your trip – both for yourself and for those you meet and travel with.

Before your visit

1. Try to get better informed

There is, of course, tons to learn – far more than anyone can easily digest. Especially before you have seen the places and the situation for yourself, things naturally can be quite a blur. But some basic background reading will give you pegs to hang things on, and will greatly increase your capacity to absorb material during your visit and to make sense of what you are told and see. 'What you know' can determine the amount of 'what you see'.

Chapters 5 to 9 above may help you in matters of Christian history and the contemporary situation, but why not supplement that with a good Bible atlas, an archaeological guidebook, a colour-illustrated picture book of the Holy Land or some books which contain real stories of people living in the Land today? Try too to get the key dates of the significant historical periods in your mind (see table on p. vii). If you do, then a quick reference from your guide to the Crusades, to Herod or the Byzantines, won't completely throw you.

2. Try to work out where you are on your spiritual 'journey'

We have emphasized how a physical journey to the Land of the Bible can, and indeed should, connect up with your own internal journey of faith. Spend some time reflecting on where you are on that journey, and where in due course you would like to be. Unlike Tom, Sarah hadn't done much background reading, but on this more 'spiritual' matter perhaps she proved to be the better prepared of the two. Ideally, you would do well to prepare in both these areas.

So what would you like the Lord to do for you? Resolve, as it were, to travel with Jesus, asking him to be your ultimate guide, and opening up yourself prayerfully to the work of his Holy Spirit for anything he might wish to do. There may be some surprises in store! – some chance encounters and conversations, or a coming together of different strands of information which suddenly connect with your own life story in a powerful way. Prepare yourself as much as you can, but also be prepared for the unexpected!

3. Begin to ask some theological questions

Chapters 1 to 4 may help here. What do I think I am doing when I go on this 'pilgrimage'? What makes this a 'Holy'

Land, or what will make this tour different from travelling elsewhere in the world? You might be really excited by seeing biblical places for the first time, but also brace yourself for an element of disappointment. Not every site will leave you on a spiritual 'high'. You may find that the contemporary situation is quite disturbing, or places are quite different from what you imagined.

4. Resolve to give, not just to get

This means, for example, accepting the fact that you will probably be travelling with other people. They will make demands on you, sharing their different experiences with you. Will you be there for them, or will you instead be lost in a reverie of your own? It also means coming to terms with the fact that you won't be able simply to visit biblical sites without meeting the local people and being affected by the complexities of their situation. Again chapters 8 and 9 may be helpful here. So don't see any scheduled visits to local institutions or churches as an intrusion on your biblical itinerary. Instead welcome these as part of a bigger tapestry which will make your visit both more real and ultimately more life-changing. Pray for these times and for the people you will meet. And why not pack a few gifts or a few things you would be ready to give away to children in need?

During your visit

5. Try to maintain a pattern of prayer each day

There may well be times scheduled in your visit for corporate prayer, but it's good to supplement these with time on your own, perhaps at the beginning or end of the day. This is an opportunity to keep walking on your inner journey, bringing your experiences before God, asking him to make sense of them and looking for his leading. And try to build in some spaces during the day, ideally at each site visited, where you can reflect a little on what you are seeing. Such 'process' time is really important, and too easily gets overlooked in a packed itinerary. Some people will find time before or after dinner each evening to write a personal journal, drawing together what they have seen with their own personal response and reflection.

6. Develop your own 'strategy' for visiting biblical sites

It can be an exciting sensation to be standing on a site mentioned in the Bible; it can be an awesome experience, affecting people quite profoundly and in a wide variety of ways. But we suggest some of the following ingredients may help.

Above all, be grateful for this opportunity which many do not have. Then try to use your imagination to transport you back into the biblical time. At the same time, as we have suggested, don't worry too much about precise issues of authenticity. That was Tom's problem at the beginning. You can still value the role these places may have played in history, acknowledging what they have meant to Christians visiting ever since and what they mean to you. Perhaps for yourself the best thing is to focus not so much on the precise *place*, as on the significance of the *event* remembered there, and the Christians who have been there for centuries before you. This may be the best way to understand what it means to talk of a 'holy place'.

In particular, when visiting Gospel sites, you will at some point have to think through your attitude towards the wonder of the Incarnation – stop to think about what this means, this awesome arrival of God in and for his world, this act of love rooted in real time and space. The world, and your world, can never quite be the same again.

And here you are in the very place where this mystery was acted out on the world stage of human history.

Finally, try to think of how the place you are visiting fits into the Bible as a whole and what biblical themes are associated with that site. In Appendix III we give a few examples of how this approach of setting sites within an overall 'biblical theology' can enrich your appreciation of the Scriptures and their message for today. This may be something you do on your own; but sometimes brief 'biblical presentations', given on site (perhaps by the tour leader), can be really helpful – especially if they don't just mention the biblical references to a site, but also apply to everyday Christian life some of the biblical themes which it raises. In this way you find yourself thinking about what it means to 'walk in his steps' not just in a geographical sense, but in the more important and ongoing spiritual sense.

7. Become aware of the perspective of your guide

The approach of your local guide will be a vital 'lens' through which you yourself encounter the Land. Invariably they do an excellent job, having been thoroughly trained and having led numerous groups before. But few westerners have obtained a permit to guide, so the vast majority are Israelis, with a mere handful of Palestinians. This means your guide is most unlikely to be a Christian. However sympathetic their approach, you may not get the spiritual input you require. Often this is supplemented by the contribution of a Christian tour leader, but not always. The guide's perspective will also affect the way the contemporary political issues are presented. After a few days you may feel able to question a few things or to see matters from a different perspective. Make sure you get a balanced diet, and also that you get a chance to think Christianly about the various sites and issues. This is part of the motivation of this book – to help Christians to think for themselves about Christian pilgrimage.

8. Seek out and talk to local people

Often there is not much free time, but invariably you will have at least some time to wander off in Jerusalem. Talking with local people can give you a perspective on the current situation which books and lectures can't. Also, there is nothing like wandering around on your own, and chatting to locals, to make you feel you understand a place a bit more. Your visit will be much the richer for having got off the tourist trail in this way.

After your visit

9. Try not to go straight back to work!

A visit to the Land of the Bible is seldom a relaxing holiday. For a start, the political situation makes the atmosphere more intense than the Costa del Sol; so too do the religious tensions between Jews, Christians and Muslims. While some people are exhilarated by Jerusalem, others find it claustrophobic and intense – even spiritually oppressive.

And, given that for many this is the visit of a lifetime, most itineraries are pretty full. People don't want to miss out on anything. It's amazing how much energy even quite elderly people can muster for nine days or so. But all this means that you will need some recovery time afterwards, to regain physical strength and to start processing and absorbing what you have received. You don't want to lose what you have been given. You will need space and time.

10. Continue your reflection and concern

During your visit, you may have encountered all kinds of important issues that previously had little bothered you. Again try not suddenly to lose all that. Maybe you have become newly aware of the issues facing Israelis and Palestinians. Watch the news, read more material, get your name on the mailing list of some of the many organizations working in the area. Or maybe your heart has gone out to some of the Christians you have met. Why not pray for them or keep in touch by letter?

However, the journey may also have brought to the surface issues in your own life. In different ways this was true for both Tom and Sarah. Some of these may now have become clearer or found a resolution; but others will be problems that need addressing. Why not talk these things through with someone you trust? Remember Christ is not confined to the Holy Land and he is just as near you once you've returned home. 'He is not here; he is risen.' But he may have spoken to you or met you on your journey to that Land and it's important not to turn away from what he has said. 'Did not our hearts burn within us as he spoke to us on the road?' So don't ignore his 'still, small voice'. In this way you can ensure that your journey to the Land of the Holy One becomes a part of your ongoing journey with that Holy One until the day when you meet him face to face in the ultimate 'holy place'. Your 'journey of a lifetime' will turn out to be just that – part of the most important journey of your entire life.

Appendix II

A SUGGESTED ITINERARY

In chapter 8 we encouraged you to see as much of the Land as you can, building in lots of variety. The following itinerary gives you one example of how the different ingredients (especially the desert) could be worked into a tour of normal length, starting on a Tuesday.

Day 1: Journey to the Holy Land
Overnight in Beersheva

Day 2: Wandering in the Wilderness
Sede Boqer, Ein Avdat, Shivte;
overnight in Arad

Day 3: The Judean Desert
Desert silence, Masada (from the west);
Dead Sea float (Ein Gedi), Qumran, approaching Jerusalem over the Mount of Olives

FOUR NIGHTS IN JERUSALEM (NEAR THE OLD CITY)

Day 4: The Way to the Cross
Palm Sunday walk from Bethphage to Holy Sepulchre and Garden Tomb
Evening meeting with Palestinian Christians

Day 5: David's Cities
Bethlehem, returning mid-afternoon via Talpiot to the Holy Land model of Jerusalem
Evening tour of Mea Shearim and Ben Yehuda

Day 6: Sharing the Lord's Day
Holy Sepulchre at dawn
variety of morning services in Jerusalem
Temple Steps/Western Wall or Yad Vashem
Israel Museum and Shrine of the Book
Evening meeting with Messianic believers

Day 7: Road to Galilee
Wadi Qelt hike, St George's Monastery
lunch in Jericho; Beth Shean

THREE NIGHTS IN TIBERIAS

Day 8: Jesus' Early Ministry
Cana, Nazareth; Sepphoris
Evening meeting for group reflections

Day 9: Around the Lake
Chorazin, Capernaum, Tabgha, Mount of Beatitudes, Bethsaida, Kursi and boat trip back to Tiberias from Ein Gev
Evening entertainment

Day 10: The Ends of the Earth

Via Mount Tabor to Megiddo and Caesarea Maritima; return flight

This itinerary has worked well and might be adapted to meet your own plans. Key elements which contribute to its success include:

- **The first forty-eight hours being spent in the quiet of the desert.** This gives space to overcome jet-lag and to attune to the vastness of the Land and its sense of history. Travellers begin to make connections with the people of Israel wandering in the wilderness, about to cross over the threshold of the promised land. There is plenty of opportunity for hiking, enjoying the wild landscapes, and also for quiet and silence either as an individual or in a group. Then we approach Masada from the west, climbing up the Roman ramp. Only then do we meet other tourists for the first time. More time is also given for desert reflection in the Judean desert after we leave the busyness of Jerusalem.

- **Approaching Jerusalem from the east.** The first view of the 'holy city' is from the Mount of Olives, having just followed Jesus' route up from Jericho. The sun is setting as the dramatic panorama of Jerusalem is spread out before you.
- **Being in Jerusalem for the weekend.** This gives the opportunity for worship with the local Christian community. Saturday, a quiet day in Jerusalem, can be spent in Bethlehem.
- **Enjoying Galilee after Jerusalem.** A chance for the dust to settle and for weary visitors to be refreshed with a little bit of 'holiday' in pleasant and more relaxing surroundings.
- **A final visit to the place from where the gospel was launched on the wider world.** Before the return flight and the pressures of normal life, it is powerful to spend a little time by the coast and reflect on Peter and Paul in Caesarea, taking the message to the Roman Empire of what had taken place in the Land.

Appendix III

BIBLICAL PREACHING AT GOSPEL SITES: THREE EXAMPLES

One way to make the Bible come alive during your visit is to have short presentations in each location of the biblical material which relates to that place. These can be useful simply as means of conveying information and facts. Yet hopefully they can do far more than that – allowing you to hear the word of God as it addresses you in quite different ways. It is surprising how the various biblical passages relating to a single place often come together in new ways to offer us powerful themes for meditation. Here again we sense the value of an overall biblical theology, which allows the Bible as a whole to speak to us. Some of these presentations can also become the basis for short sermons in acts of worship. Celebrating communion together can also be a powerful experience – whether on the shores of Galilee, in the shepherds' fields, or in the desert.

Below we offer you in outline the kind of thing that we have in mind. For reasons of space only three examples have been selected, but these may be sufficient to provide a useful model for you then to do something similar with other Gospel sites. Several sites in Jerusalem have been covered in 'The Pilgrims' Tale'. So here we leave Jerusalem and consider three quite different sites: Bethlehem (mentioned frequently in the Old Testament), Tabgha (a place where several Gospel episodes have been brought together) and Caesarea Maritima (which Jesus never visited, but which introduces us to the Book of Acts and the spread of the gospel to the wider world).

BETHLEHEM

Bethlehem (or 'House of Bread' in Hebrew) lies seven miles to the south of the Old City of Jerusalem. According to the Gospels (Matthew and Luke), this was the birthplace of Jesus – some time between the years 7 and 4 BC. From as early as the third century it was noted that 'house of bread' was a fitting name for the birthplace of Jesus, the 'Bread of Life': 'Jesus accords to Bethlehem the true meaning of her name', Origen wrote, 'by being born within her walls'. Even before him (early in the second century AD), the exact place of Jesus' birth was identified as a 'cave', over which in 326 Constantine ordered the construction of a basilica – the oldest continuously used church in Christendom.

So as a modern visitor you come at the end of a long line of pilgrims. They have come, like latter-day Magi, to 'worship him who was born King of the Jews', and to marvel at the mysteries of the Incarnation and of the Virgin Birth. Here the 'Word was made flesh' (John 1:14). If Jesus was 'made sin' at Calvary, it was only because he was first 'made man' in Bethlehem. To visit Bethlehem is to be challenged with the mystery of the gospel.

But, unlike some other New Testament sites, Bethlehem also features quite prominently in the Old Testament. Noting the role of Bethlehem within all the Scriptures can add greater depth to your visit:

Genesis 35:16–20	Jacob's wife Rachel dies on the way to Ephratha/Bethlehem in giving birth to Benjamin.
Ruth	Ruth the Moabitess comes here with her mother-in-law, Naomi. She marries Boaz and becomes the grandmother of King David.
1 Samuel 16:1–13	Samuel anoints the young shepherd boy, David, as king.
2 Samuel 23:13–17	Three of David's 'mighty men' steal into Bethlehem (when occupied by the Philistines) to get a drink of water for David.
Micah 5:2–4	The prophet foretells that a ruler of Israel will come from Bethlehem, even though the village is 'small among the clans of Judah' (quoted later to Herod in Matthew 2).
Matthew 2:1–18	The Magi visit first Herod and then the infant Jesus, resulting in the flight to Egypt and the 'massacre of the innocents'. Matthew quotes Jeremiah 31:15, which pictures Rachel weeping for her children in exile.
Luke 2:1–20	Mary and Joseph journey from Nazareth and Jesus is born. As instructed by the night-time angels, the shepherds go to find Jesus placed in a manger.
John 7:42	People in Jerusalem dispute Jesus' Messiahship, questioning his birth in Bethlehem.

So Bethlehem, though a tiny village, has a long biblical pedigree. Note how it proves to be

- **A place of danger but of hope.** This was the case for Rachel and David's mighty men, for the Holy Family and the young children; but through the tragedy and pain come new beginnings – the birth of Benjamin, the anointing of David, the end of exile, the coming of the Messiah. Naomi (which means 'pleasant') wished to be renamed 'Mara' (meaning 'bitter'), but her bitterness was turned to rejoicing. It is a house of sorrow, but also a house of joy.
- **A place of sacrifice.** We see this in the story in 2 Samuel. When his 'mighty men' return with his desired water, David refuses to drink it: 'Far be it from me to do this; is it not the blood of men who risked their lives?' So the water offered to David and the wine offered by Jesus in the Last Supper are both referred to as 'blood'. David's men had gone forth *to* Bethlehem, risking their lives for David; Jesus went forth *from* Bethlehem to give his life for us. If David refused in the end to drink it, then that can be a sign to us of the importance of what we do in communion: it is no small thing to drink the 'blood' of another.
- **A place of shepherd–rulers.** The parallels between David and Jesus can also be seen in that both these sons of Bethlehem, in their different ways, were kings and shepherds. David, the greatest king in Israel, starts as a shepherd on the hills outside Bethlehem. Jesus' birth is announced to shepherds in those same fields, and he is later described as the 'great shepherd of the sheep' (Hebrews 13:20; cf. 1 Peter 2:25; John 10:11). The parallels between David and Jesus continue throughout Scripture, as Jesus is recognized as the true Messiah, the long-awaited King, the royal 'son of David' – indeed 'great David's greater Son'.

- **A place of divine reversal.** Above all, Bethlehem in the Bible is the place where human expectations are overturned. David was the youngest of eight sons, a grandson of a Moabitess; he was small and 'ruddy'; but, if humans consider outward appearances, 'the Lord looks on the heart' (1 Samuel 16:7). So too Jesus was born not in a Jerusalem palace but in a cave on the edge of tiny Bethlehem, and visited by shepherds who were often on the very edge of society. The 'ruler of Israel' indeed came from the 'least of the tribes of Judah'. So God's foolishness proves to be wiser than human wisdom. Here is a complete divine reversal of our expectations. He is indeed a God of surprises, with whom the first will be last.

And what of our response? Will we react like King Saul in the Old Testament? He was dismissive of the son of Jesse, but at the end of his life he admitted, 'I have played the fool' (1 Samuel 26:21). Or will we react like the Saul of the New Testament? Initially he too was dismissive of Jesus and his cross, but then he humbled himself before God's unexpected revelation; at the end of his life, he could proclaim: 'I have fought the good fight, I have kept the faith' (2 Timothy 4:7). The God of the Bible brought important things to pass in humble Bethlehem. Will we be too proud to respond?

As you approach Bethlehem's Church of the Nativity you will have to stoop down to enter through the low door into the building. In the same way, people from all over the world are called to humble themselves before what God has done in Bethlehem – his mighty power revealed in a helpless baby, the 'Ancient of Days, but an hour or two old'. 'Consider the grace of the Lord Jesus Christ, who though he was rich, yet for your sake became poor, so that through his poverty you might become rich' (2 Corinthians 8:9). Bethlehem, the tiny poor village, the place of humble beginnings, requires us too to be humble as we follow the shepherd-King.

Suitable hymns:

> Christmas carols and Epiphany hymns, including:
> *Of the Father's love begotten*
> *Thou who was rich beyond all splendour*
> *O little town of Bethlehem*
> *Hail to the Lord anointed*

TABGHA

Tabgha is the Arabic name for the area on the north-western shore of the Sea of Galilee, a mile to the west of Capernaum. Its name is derived from the Greek for the 'seven springs' (*Heptapega*) which can be found in the area. Fourth-century Christians found this a convenient site to remember two biblical events: first, the lakeside Resurrection-appearance of John 21 and Jesus' conversation with Simon Peter (which plausibly *could* have been in this vicinity); secondly the feeding of the five thousand (which almost certainly was located instead on the north-eastern side of the lake).

It also lies just beneath the 'Mount of Beatitudes', at the foot of which is a cave, where the Byzantines recalled Jesus' Sermon on the Mount. So at least three Gospel episodes came to be remembered in this one location. At a later point, attention was also given to Jesus' other interchanges with Peter – hence the church of 'Saint Peter's Primacy', built over a suitable 'rock' (cf. Matthew 16:16). Today the focus tends to be primarily on the feeding miracle (recounted in each of the Gospels: see especially Mark 6 and John 6) and the Resurrection-appearance (John 21, foreshadowed perhaps in the earlier miraculous catch of fish recounted in Luke 5).

What biblical themes emerge when we put these two

Gospel episodes alongside one another in Tabgha? In both, of course, there is profound teaching about the identity of Jesus (the Great Teacher, the Worker of miracles, the Bread of Life, the Risen Lord), but visitors can also learn important lessons about what it means to follow this Jesus today:

- **Jesus' commitment to teaching.** Even though he and the disciples were tired, needing to collect themselves, Jesus was moved with compassion when he saw the crowds like 'sheep without a shepherd'. And his response was to 'teach them many things'. There is nothing like the truths of God to give healing and guidance. So the true shepherd, who like Peter is called to 'tend Jesus' sheep', does not just care for them in practical ways, but also resolves to teach them the truths of Christ (cf. Paul's example in Acts 20 and Peter's own teaching in 1 Peter 5). We must all welcome the word of God in our lives and, especially if called to be 'pastors', we must also endeavour to pass it on to others. 'Let the Word of Christ dwell in you richly' (Colossians 3:16).
- **Jesus' training of his disciples**. Simon Peter (who in Luke 5 was made so acutely aware of his sinfulness) was hurt to be asked three times about his love for Jesus; it so clearly echoes his threefold denial of Jesus in Jerusalem. The disciples were teased and stretched by Jesus' command to feed the multitude. But once their pride, their failings and their incapacity had been highlighted, they were quickly used again in the Master's service. They distribute the food to the multitudes; Peter is recommissioned and given a new responsibility. In the service of this Jesus we come across these profound paradoxes: when we come to the point of helplessness, we may be able to help others; when our weaknesses are exposed, then we can begin to be made strong; when we have

nothing left to give, Jesus can take even the little that we do have and use it to bless others. He can take us as we are, not as we ought to be. There is also room for mistakes. But Jesus can take us back to those places of failing or pain. Surely that's why Jesus prepared a charcoal fire on the shore – the smell would immediately take Peter back to the fire in the courtyard of the High Priest, the scene of his bitterest memory. But once we are healed there, we are free once again to move forward into his future.

- **Jesus' mission and agenda**. Both episodes draw upon the two imageries of fish and sheep. The fish need to be caught; the sheep need to be cared for and fed. So too the people of Jesus are involved in both mission and nurture – drawing people into the net of God's Kingdom-rule through the gospel, and then helping each other grow into maturity through the love of Christ. In both fishing and feeding, it is also imperative to follow Jesus' directions; only so will the people be fed, only so will the fishing be successful. We often want to squeeze Jesus on to our own preferred agenda, but when the crowds wished to make him King (John 6:15), Jesus resolutely refused to co-operate. If we are to be his followers today, then Jesus must remain in charge. It is his mission, not ours – to be conducted in his way, not ours.
- **Jesus' questions**. In his training of the disciples we note Jesus' capacity to put his finger on the point of need. In particular, his threefold question to Peter echoes down the centuries. Do we love him above all other things and people? It is so easy for other idols to capture our hearts, to have independent pockets of our lives to which we return for comfort in the hope that we are safely out of his gaze. But the modern follower of Jesus, the visitor to Tabgha, is called to love him with a whole heart. Peter did not

know the precise details of the future, nor does the Christian pilgrim returning home from a visit to beautiful Galilee, but through it all there come those words from the Lord: 'Follow ME!'

Suitable hymns:

O Jesus I have promised
Break thou the Bread of Life

CAESAREA MARITIMA

This Caesarea, mentioned in the book of Acts, is not to be confused with Caesarea Philippi (the place near where Peter confessed Jesus as the Messiah: Mark 8:27). Both were named in honour of the Roman emperor, Augustus Caesar. Caesarea Maritima ('on the coast') was built by Herod the Great between 22 and 10 BC. It was a remarkable achievement. Until you reached the bay at modern Haifa, there was no natural port on the western shore of Palestine. So Herod built a massive harbour with breakwaters reaching far out to sea, making use of a useful recent invention – concrete! He also built a complete underground sewage system for his new city; twice a day it was flushed out by the incoming tide.

The city soon established itself as a major hub of trade and as the administrative capital of the Roman province. After New Testament times it eclipsed Jerusalem in importance for several centuries and the modern visitor can easily sense the contrast between these two cities: the religious, numinous city up in the hills compared to the more secular, trading city on the coast; the Jewish city focused on the things of God, the Graeco-Roman city looking out on the Mediterranean and the wider Roman world. So it is no accident that the gospel of Jesus first encountered Gentiles in this city. This was where Peter came to meet the

Roman centurion, Cornelius (Acts 10:1–48); this too was where Paul was taken, after his arrest in Jerusalem, to await his sentence from the provincial authorities (Acts 23:23–27:2).

So it can be a powerful place to visit, especially at the end of your tour, as you reflect on all that you have witnessed in 'Galilee and Judea' (Acts 10:37) and as you prepare, like Paul, to leave the shores of the Land – a good last stop before the airport! What biblical themes should guide your reflection in this place?

- **An overview of the gospel message.** Peter's speech in Acts 10:34–43 is a brilliant summary of what the apostles saw as the essence of the gospel: the Spirit-filled ministry of Jesus in Galilee and Jerusalem, his death and resurrection, the resultant message that Jesus is Lord and Judge, the one who brings the good news of peace for Israel and forgiveness of sins to all those who believe in him. Similar summaries are found on Paul's lips in his various defences: he speaks of 'righteousness, self-control and the judgement to come' (Acts 24:25), but he especially emphasizes Jesus' resurrection and the fact that this is fully in keeping with the prophetic hope of Israel (Acts 24:14–15; 25:19; 26:6–8; 26:22–3). This is the message that we too need to receive and pass on to others.
- **God's inclusion of the Gentiles.** Some refer to Acts 10 as a 'Gentile Pentecost'. Consider the drama of this unique moment in God's purposes when the gospel at last broke out into the Gentile world. There had been clear hints in the ministry of Jesus that God's Kingdom would include the Gentiles (his praise of the Roman centurion, his welcome to all including the Samaritans, his table-fellowship with those deemed 'unclean'), but his own focus was on the 'lost sheep

of Israel' (Matthew 10:6; 15:24). He had to do in and for Israel what God had promised; only then could the blessing go out to the nations – as a 'light to the Gentiles'. Peter and others were initially cautious, perhaps fearing the reaction of their fellow Jews or perhaps expecting some further sign of Israel's being 'restored'. Hence the need for the clear and demonstrable work of the Holy Spirit. Paul, however, the apostle to the Gentiles, was convinced that this was in God's plan – perhaps even from the moment of his conversion (Acts 26:17). Does this mean God continues to break out from the confines of his revealed will in Scripture, doing lots of new things? No, for the New Testament writers quickly saw this particular 'new' event as truly in God's eternal purposes; after all, the call of Abraham was always to undo the sin of Adam and to be the 'father of many nations'. But Caesarea is the place where this was made clear, beyond doubt. 'God does not show favouritism' and through the gospel accepts people from 'every nation' (10:34–5); he has 'granted to the Gentiles repentance unto life' (11:18). Believers from a Gentile background should always be grateful for the events located in Caesarea. This was the moment when 'we' came fully into the story.

- **God's purposes towards Paul**. It can be a powerful thing to act out some of Paul's trials in the theatre at Caesarea, or to watch the ocean waves and think of him looking out on those same waves from behind prison bars for two whole years. For this energetic missionary, who longed to plant new churches and visit ones already established, this must have been so frustrating! And what an outcome for someone who had only returned to the dangers of Jerusalem because he wished to bring a love-gift of money for the Jewish believers. But it was a place where he made important decisions; he would not allow himself to be sent back to Jerusalem, but rather would appeal to Caesar. That way he would realize his long-awaited dream of reaching Rome – even if in chains. This would symbolize the spread of the gospel of Jesus from 'Jerusalem to the ends of the earth' (Acts 1:8). Paul was convinced that God could still be at work in the midst of his frustrations and in the face of adversity.

- **Reflections from the Land**. Something else, too, of great value may come from that two-year period when Paul was in prison. Paul's friends, who had travelled to Palestine with him, were allowed to visit him (24:23); one of these was Luke the physician. Almost certainly this is the same man who wrote both Luke and Acts. If so, those two years of waiting for Paul may have been put to good use: conceiving his two-volume work and going on research trips to Jerusalem and elsewhere. So we see that visits to the Land of the Holy One can be exciting – and worth writing up when you get home!

Suitable hymns:

We have a gospel to proclaim
I the Lord of sea and sky
Men of faith, rise up and sing

Appendix IV

FOR FURTHER READING

There are many, many books on the Holy Land. The following is just the briefest selection to get you started and includes those we have referred to in the book. They are divided up into different sections, but this is not watertight, since some books naturally cover more than one issue.

Theological issues

J.G. Davies, *Pilgrimage Yesterday and Today: Why? Where? How?* (London: SCM, 1988)

W.D. Davies, *The Gospel and the Land* (Berkeley: University of California, 1974)

S. Hauerwas and W. Willimon, *Resident Aliens: Life in the Christian Colony* (Nashville: Kingdom Press, 1989)

D.E. Holwerda, *Jesus and Israel: One Covenant or Two?* (Leicester: Apollos, 1995)

S. Motyer, *Israel and the Plan of God: Light on Today's Debate* (Leicester: IVP, 1989)

O.P. Robertson, *Understanding the Land of the Bible: a Biblical and Theological Guide* (Westminster: Presbyterian and Reformed, 1995)

P.W.L. Walker, *Jesus and the Holy City: New Testament Perspectives on Jerusalem* (Grand Rapids: Eerdmans, 1996)
P.W.L. Walker and P.S. Johnston (eds.), *The Land of Promise: Biblical, Theological and Contemporary Perspectives* (Leicester: IVP, 2000)
P.W.L. Walker, M. Wood and L. Loden (eds.), *The Bible and the Land – an Encounter: Western, Jewish and Palestinian approaches* (Jerusalem: Musalaha, 2000)

Historical issues

S. Aburish, *The Forgotten Faithful: the Christians of the Holy Land* (London: Quartet, 1993)
K. Armstrong, *A History of Jerusalem* (London: HarperCollins, 1996)
K. Cragg, *Palestine: The Prize and Price of Zion* (London: Cassell, 1997)
—*The Arab Christian* (London: Cassell, 1991)
W. Dalrymple, *From the Holy Mountain* (London: HarperCollins, 1997)
Eusebius of Caesarea, *Ecclesiastical History* (trans. G.A. Williamson; Harmondsworth: Penguin, 1965)
—*The Life of Constantine* (ed. A. Cameron and S.G. Hall; Oxford: Clarendon, 1999)
S. Graham, *With the Russian Pilgrims to Jerusalem* (London: T. Nelson, 1919)
B. Hamilton, *The Crusades* (Stroud: Sutton, 1998)
E.D. Hunt, *Holy Land Pilgrimage in the Later Roman Empire AD 312–460* (Oxford: Clarendon Press, 1982)
J.N.D. Kelly, *Jerome: His Life, Writings and Controversies* (London: Duckworth, 1975)
L.P. McCauley and A.A. Stephenson, *The Works of Saint Cyril of Jerusalem* (Washington: Catholic University Press of America, 1970)
J. Murphy O'Connor, *The Holy Land: an Archaeological Guide* (4th ed., Oxford: OUP, 1998)

A. O'Mahony (ed.) et al, *The Christian Heritage in the Holy Land* (London: Scorpion Cavendish, 1995)
R.N. Swanson (ed.) *The Holy Land, Holy Lands and Christian History* (Woodbridge: Boydell, 2000)
P.W.L. Walker, *Holy City, Holy Places? Christian Attitudes to Jerusalem and the Holy Land in the Fourth Century* (Oxford: OUP, 1990)
P.W.L. Walker, *The Weekend that Changed the World* (London: Marshall Pickering, 1999)
R.T. Wilken, *The Land Called Holy* (New Haven: Yale University Press, 1992)
J. Wilkinson, *Egeria's Travels* (2nd ed., Warminster: Aris and Phillips, 1982)

The Desert

E. Abbey, *Desert Solitaire* (New York: Ballantine, 1992)
D. Burton-Christie, *The Word in the Desert: Scripture and the Quest for Holiness in Early Christian Monasticism* (New York: OUP, 1993)
D. Chitty, *The Desert a City* (New York: St Vladimir's Seminary Press, 1966)
H. Nouwen, *The Way of the Heart: Desert Spirituality and Contemporary Ministry* (London: DLT, 1981)
D. Praill, *Return to the Desert: A Journey from Mount Hermon to Mount Sinai* (London: HarperCollins, 1995)
B. Ward, *The Sayings of the Desert Fathers* (London: Mowbray, 1981)
—*The Wisdom of the Desert Fathers* (Oxford: SLG Press, 1986)

Contemporary Middle East

G. Burge, *Who are God's People in the Middle East?* (Grand Rapids: Zondervan, 1993)
E. Chacour, *Blood Brothers* (Eastbourne: Kingsway, 1984)

C. Chapman, *Whose Promised Land?* (2nd ed., Oxford: Lion, 1989)

K. Crombie, *For the Love of Zion* (Sevenoaks: Hodder & Stoughton, 1991)

N. Finkelstein, *The Image and Reality of the Israel/Palestine Conflict* (New York/London: Verso, 1995)

G. Hewitt, *Pilgrims and Peacemakers: A Journey through Lent towards Jerusalem* (Oxford: Bible Reading Fellowship, 1995)

N.A. Horner, *A Guide to the Christian Churches in the Middle East* (Elkhart: Mission Focus Publications, 1989)

B. Morris, *The Righteous Victims: A History of the Zionist/Arab Conflict 1881–1999* (London: John Murray, 2000)

S. Munayer (ed.), *Seeking and Pursuing Peace: the Process, the Pain and the Product* (Jerusalem: Musalaha, 1998)

E. Said, *The Politics of Dispossession: the Struggle for Palestinian Self-Determination 1969–1994* (New York: Pantheon, 1994)

B. Skjott and K. Kjaer-Hansen, *Facts and Myths about the Messianic Congregations in Israel* (Jerusalem: UCCI, 1999)

D. Wagner, *Anxious for Armageddon* (Ontario: Herald, 1995)

Christian guidebooks for visiting the Holy Land

E.M. Blaiklock, *Eight Days in Israel* (London: Ark, 1980)

R. Brownrigg, *Come, See the Place* (Sevenoaks: Hodder & Stoughton, 1985)

A. Hilliard and B.J. Bailey, *Living Stones Pilgrimage: with the Christians of the Holy Land* (London: Cassell, 1999)

M. Prior (ed.), *They Came and they Saw* (London: Melisende, 2000)

S. Sizer, *A Panorama of the Holy Land* (Guildford: Eagle, 1998)

N.T. Wright, *The Way of the Lord* (London: SPCK, 1999)

ACKNOWLEDGEMENTS

PLATE SECTION CREDITS

1. © Graham Tomlin
2. © Terry Clark
3. © Graham Tomlin
4. © Peter Walker
5. © Peter Walker
6. © Garo Mabaldian
7. © Graham Tomlin
8. © Graham Tomlin
9. © Terry Clark
10. © Peter Walker
11. © Graham Tomlin
12. © Graham Tomlin
13. © Terry Clark
14. © Graham Tomlin
15. © Graham Tomlin
16. © Graham Tomlin
17. © Sami Awwad
18. © Brian C. Bush

FIGURE CREDITS

5. © Ancient Art and Architecture Collection
7. © From Claire Amos, *A Many-coloured Mosaic,* 1984
9. © From O.P. Robertson, *Understanding the Land of the Bible* (Westminster: Presbyterian and Reformed, 1995)